Political Corruption and Governance

Series Editors
Dan Hough
University of Sussex
Brighton, United Kingdom

Paul M. Heywood
University of Nottingham
Nottingham, United Kingdom

This series aims to analyse the nature and scope of, as well as possible remedies for, political corruption. The rise to prominence over the last 20 years of corruption-related problems and of the 'good governance' agenda as the principal means to tackle them has led to the development of a plethora of (national and international) policy proposals, international agreements and anti-corruption programmes and initiatives. National governments, international organisations and NGOs all now claim to take very seriously the need to tackle issues of corruption. It is thus unsurprising that over couple of decades, a significant body of work with a wide and varied focus has been published in academic journals and in international discussion papers This series seeks to provide a forum through which to address this growing body of literature. It invites not just in-depth single country analyses of corruption and attempts to combat it, but also comparative studies that explore the experiences of different states (or regions) in dealing with different types of corruption. We also invite monographs that take an overtly thematic focus, analysing trends and developments in one type of corruption across either time or space, as well as theoretically informed analysis of discrete events.

More information about this series at
http://www.palgrave.com/series/14545

Roxana Bratu

Corruption, Informality and Entrepreneurship in Romania

palgrave
macmillan

Roxana Bratu
University College London
London, United Kingdom

Political Corruption and Governance
ISBN 978-3-319-66666-2 ISBN 978-3-319-66667-9 (eBook)
https://doi.org/10.1007/978-3-319-66667-9

Library of Congress Control Number: 2017955214

Cover illustration: Evgenii Zadiraka / Alamy Stock Photo

Printed on acid-free paper

This Palgrave Macmillan imprint is published by Springer Nature
The registered company is Springer International Publishing AG
The registered company address is: Gewerbestrasse 11, 6330 Cham, Switzerland

Acknowledgements

This book took a long time to complete. During this process, I was fortunate enough to be supported by wonderful friends and collaborators who strongly encouraged me on the way. I am firstly in debt to all the 'research participants' who have gracefully shared their knowledge and experiences with me. My gratitude goes beyond the customary thanks because most of the 'research participants' have been my close friends and family members. They shall remain anonymous for health and safety reasons.

This book is based upon my doctoral research conducted at the London School of Economics and Political Science (LSE) in the Department of Sociology, and substantially rewritten during my postdoctoral years at University College London (UCL), School of Slavonic and East European Studies (SSEES). While at UCL, I was fortunate to be part of the largest (at the time!) social science project ever funded by the European Commission through FP7: *Anticorruption Policies Revisited: Global Trends and European Responses to the Challenge of Corruption* (ANTICORRP). I am grateful to have been part of this phenomenal intellectual endeavour that aimed to change no less than the contemporary corruption paradigm.

Several people, networks and institutions have supported me along the way. At the LSE, Wicher Bergsma, Marianne Colbran, Cecilia Dinardi, Janet Foster, Frances Heidensohn, Dick Hobbs, Paul Rock and Fran Tonkiss. At UCL, Alena Ledeneva was my boss, mentor and close work companion. Philipp Koeker has been a wonderful officemate. Other friends and colleagues have enriched my life, supported my endeavours and challenged me on the way: Anna Bailey, Costanza Curro, Pete Duncan,

Slavo Radosevic, Allan Sikk, Elizabeth Teague, Barbara Wiley and Andrew Wilson. In Romania, my former colleagues Aurora Liiceanu, Doina Saucan and Octavian Rujoiu made a world of difference in terms of joy and sanity. From the ANTICORRP project, I am particularly in debt to my colleagues from working packages 3, 4, 6, 8 and 11: Ioana Avadani, Monika Bauhr, Alessio Cornia, Ramin Dadašov, Valentina Dimulescu, Mihály Fazekas, Marcia Grimes, Iveta Kazoka, Aram Khaghaghordyan, Paolo Mancini, Marco Mazzoni, Natalia Milewski, Alina Mungiu-Pippidi, Dimitri A. Sotiropoulos, Andrej Školkay, Zoltán Szántó, István János Tóth and Davide Torsello.

I am grateful to the series editors, especially to Paul M. Heywood, who has been an amazing supporter of this project. At Palgrave, Ambra Finotello and Imogen Gordon Clark have been excellent and patient editors.

Close friends and family members supported me along the way. Hence, my heartfelt thanks to my parents and Amina Aitsi-Selmi, Ligia Birdici, Gabriela Bucataru, Madalina Baetii, Ioana Burtea, Denis Binisor, Daniela Ciurus, Katy Littlewood, Andreea and Radu Oniga, Carla Osman, Ioana Preda, Narcisa Petre, Marsha Providence, Smaranda Schiopu, Pedja Sovilj and Sister Monica. My parents deserve to be singled out as champions of love for and faith in me.

Finally, I am grateful to the funding bodies who considered this research worth pursuing. I was fortunate to be fully funded as a student by the LSE Sociology Department, which awarded me first a four-year scholarship and then two more research studentships. The Ratiu Family Foundation awarded me a grant in my first year and Goodenough College has given me three bursaries over the years.

London 2017

Contents

Acronyms

ANI	National Agency for Integrity (Agentia Nationala de Integritate)
APDRP	Agency for Payment for Rural Development and Fishing (Agenţia de Plăţi pentru Dezvoltare Rurală şi Pescuit)
APIA	Agency for Payment and Intervention in Agriculture (Agentia de Plati si Interventie pentru Agricultura)
CAP	Agricultural Cooperative for Production (Cooperativa Agricola de Productie)
CC	Constitutional Court (Curtea Constitutionala)
CNI	National Council for Integrity (Consiliul National de Integritate)
DCA	Directorate for Control and Antifraud (Directia Control si Antifrauda)
DGA	General Anticorruption Directorate (Directia Generala Anticoruptie)
DGPA	General Directorate for Protection and Anticorruption (Directia Generala pentru Protectie si Anticoruptie)
DLAF	Department for Fight Against Fraud (Departamentul de Lupta Antifrauda)
DNA	National Anticorruption Directorate (Directia Nationala Anticoruptie)
EC	European Commission
EU	European Union
GNP	Gross national product
GRECO	Group of States Against Corruption
ISPA	Instrument for Structural Policies for Pre-accession
MAI	Ministry of Administration and Interior (Ministerul Administratiei si Internelor)
MCV	Mechanism of Cooperation and Verification
OECD	Organisation for Economic Co-operation and Development
OLAF	European Anti-fraud Office (Office Européen de Lutte Antifraud)
OPCP	The Office for PHARE Payments and Contracts

PHARE	Poland and Hungary: Assistance for Restructuring Their Economies
PSD	Social Democratic Party (Partidul Social Democrat)
SAPARD	Special Accession Programme for Agriculture and Rural Development
SNA	National Anticorruption Strategy
UEFA	Union of European Football Associations
UN	United Nations
UNCAC	United Nations Convention Against Corruption

List of Figures

List of Tables

CHAPTER 1

Corruption European Union Funding: Transnational Policies Versus Local Praxis

In the aftermath of the 2008 financial crisis and the Brexit vote that put the euro under strain and called into question the viability of the Union itself, the gaps between transnational-led policies and national interests, political priorities and cultural identities have become wider due to the declining trends of economic growth and unsustainable social promises. This book offers new insights into the challenges and opportunities brought by EU integration policies by taking as a case study the process of accessing EU funding in Romania and its impact on the performance and reproduction of contemporary entrepreneurial identities.

After joining the EU in 2007, Romania could access up to €20 billion by 2013 (The Economist 2012) through EU funding structural and cohesion programmes and a further €23 billion by 2020. In May 2017, the Romanian Minister for EU funding reported a 90% access rate for 2007–2013 in a conference regarding the impact of EU funding in Romania organised on Europe Day. She further added that EU funding had a net positive effect on the economy, having positively contributed to the national gross domestic product by 13.6%, lowered the unemployment rate by 3.7% and created approximately 100,000 jobs.[1]

This success story was somewhat toned down by the European Commissioner for Regional Policy, Corina Cretu, who urged the Romanian authorities to "move from talking to acting" as "time is running out of patience": "2017 is a crucial year. I assure you that if I could implement

R. Bratu, *Corruption, Informality and Entrepreneurship in Romania*, Political Corruption and Governance,
https://doi.org/10.1007/978-3-319-66667-9_1

[projects], I would go myself to the construction sites, but unfortunately, I have nowhere to work because […] for example, the most advanced [highway] project is not yet in the construction phase." Corina Cretu further noticed: "EU funds represent the only way to reach the average standard of living from the Western countries."

The president of the Romanian Chamber of Commerce and Industry argued for reducing the bureaucratic formalities necessary for accessing this type of funding making reference to his own experience: "the man speaking to you has [personally] signed and stamped page by page [a project of] 26,200 pages for a trans-border project in Constanta. The management authority [which meant] four people in the same office asked for one original document each. I was right to tell them that I deserve a van to carry the papers (…) I do believe in resetting the formalities that need to be done." The president of the Federation of unions of construction companies said: "The workforce in construction is 300,000 workers. 100,000 is allegedly not qualified. In two years, we are going to need over half of million workers and we are not going to have them on the market. There is no legislation to bring contingents from outside the EU. The legislation for professional development, fiscal inefficiencies and public acquisitions and the release of construction authorisations will have minimal results. The consequence is that the [EU funded] projects will be blocked." Last but not least, the vice president of the Economic and Social Council summed it up: "…the money circulates from West to East and the workforce from East to West. EU funding should mediate this situation. The problem is that people are losing confidence in EU funding. The Ministry should rebuild trust in these institutions and in the capacity of EU funds to solve development issues. The dangers for 2014–2020 are not related to the commencement of the project bids. In 2018 we anticipate a major deficit of liquidities."

These accounts nicely sum up some of the main issues around the topic of EU funding in Romania—the access rate, the economic impact of this funding, the failures encompassed by the inevitable delays, the excessive bureaucracy, the dissatisfaction associated with it and the enhanced levels of distrust in this funding. All these issues should be interpreted in the context of scarce workforce, lack of liquidities, institutional development and political transition.

Furthermore, official reports and journalists' reports have uncovered dubious arrangements that involved high-level officials, stories of fraud or misuse of funds and entire projects fully funded by the EU that existed only on paper. Probably the most famous case involved the former minister of European Integration—Hildegard Puwak—who distributed EU funds to firms controlled by her husband and her son.[2] The ongoing investigation had started in 2003, and she had to answer not only to accusations of fraud but also to accusations of corruption.[3] Another high-profile figure accused of EU funding misuse by the Romanian Anti-corruption Directorate is the Archbishop of Tomis. He was put under judicial control in May 2017. The anti-corruption prosecutors even requested the measure of house arrest, but the judges rejected the request.

However, beyond these (sometimes) scandalous accounts and dry quantitative assessments, there is little research about the people and practices of accessing EU funding. How do EU anti-corruption policies, practices and assumptions frame the process of accessing EU funding in Romania? What does 'corruption' mean in this context? How much corruption is there in the area of EU funding? This book aims to fill this gap by providing an ethnographic account of EU funding in Romania. In doing so, it pushes forward the understanding of EU funding as a space of interaction between global, European and local forces, while unpacking the assumptions, policies and practices behind the regulations that govern it.

This is a very timely project both practically and theoretically. Firstly, it has direct implications for particular geographical areas—for example, Central and Eastern Europe, which reflects indirectly on Western Europe as the main EU funding policy centre, while discussing potential governance implications for Eastern Europe. In its latest anti-corruption report issued in February 2014, the European Commission stated its concern regarding the mismanagement of EU funding warning that it "can lead to interruption and/or suspension of payments until appropriate corrective measures have been taken by the Member State, including the strengthening of the management and control systems" (EC 2014: 26).[4]

Secondly, a striking feature of the booming literature on EU funding and deviance is how the comparatively small number of ethnographic studies is easily overshadowed by quantitative assessments, policy papers and secondary sources. For example, a recent World Bank review noticed that only 2% of the relevant scientific literature on corruption is covered by anthropological studies (in Torsello 2012). This book contributes to this line of ethnographic fieldwork-based studies, following the contemporary, but not-yet-established, practice of hyper-comparative trans-local ethnographies that analyse a concept while retaining the sensitivity to the context and that deconstruct the moral indignation associated with big concepts like organised crime (Hobbs 2013), (il)legal trades (Nordstrom 2007) or corruption (Ledeneva 2013b). Such studies are based on flexible, distinctively qualitative methodologies, while retaining an 'ethnographic attitude' (Haraway 1997) not confined to a set of methods. To a certain degree, they are similar to studies from the sociological tradition of the Chicago School (Cressey 1932; Polsky 1971/1967) and its followers (e.g., Cohen 1971; Downes 1966; Hobbs et al. 2003) that are based on sustained critical effort to understand the context-specific social interactions and interpretative schemas of people's 'worlds' (van Maanen 1995). In the same fashion, this research was conducted from an appreciative position hoping to present EU funding as a complex, exciting, dull and messy space of interaction.

I conceptualise EU funding as an arena of transnational policy construction that allows for interaction between new institutions and entrepreneurial practices, political gestures and vernacular routines of doing business. This analytic perspective is particularly apt to catch innovation in practices employed or the emergence of new actors and markets (e.g., EU funding consultancy) that are both a product and a source of wider societal changes. The main argument of the book is that EU funding—as an economic process shaped by EU anti-corruption practices, policies and assumptions—configures new political and economic subjects through intertwined vocabularies of corruption and crime, a mix of formal and informal entrepreneurial practices and commodification of finance. This dynamic process concomitantly enables Romania's top-down integration into the EU through the adoption of transnational regulations, institutions and anxieties *and* Romania's bottom-up integration into the EU through the assimilation of the EU funding regulations into the vernacular practices of doing business.

Even since the inception of the EU, one of the most important issues faced by the European leaders envisaged sustaining the EU's expanding agenda and development policies encompassed in EU funding while protecting its financial interests. Historically, at the transnational level, anxieties associated with EU funding misuse have materialised in heightened regulations that employ the vocabularies of crime and corruption. In 2007 after the second Eastern Enlargement, when Romania and Bulgaria joined the EU, these anxieties reached paroxysm because in these countries corruption was perceived as a societal *condition*. Such a medicalised view called for vigorous treatment, and the European Commission imposed a set of 'conditionalities' that entailed enhanced surveillance in order to curb corruption while designing even stricter regulations for EU funding eligibility and control. This book assesses for the first time the effects of such heightened regulations on the process of accessing EU funding and on corruption, showing that their main effect is to increase the costs associated with accessing EU funding and thus exclude a wide range of applicants. By discussing the association between corruption and EU funding regulations in Romania, this book shows that EU funding as a *development theme* was metamorphosed into corruption, a *crime theme*. The book investigates the *rebranding mechanisms*—that created new labels for vernacular ways of doing things, changing the meanings associated with contemporary entrepreneurial practices or reporting the present in a language compatible with global anxieties related to corruption.

Even though transnational entities and the state proved their potency by imposing regulatory control over the EU funding economy, they failed to make it accessible. Hence, a new market force took over this task: consultancy appeared at the intersection of bureaucracy and local entrepreneurship in order to mediate between the two spaces and decode the highly technical eligibility idioms of EU funding. As market-makers, consultants commodify EU funding, treating eligibility criteria as production factors. In this sense, the growing transnational articulation of European integration is not a form of cultural domination by the EU over the local, but finds its embodiment in the appropriation by the local elements of EU funding in order to formulate new and innovative economic and social forms. Consultants are unique elements in this equation, as they are deeply embedded in the local histories, thus familiar with the inclusive morality of informality, but also highly literate in the exclusive idioms of EU funding. By discussing this unanticipated process of market-making through EU funding, this book contributes to economic sociology debates about economic coordination mechanisms, money, markets and modes of exchange.

EU funding is an essentially interactive phenomenon governed transnationally, but I have been concerned to situate it within the local context. Aware that the post-socialist context is a complex interpretative terrain (Humphrey and Mandel 2002), where Western concepts such as 'market', 'civil society', 'Europeanisation' take on distinctly different meanings from those applied by policy makers, my approach was to deconstruct and recontextualise accounts that seemed at first glance exaggerated. My aim was not to impose a moral or theoretical template, but "to comprehend and to illuminate the subject's view and to interpret the world as it appears to him" (Matza 1969: 25). Despite the new legislation (starting 2000) that effectively rebranded as corruption typical economic practices in Romanian society, entrepreneurs use them in daily work routines. The entrepreneurial culture described in the book is an unremarkable characteristic of the local work routines. Fundamentally, this economic activity is a hectic space in which the use of old solidarity networks, favour and gift exchange or informal arrangements coexist with complex risk assessments, business plans and feasibility studies. By looking at mundane practices of accessing EU funding in Romania, this book gives an intimate view into an economy and its shifting values contributing to the academic debates about post-socialist and transition economies.

This book employs a mid-level instrument of analysis that explores three modes of coordination of social and economic life: markets, hierarchies and networks (Thompson et al. 1991). It argues that EU funding is a hybrid space, based on a plurality of coordinating mechanisms that aims to accommodate transnational regulations with vernacular practices. Broadly, the network provides the overarching model of analysis due to its flexible nature, thus embedding hierarchies and markets in the social. Particular attention is paid to transnational and national regulations and their role in framing the economic process. I rely on the concept of entrepreneurship well grounded in economic sociology and the sociology of deviance literatures. Building on these links, the book contributes to the sociological debates by analysing the blurred boundaries between legal, informal and illegal economic activities in the area of EU funding.

The book is based on my direct involvement with EU funding policies—having acted as a consultant in my own firm for 16 months, rich ethnographic research updated yearly after 2012, as well as statistical analysis, institutional research and reach ethnographic interviews. To my knowledge, this is the first monograph of EU funding in a post-socialist country that would trace its history as well as the sociology of its governance. Throughout the book, I often open up my personal archives for the readers and engage with methodological debates about what it means to do ethnography in the contemporary world and with the current academic ethical standards. My ethnographic journey was an *iterative* process mixing inductive with deductive strategies in an attempt to go beyond the official data and innovate the theoretical framework surrounding the world of EU funding. In discussing the choices made and dilemmas raised by fieldwork activities, I show that this endeavour was an interactive and transformative framework in which ethics, danger and risk were *processes* and not *codes of action*.

Outline of the Book

Chapter 2 conceptualises EU funding as a mode of coordinating economic and social life that aims to accommodate transnational regulations with vernacular economic practices bearing in mind Weber's remark that "legal order of legal theory has nothing directly to do with the world of real economic conduct, since both exist on different levels. One exists in the realm of the *ought*, while the other deals with the world of the *is*" (Weber [1922] 1968: 312). The gap between *is* and *ought* is further explored through the concept of entrepreneurship, which I define as a form of co-creative practical competence that allows actors to transform the arenas they come in contact with, through hybrid activities that break the imagined boundaries between legality, morality and legitimacy.

In the second part of the chapter, I look at the 'ought' through the literature regarding new technologies of governing promoted in relationship to development, Europeanisation and international aid. Recently, international development has widened its scope to incorporate donors' ideas about social and cultural intervention that condition foreign aid by institutional redesign at central and local levels, driving the implementation of new technologies of government as part of a 'modernisation' process. In this context, the anti-corruption agenda plays a major role, aiming at restraining bureaucratic discretion and strengthening external oversight, through a credible, apolitical monitoring system (Rose-Ackerman 1999; Klitgaard 1988). I offer a critique of the contemporary paradigm of corruption and show that the dynamics of corruption rhetoric and anti-corruption practices are part of a wider political economic context whose relevance is critical for the understanding of EU funding.

The third part of the chapter turns to the 'is' by looking at the literature regarding post-socialist transformations (Eyal et al. 1998; Humphrey and Mandel 2002; Kornai 1992; Verdery 2004) that deal with re-establishment of property rights (Alexander 2004); privatisation of state-owned factories (Verdery and Humphrey 2004); forced deindustrialisation and the apparent change in the local elites, emergence of robber barons and local oligarchs (Ledeneva 2006); development of informal networks of support which led to the privatisation of public life through the hybrid forms of economic practice (e.g., *blat/guanxi*), which enhanced horizontal solidarity (Yang 1994), while vertical solidarity was developed through patronage (Wedel 2003; Ledeneva 2013a) and corruption (Mungiu-Pippidi 2009). My work is informed by post-2008 crisis material and EU enlargement and contends that while the transition approaches mentioned above are informative, they are not appropriate to capture the contemporary landscape of Romania. Thus, I include material regarding cosmopolitanism, globalisation and transnational capitalism and their impact on the workplace, everyday routines and economic practices, which have largely been excluded so far (Hobbs 2013; Ruggiero 2013).

Chapter 3 interrogates the construction of the anti-corruption and EU funding establishment by looking at the institutions and practices that constitute its governance. The first part of the chapter looks comparatively at EU funding use in various European countries. It further focuses on emergent vocabularies of crime related to the protection of the financial interest of the EU. The link between EU funding and corruption is established, as the chapter shows that, historically, at the EU level, concern with corruption was rooted in the need to protect the financial interests of the EU. Analysed from a comparative and historical perspective, the development of EU funding institutional establishment is shown to be associated with global and European anxieties, assumptions and stereotypes related to the impact of new member states on the EU.

The second part situates EU funding within sociopolitical context of post-communist Romania. I contend that two histories are particularly relevant: one relates to gradually blurring the differences between the European east and west through a top-down process (e.g., the adoption of the acquis communautaire). Part and parcel of this process, EU funding as an ideal type of economic activity, shaped by Brussels bureaucrats' assumptions, anxieties and policies, entailed the creation of a new institutional setting designed to administer economic opportunities differently at the national level. This was based on transfer of 'good practices' from the EU to Romania that involved a 'one size fits all' approach, which put in place impersonal institutions that failed to take into account the elements of time, space, biography and context and inevitably failed to achieve the expected results. The second story relates to the emergence of new categories of differentiation, among which corruption is the most prominent. I offer an institutional history of the emerging 'corrupt Romania' by examining how 'corruption' was symbolically created in the first place and how anti-corruption came to life institutionally. I also look at the emergence of anti-corruption industry (Bryane and Bowser 2009; Sampson 2010), showing how local actors adapted to the political environment and its dominant discourse becoming conjunctural anti-corruption entrepreneurs. The chapter argues that as opposed to the European historical trend, in Romania, anxieties regarding corruption have preceded preoccupations regarding safeguarding the financial interests of the EU.

Chapter 4 draws on respondents' experiences to offer a sociological account of the process of accessing EU funding in Romania. Contrary to the media reports that portray it as a world populated by corruption or fraud and the official narratives that display a sanitised uncomplicated process, the fieldwork experiences show that this is a complex, emotional process marked by confusion, ambiguity, miscommunication and struggles. Following the actors, the dynamics of the local markets and the interaction between various economic, social and political forces, Chap. 4 focuses on the interplay between institutional demands that aim to destroy the routines of economic activities presumed to be marked by corrupt practices and vernacular practices of doing business. It shows that the process of accessing EU funding as imagined by the EU or Romanian bureaucracy has very little in common with the practice of accessing EU funding as employed by Romanian entrepreneurs. Actors who apply for EU funding are influenced by multiple frames of meaning (technological, regulatory, political, economic), act at the intersection of different markets (e.g., market for consultancy, market for tourism, market for construction), move between registers of ***eligibility***, ***compliance*** and ***profitability*** and, in doing so, use a wide range of economic and social practices.

The process of accessing EU funding is a complex economic endeavour, complicated on the one hand by eligibility rules' ambiguity and rigidity and on the other hand by fluctuating business conditions and political instability. In order to reduce the risks and enhance profitability, actors disregard the theoretical public-private divide (Gupta 1995; De Sardan 2005) and rely on formal and informal arrangements, old solidarity networks (Yang 1994; Ledeneva 2013a; de Sardan 1999), transfer of capital, favour and gift exchange (Henig and Makovicky 2015) which are adjusted and included in the new repertoire employed for EU funding, thus making the distinction between legal, illegal and informal spheres superfluous (as shown by Nordstrom 2007; Hobbs 2013 for different contexts). Contrary to the effects anticipated by the EU bureaucrats, this type of funding does not fundamentally change the practices of doing business in Romania, but leads instead to emerging syncretic cultures of entrepreneurship. This chapter sets the stage for the next chapters which follow the logic of the process by looking at various actors as they become involved with EU funding and undertake different work roles.

Drawing on participant observation and ethnographic interviews, Chap. 5 pencils the world of consultants and experts that have appeared as a direct consequence of the need to 'enter Europe'. Engaging with topics like clientelism (Wedel 2003), informality in economic transactions (Henry 1978; Mars 1994), brokerage and its role (Blundo and De Sardan 2006), Chap. 5 argues that EU funding is commodified by consultants through the exploitation of its symbolic, technical and economic space as a terrain on which to (re)construct market relations. Entrepreneurs who want to access these funds are taken aback by highly elaborate technical idioms employed in the rules that grant access to EU funding. Historical low levels of trust in local bureaucracies and the need to make profit cause them to turn to consultants who teach them to become *beneficiaries* by decoding and performing eligibility requirements. In this way, consultants act as agents of change, being both by-products of this tectonic shift of EU integration and its exponents. As by-products of European integration, but also entangled in local contexts, consultants decode and transmit information regarding EU funding to the applicants. As exponents of European integration, consultants act as market-makers by treating criteria of eligibility as production factors.

This chapter shows that consultants are chameleonic actors who capitalise on their social status and role to construct themselves as professionals. In the absence of formal training and faced with the impossibility of getting on-job training, consultants make use of transfer of capital from their previous professional positions to claim expertise in this new line of work. Typically, established consultancy firms have on their boards retired high-level bureaucrats who act as brand names. The vernacular interpretation of this fact can be anything from assuming knowledge, putting in a 'good word', opening doors and getting insider information. Even though not illegal, rarely investigated and never convicted, such interpretations increase the perceived levels of corruption. The chapter explores the porous boundaries between corruption and informality in the creation of a new market—consultancy.

Following Becker's (1963) classical criminological command of analysing not only the deviant subcultures but also the legal and political authorities who are both the official interpreters of the florid cultures of deviance and the ones who attach the criminal labels, in Chap. 6 I turn to the compliance register. The chapter is based on over 50 interviews with actors working in the area of compliance and anti-corruption (mainly controllers, prosecutors, judges and police officers) and participant observation. This empirical analysis indicates that transnational anxieties regarding possible abuses of EU financial interests have put in place an extraordinary multi-level control system with ambiguous effects. The new legal-institutional order is sustained by emerging bureaucratic identities connected to high-profile anti-corruption and anti-fraud institutions constructed as 'elite squads'. The institutional design of EU funding control is sustained by the specialisation of the justice circuits based on the systematic association between corruption and protection of the financial interests of the EU, which have effectively become the new political spotlights.

However, the chapter shows that the attempt to implement technical solutions (e.g., the 'one size fits all' anti-corruption discussed in Chap. 3) in a rather political environment is bound to have mixed results. On the one hand, the pressure put on the control apparatus leads to unexpected forms of resistance like 'signature strikes' in which civil servants refuse to sign any papers thus blocking the bureaucratic flow. On the other hand, the transnational-led control framework clashes with vernacular work routines creating its own informality because on the ground, compliance takes the form of interpersonal bargaining for licences and permits in morally uncertain territories. The unanticipated consequences of the establishment of EU funding control are analysed through three paradoxes: the discursive power of EU funding and how it became a semantic of governance, informality in constructing compliance narratives and the costs of compliance which show how this culture of control (Garland 2002) deters not only crime but also positive action to access this type of funding.

The last empirical chapter turns to the heterogeneous world of actors who try to access EU funding. It shows that the high levels of regulation that accompany financial participation cause EU funds to have perverse effects in Romania, allowing access mainly to actors who are already endowed with high levels of financial, political and social capital, thus reinforcing economic gaps in the society by making the rich richer and excluding the poor from this process. Making use of life histories, this chapter profiles the winners of this funding as *serial entrepreneurs*, involved in multiple businesses simultaneously, for whom EU funding is a sideline activity. It shows that EU funding is enacted through vernacular practices of entrepreneurship, decoded through work routines which are a direct result of the social and economic context, carrying the characteristics of the communist regime and the traits of a newly born capitalism. Whereas the EU regulations will provide only one way of conducting transactions, entrepreneurs will try to make them as personal as they can, by entering informal arrangements, bribing, getting discounts and using their social capital to get favours. Such practices might lie outside the orthodoxy of the market exchange as understood by the EU Agencies, but they do not challenge the conventions of the local markets. In itself the context favours the existence of nuanced ethical systems due to the blurring boundaries between legal and illegal. However, the best actors gain not only from the context but also from their particular competence to politically embed their economic activity. EU funding favours the emergence, proliferation and democratisation of novel forms of entrepreneurial patterns of action.

The Conclusion chapter reassesses the gaps between political and social orders of EU funding drawing wider implications regarding corruption and informality in relationship to transnational aid flows in a globalised world. Firstly, I summarise the key theoretical and empirical concepts of EU funding (as a space of transnational policy construction that allows for interaction between new institutions and entrepreneurial practices, political gestures and vernacular routines of doing business, out of which everybody hopes to gain something—hence the title of the book) and entrepreneurship (as a form of co-creative praxis). Secondly, I examine how these concepts have been used to explore the boundaries between corruption and informality in this context and thus challenge the conventional paradigm about corruption. Furthermore, I examine the wider sociological and criminological implications regarding formal and informal economic practices, corruption, development and their cultural determinants (gift, patronage, clientelism). Thirdly, I tie together how looking at the past and at the future of corruption and informality in the area of EU funding in Romania can engage readers with the main arguments that emerged from this book in the wider European and global contexts. Finally, this chapter concludes with a reflection on the research still to be done on aid flows and corruption, and its implications for the transnational development policies and anti-corruption agenda.

Notes

1. https://www.antena3.ro/economic/biz-news/intact-professional-debates-fonduri-europene-2017-un-nou-inceput-412518.html.
2. http://www.9am.ro/stiri-revista-presei/Politica/17577/Procurorii-PNA-au-redeschis-dosarul-fostului-ministru-al-integrarii-Hildegard-Puwak.html.
3. http://www.mediafax.ro/social/procurorii-cer-arest-la-domiciliu-pentru-arhiepiscopul-tomisului-ips-teodosie-prelatul-la-instanta-suprema-de-la-prima-ora-16391700.
4. https://ec.europa.eu/home-affairs/sites/homeaffairs/files/e-library/documents/policies/organized-crime-and-human-trafficking/corruption/docs/acr_2014_en.pdf.

Bibliography

Alexander, C. 2004. Value, Rights, and Changing Bodies: Privatization and Property Rights in Kazakhstan. In *Property in Question. Value Transformation in the Global Economy*, ed. Katherine Verdery and Caroline Humphrey, 251–273. Oxford: Berg.

Becker, H. 1963. *Outsiders Studies in the Sociology of Deviance*. New York: Free Press.

Blundo, G., and O. De Sardan. 2006. *Everyday Corruption and the State. Citizens and Public Officials in Africa*. London and New York: Zed Books.

Bryane, M., and D. Bowser. 2009. The Evolution of the Anti-corruption Industry in the Third Wave of Anti-corruption Work. http://works.bepress.com/bryane_michael/50

Cohen, S. 1971. Introduction. In *Images of Deviance*, ed. S. Cohen. Harmondsworth: Penguin.

Cressey, P. G. 1932. *The Taxi-Dance Hall: A Sociological Study in Commercialized Recreation and City Life*. Chicago, IL: Chicago University Press.

De Sardan, J.P. Olivier. 1999. A Moral Economy of Corruption in Africa? *The Journal of Modern African Studies* 37 (1): 25–52.

De Sardan, J.P. Olivier. 2005. *Anthropology and Development. Understanding Contemporary Social Change*. London and New York: Zed Books.

Downes, D. 1966. *The Delinquent Solution: A Study in Subcultural Theory*. London: Routledge and Kegan Paul.

European Commission. 2014. Report from the Commission to the Council and the European Parliament. EU Anti-corruption Report. https://ec.europa.eu/home-affairs/sites/homeaffairs/files/elibrary/documents/policies/organized-crime-and-human-trafficking/corruption/docs/acr_2014_en.pdf

Eyal, G., I. Szelenyi, and E. Townlsey. 1998. *Making Capitalism Without Capitalists: Class Formation and Elite Struggles in Post-Communist Central Europe*. London and New York: Verso.

Garland, D. 2002. *The Culture of Control: Crime and Social Order in Contemporary Society*. Oxford: OUP.

Gupta, A. 1995. Blurred Boundaries: The Discourse of Corruption, the Culture of Politics, and the Imagined State. *American Ethnologist* 22 (2): 375–402.

Haraway, D. J. 1997. The Virtual Speculum in the New World Order. *Feminist Review* 55 (Consuming Cultures): 22–72.

Henry, S. 1978. *The Hidden Economy: The Context and Control of Borderline Crime*. Oxford: Martin Robertson.

Henig, D., and N. Makovicky. 2015. *Economies of Favour After Socialism*. Oxford: OUP.

Hobbs, D. 2013. *Lush Life. Constructing Organized Crime in the UK*. Oxford: Oxford University Press.

Hobbs, D., P. Hadfield, S. Lister, and S. Winlow. 2003. *Bouncers : Violence and Governance in the Night-Time Economy*. Oxford: Oxford University Press.

Humphrey, C., and R. Mandel. 2002. The Market in Everyday Life: Ethnographies of Postsocialism. In *Markets and Moralities*, ed. R. Mandel and C. Humphrey, 1–18. Oxford: Berg.

Klitgaard, R. 1988. *Controlling Corruption*. Berkeley: University of California Press.

Kornai, J. 1992. *The Socialist System: The Political Economy of Communism*. Oxford: Clarendon Press.

Ledeneva, A.V. 2006. *How Russia Really Works. The Informal Practices That Shaped Post-Soviet Politics and Business*. Ithaca and London: Cornell University Press.

Ledeneva, A. 2013b. *Can Russia Modernise? Sistema, Power Networks and Informal Governance*. Cambridge: Cambridge University Press.

———. 2013c. A Critique of the Global Corruption "Paradigm". In *Postcommunism from Within. Social Justice, Mobilization and Hegemony*, ed. Jan Kubik and Amy Linch, 297–332. New York and London: New York University Press.

Mars, G. 1994. *Cheats at Work: An Anthropology of Workplace Crime*. Aldershot: Dartmouth Publishing.

Matza, D. 1969. *Becoming Deviant*. Englewood Cliffs, NJ: Prentice Hall.

Mungiu-Pippidi, A. 2009. Romania: Outsmarting The EU's Smart Power. In *Democracy's Plight in the European Neighbourhood*. Brussels: Centre for European Policy Studies (CEPS).

Nordstrom, C. 2007. *Global Outlaws*. In *Crime, Money and Power in the Contemporary World*. Berkeley, Los Angeles and London: University of California Press.

Polsky, N. 1971. *Hustlers, Beats and Others*. Harmondsworth: Pelican.

Rose-Ackerman, S. 1999. *Corruption and Government. Causes, Consequences and Reform*. Cambridge: Cambridge University Press.

Ruggiero, V. 2013. *The Crimes of the Economy. A Criminological Analysis of Economic Thought*. New York: Routledge.

Sampson, S. 2010. The Anti-corruption Industry: From Movement to Institution. *Global Crime* 11 (2): 261–278.

The Economist. 2012. https://www.economist.com/blogs/easternapproaches/2012/06/eu-funds-absorption-romania

Thompson, G., J. Frances, R. Levacic, and Jeremy Mitchell, eds. 1991. *Markets, Hierarchies and Networks. The Coordination of Social Life*. London, Thousand Oaks, and New Dehli: Sage.

Torsello, D. 2012. The New Environmentalism? Civil Society and Corruption in the Enlarged EU. *Urban Anthropology*, ed. , G. Prato and I. Pardo. Surrey: Ashgate.

Van Maanen, J. 1995. *Representation in Ethnography*. London: Sage.

Verdery, K. 2004. The Obligations of Ownership: Restoring Rights to Land in Postsocialist Transylvania. In *Property in Question. Value Transformation in the Global Economy*, ed. K. Verdery and C. Humphrey, 139–159. Oxford: Berg.

Verdery, K., and C. Humphrey, eds. 2004. *Property in Question. Value Transformation in the Global Society*. Oxford: Berg.

Weber, M. 1968. *Economy and society*. Vol. 1. New York: Bedminster.

Wedel, J. 2003. Clans, Cliques and Captured States: Rethinking 'Transition' In Central and Eastern Europe and the Former Soviet Union. *Journal of International Development* 15: 427–440.

Yang, M. 1994. *Gifts, Favours and Banquets. The Art of Social Relations in China*. London: Cornell University Press.

CHAPTER 2

A Dance of the (Il)legal: Transnational Aid Flows, Entrepreneurship and Corruption

This chapter situates the process of accessing EU funding within a broad economic sociology framework by employing a mid-level instrument of analysis that explores three modes of coordination of social and economic life: markets, hierarchies and networks. It argues that EU funding is a hybrid space based on a plurality of coordinative mechanisms that aims to accommodate transnational regulations with vernacular practices. The chapter is divided into four sections. The first section discusses markets and hierarchies and emphasises the importance of networks in understanding the coordination of any social and economic process. The second section looks at the impact of law and regulation on the economic process, touching upon issues of transnational governance and development aid. The third section focuses on entrepreneurship and vernacular entrepreneurial culture by connecting insights from economic sociology and the sociology of work. Building on these links, the fourth section turns to analyse the blurred boundaries between legal, informal and illegal economic activities linking economic sociology with sociology of deviance and criminology.

Coordinating Economic and Social Life: Markets, Hierarchies and Networks

This section looks at *markets*, *hierarchies* and *networks*—which act as mapping devices that explain the organisation of contemporary social, economic and political life. This mid-level instrument of analysis explains not

R. Bratu, *Corruption, Informality and Entrepreneurship in Romania*, Political Corruption and Governance,
https://doi.org/10.1007/978-3-319-66667-9_2

only domestic arrangements but also international relationships between states and the impact of transnational regulations on domestic affairs and practices of doing business. The 'coordination of social life' means relating otherwise disparate activities (Thompson et al. 1991), making them compatible and efficient, ordering (Weber [1922] 1968) various agents and agencies. The market, some argue (Von Hayek 1989), is the best way to achieve coordination via its 'invisible hand' (Smith 1826) of exchange and price system supported by self-interested, individually motivated individuals. Against this view, others (Weber [1922] 1968) contend that such 'unconscious mechanisms' should be replaced by administrative means that exercise overt control through hierarchies. Promoters of the network approach (Granovetter 1974) criticise the previous positions because they neglect the informal mechanisms that govern the cross-cutting chains of relatively independent networks of social, political and economic relationships. Despite the fact that the economic sociology literature presents them as alternative ways to achieve coordination, the section argues that markets, hierarchies and networks complement each other in order to transgress their individual limits.

Markets

In the neoclassical version, markets bring together strangers in the act of exchange (Marshall 1936 in Thompson et al. 1991). This is a purely economic model of exchange where social or political goals are less important than economic goals. Polanyi (1954) argued that in the market, goods are commodities exchanged for profit according to the law of supply and demand that determine the price tag. In order to maximise their profit, decision-makers who are in possession of required information adapt their behaviour to the price. The markets are characterised by 'perfect competition' (large number of buyers and sellers with no direct control of the prices) and a Pareto type of equilibrium (for every person that is better off, another participant to the market must be worse off). By contrast, the neo-Austrian school (Krizner 1973) puts forward a dynamic understanding of the market as a process characterised by disequilibrium, emphasising its competitive nature. In this view, the situation of monopoly is not necessarily wrong as it results from past successful entrepreneurial initiatives fostered by dynamic competition. The imbalances created by price disequilibrium are considered transitory, soon to be regulated through the free market process of 'creative destruction' (Schumpeter 1942).

This debate introduces essential concerns that influence a key issue for this book: *profitability*. Prices and costs determine the profit of any economic activity, ensuring that an enterprise can reproduce itself financially. The supreme advantage of the price system allows for 'consumer sovereignty' which lies at the foundation of the market. Prices act as a signalling device that suits a decentralised decision-making environment, potentially harmonising any conflicts so that *all* could benefit. If the market allows for competition, the price is determined by the interaction of buyers and sellers, thus "the price is set *by* or in the market" (Thompson et al. 1991: 7). In a monopoly, the dominant agent sets the prices because "the monopoly *is* the market" (Thompson et al. 1991: 7). Between the two extremes there are a number of monopolistic or oligopolistic situations of competition in which large enough agents have some influence over market prices.

Profitability, however, is not only defined by an enterprise's pricing strategy but also by its investment strategies and its relationship with government agencies through grants, subsidies or government procurement contracts. An interesting combination of markets and hierarchies are the 'quasi-markets' in which a market model is applied *within* an organisation. For example, in the UK, the NHS has been transformed in the past decades in order to coordinate better its internal activity and increase its productivity and service quality, maintaining a low price for a publicly provided service (Mullen 1990). The market model has been extremely appealing for designing *new markets*, like the EU market. Remnants of the neoclassical paradigm can be traced in the design of EU funding.

Sociological and anthropological accounts have pleaded for a more nuanced approach to markets arguing that economic activity is embedded in social activity (Granovetter 1973; Hart 2000; Thrift 2001). Moreover, each market and marketplace has its specific cultural logics, processes and representations which are sustained and reinforced by social relations (Granovetter 1973). Baker (1981) advocated for a middle range theory of markets-as-networks, showing that markets were not homogeneous beings, but socially constructed. "Since 'market' is typically assumed, not studied, economic analysis implicitly characterises the 'market' as a 'featureless plane'" (1981: 211 in Smelser and Swedberg 2005: 247). White's model (1970) contrasts markets with networks testing the concept of 'vacancy chains'—when a person gets a new job, a vacancy is created which has to be filled, thus creating a new vacancy and so on. The most successful application of network analysis so far is Granovetter's (1973) study of the social mechanisms through which people find employment. He wanted to know if the economists were right in assuming that the labour market allowed for free circulation of information that reached all participants. His results showed that 56% of the people got their job through contacts, 18.8% through direct application and 18% through formal means. Granovetter concluded that "perfect labour markets exist only in textbooks" (1974: 25) and the economists' idea of a rational job search is not validated empirically. An interesting add to the literature is Brian Uzzi's contribution (1997) which draws on ethnographic material collected from 20 firms in the apparel industry in New York. He found that firms tended to distinguish between 'market relationships'—the embodiment of standard economic analysis—and 'close or special relationships', which reflect Granovetter's embeddedness. He concluded that successful businesses strived to achieve a balance in their interactions between market and embedded ties reaching for an 'integrated network'. This strand of literature is a good starting point for discussing the way in which EU funding, as an economic activity, is shaped by context.

Hierarchies

Markets usually stand in stark opposition to hierarchies. According to Weber ([1922] 1968), bureaucratic rationality is a modern way of introducing order into the world through systematic administrative control characterised by specialisation of functions, hierarchical authority and progressive breaking down of complex tasks in order to ensure coordination according to a fixed set of rules. Administrating an internal hierarchy involves particular practices made available through edicts, orders, statutes and specialised techniques designed to 'govern' which means exercise power and authority.

The literature regarding public administration and bureaucratic spirit (Selznick 1949; Du Gay 2000; Gouldner 1964) shows that bureaucracies are inefficient due to inflexible decision-taking mechanisms (Merton 1957), civil servants' lack of initiative and goal displacement (Gouldner 1964) or insensitivity to public opinion (Du Gay 2000). Survival in this environment equates with internalising its norms, ethics and aspirations through self-adaptation (Benveniste 1977). The main advantage of the hierarchical modes of coordination (Jaques 1990) is consistency of decision-taking achieved through the implementation of a clear set of rules which reduces discretion, increases accountability and allows for large-scale tasks to be coordinated. Douglas North (1981) added to this analysis by suggesting that institutions can be defined as rules on which organisations play. This strand of literature that analyses internal hierarchies is useful for uncovering the internal workings of EU funding bureaucratic system in Romania.

External hierarchical coordination refers to the relationships between different organisational units (Thompson et al. 1991), which may involve nation states, the EU or transnational corporations. At a macro level, central planning common to Soviet Union and Eastern Europe from late 1940s until the early 1990s was a 'consciously' managed, rigidly organised coordination mechanism based on a predetermined assessment of population needs and demands which shaped production and excluded market competition. The post-war Western economic development took the form of 'indicative planning' (Sartori 1987) which enhanced a dialogue between the state and the private sector in order to ensure the growth of the economy as whole, without altering the ownership structure. Another form of macroeconomic coordination is 'semi-hierarchical planning' which essentially requires the government to be the major decision factor and influence the private sector through fiscal and monetary policies (Sartori 1987). All these forms of external hierarchical control are rather attempts to regulate the market systems and for this reason important additions to the conceptualisation of EU funding.

Governments also have a series of techniques for ensuring coordination at lower levels—for example, nationalisation, regulation and subsidisation. When previously nationalised industries that have been dismantled and privatised turned into private monopolies, governments put forward new sets of regulatory devices to control the pricing and protect the consumers from potentially undesirable effects of the market changes. Alternatively, previously unregulated arenas of economic activity have been regulated in order to protect consumers. Through subsidisation, governments direct economic resources into areas that are beneficial to society but lack investments from the private sector, thus creating a form of 'state capitalism' (Bremmer 2010; Aligica and Tarko 2012). These two mechanisms are essential for understanding the process of accessing EU funding. As detailed in Chap. 5, the design of EU funding is highly regulated, while being presented as a subsidy—thus making this area a new, hybrid form of intervention designed by transnational regulatory bodies and implemented by national governments. When EU-funded projects are used to enhance the political legitimacy of the local or national governments and increase their financial capital, one can talk about 'capitalism pe banii UE' ('transnational/EU funded capitalism'—Chap. 8).

The dichotomous view of markets and hierarchies (Coase 1937; Williamson 1975) emphasises the sharp boundaries of firms seen as "islands of planned coordination in a sea of market relations" (Richardson 1972 in Powell 1990: 266). In response to the empirical evidence that documents patterns of change rejecting the vertical integration thesis *and* the arm length's market contracting, scholars introduced the idea of continuum market transactions (Thompson et al. 1991). This view situates market transactions at one pole and highly centralised organisations at the other, with a range of hybrid forms in between, thus implying that the market would be the basic form of exchange from which all other methods would evolve. Anthropological and historical evidence contradicts this assumption. Finley (1973) shows that the market, in a modern sense, did not exist in the classical world and that economic activities emerged out of a dense web of political, religious and social interactions and affiliations. Thompson (1971) described the 'moral economy' as a system of symbolic expectations surrounding eighteenth-century British marketplaces, while Agnew (1986) documented the highly hierarchical, symbolic and personal nature of the medieval England marketplaces. The modern understanding of the market, as a timeless and boundless arena of buying and selling, thus separated from the marketplace, only penetrated the British-educated class around the end of the eighteenth century (Agnew 1986). Similarly, hierarchies are not the endpoint of economic evolution, as proven by Braudel (1982) and Polanyi (1954). The history of modern commerce is recounted through family businesses, cartels, guilds and essentially all enterprises with highly permeable boundaries.

Networks

A third mode of coordination of social and economic activity is represented by the network, interpreted here as a flexible entity, a source and resource for information and capital (Callon 1998). Networks are highly positive social arrangements that lubricate the coordination of social life through social relations based on cooperation, loyalty and trust (Lorenz 1989). A new trend derived from the uncertainty associated with technological developments and economic conditions of modern markets has been the disintegration of big corporations that tend to concentrate on core activities and outsource the rest. Divesting peripheral activities created new networks of small- and medium-sized enterprises (SMEs) that act as subcontractors for the main business (Lorenz 1989). These new developments enhance network-based coordination mechanisms of economic activity because the new small enterprises do not return to a market model based on price competition, while the relationship with the big corporation is also not conducted on the basis of hierarchical administrative relations.

Networks are looked upon with suspicion because they are associated with informality and illegality, which impact negatively on formal accountability mechanisms. Corruption, for example, can be one of the most potent mechanisms of coordination in social and economic life (Mandel and Humphrey 2002; Ledeneva 1998; Wedel 1986; Yang 1994). As fluid, highly adaptable entities, strengthened by kinship, ethnicity, social proximity and economic affairs, networks are most suitable for illegal partnerships (Hobbs 2013). Hierarchies are discarded in favour of fluid networked models which "make it harder for law enforcement to infiltrate, disrupt and dismantle. Many organised crime groups opportunistically form around specific short term schemes and may outsource portions of their operations rather than keeping it all in house" (Bjelopera and Finklea 2010: 1 in Ruggiero 2013). This favours the establishment of "dirty economies and fuzzy business careers" (Ruggiero 2013) where licit and illicit operations are simultaneously carried out.

Despite its negative connotations, the network model has come to shape the modern understanding of coordination mechanisms. Social and political scientists (Alvesson and Thompson 2005; Reed 2005) talk about post-bureaucratic organisations which are described as 'networked' (Castells 1996), 'entrepreneurial' or 'market-led', manipulated by corporate cultures featuring organic or indirect forms of control. The post-modern factory (Drucker 1992) has changed from a traditional battleship to a flotilla "a set of modules centred around stages in the production process or closely related operations." The network enterprise (Castells 1996) uses flexible rather than mass production through horizontal integration with other corporations. Cascio (2000) describes virtual organisations as post-bureaucratic forms of coordination in which people are not physically located in the same place but cooperate with management and co-workers in a virtual workplace. However, these new forms of post-bureaucratic arrangements do not announce the premature death of bureaucratic organisation (Alvesson and Thompson 2005)—rather they emphasise that contemporary changes are hybrid forms of traditional hierarchical organisational principles, which rejuvenate rather than supersede bureaucracy (Courpasson and Clegg 2006). This argument applies to public management. For example, Farrell and Morris (2003) show that increased 'marketisation' of public services leads to the emergence of a 'bureaucratised market form' or 'neo-bureaucracy' which is a simultaneously centralised and decentralised hierarchical forms of coordination.

Hybrid Orders of Coordination

How can the three models explain complex patterns of coordination and interaction of social and economic life? Table 2.1 (Powell 1990) summarises some of the key differences between the three models by looking at seven categories.

Table 2.1 Stylised comparison of forms of economic organisation

Key features	*Forms*		
	Markets	*Hierarchies*	*Networks*
Normative basis	Contract-property rights	Employment relationship	Complementary strengths
Means of communication	Prices	Routines	Relational
Methods of conflict resolution	Haggling—resort to courts for enforcement	Administrative fiat—supervision	Norm of reciprocity—reputational concerns
Degree of flexibility	High	Low	Medium
Amount of commitment among parties	Low	Medium to high	Medium to high
Tone or climate	Precision and/or suspicion	Formal, bureaucratic	Open-ended, mutual benefits
Actor preferences or choices	Independent	Dependent	Interdependent
Mixing of forms	Repeat transactions (Geertz 1978)	Informal organisation (Dalton 1959)	Status hierarchies
	Contracts as hierarchical documents (Stinchcombe 1985)	Market-like features: profit centres, transfer pricing (Eccles 1985)	Multiple partners
			Formal rules

Source: Powell (1990) in Thompson et al. (1991)

By comparing and contrasting *markets*, *hierarchies* and *networks*, Powell (1990) shows that the process of exchange is shaped differently in each model: in market transactions, the goods are clearly specified in agreements based not on mutual trust, but on legal contracts; in hierarchies, it is shaped by concerns for career mobility, a history of previous interactions and detailed information about the other party; and network-based exchanges entail indefinite transactions within the general pattern of interactions, using normative rather than legal mechanisms of enforcement, creating indebtedness and reliance rather than immediate one-off interactions. In markets, communication is conducted through prices, in hierarchies through regulations and in networks through relations. Kaneko and Imai (1987 in Powell 1990) show that information obtained from network contacts is 'thicker' than obtained on the market and 'freer' than obtained from bureaucracy, which makes networks in particular adapt for exchanges that are not easily measured and priced (e.g., know-how, technological abilities, spirit of experimentation).

Central to the issue of network-exchange is the concept of reciprocity, typically discussed by the sociological and anthropological literature in the form of indebtedness. Mauss (1925) showed that the obligations to give, return and receive did not only involve rational calculations, they carried cultural understandings of the implications involved in the act of exchange. Sahlins (1972) regarded indebtedness as a measure of imbalance that sustained social partnerships and interactions, by compelling further meetings, thus connecting the parties in the future. In the game theoretical literature, reciprocity was proven to enhance individual interests through cooperation (Axelrod 1984; Keohane 1986). In the neoclassical understanding, markets ensure a high degree of flexibility, through the anonymity of encounters (Callon 1998), while bureaucratic arrangements and network-based interactions are restricted by administrative or social norms. Networks essentially create interdependencies through embeddedness with social and cultural settings, while markets tend to disembed actors.

Powell's typology is most useful for understanding the differences between *markets*, *hierarchies* and *networks*, as *ideal types* (Weber [1992] 1968), but it hardly captures the complexity of contemporary social and economic arrangements. Admittedly, in the last row of his table, he acknowledges the existence of mixed forms of coordination, citing a range of anthropological and sociological studies that essentially document the messiness of social arrangements. This book starts exactly where Powell ends, building on the observation that modern life is not easily convertible

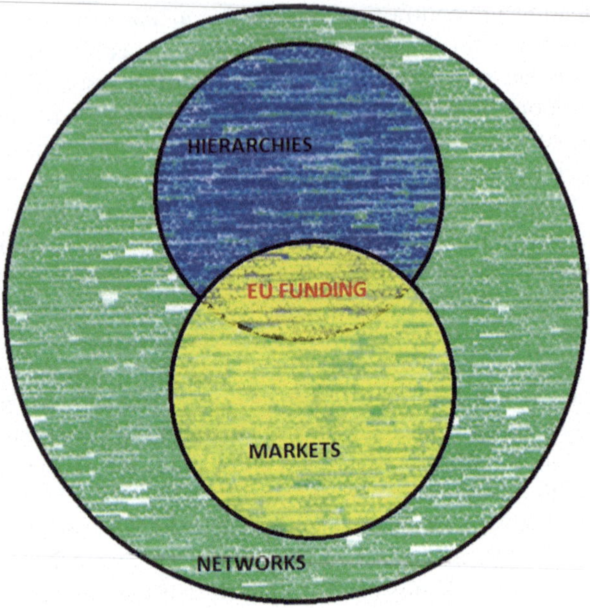

Fig. 2.1 The coordination of economic and social life

into categories and typologies due to its chaotic and unpredictable nature (Hobbs 2013; Ruggiero 1996). Instead of assuming *stability* as Powell did, I employ *change* as the dependent variable, thus discussing EU funding as space that allows for a plurality of coordinative mechanisms rather than their mutual exclusivity. Broadly, the network provides the overarching model of analysis due to its flexible nature, as shown in Fig. 2.1.

Governing Through Economics: The Role of Transnational Governance in Coordinating Social and Economic Life

The role of the state for the economy has been conceptualised within economic sociology by Neil Fligstein (1996, 2001) through 'Markets as Politics' and 'Architecture of Markets'. "I view the formation of markets as part of state-formation" (1996: 657) he argued, showing that the state constructs markets through property rights, governance structures and rules of exchange. In relationship to the role of conflict in the market,

Fligstein argued that modern states would regulate competition in order to secure the *stability* of markets. Once in place, these structures would influence the future economic development of the country, ensuring that governance rules stabilise the market for the largest firms. The state can not only create the market in structural terms as Fligstein (1996, 2001) remarked, but also in very direct ways. Hidden exchanges between entrepreneurs and politicians presented as *lobbying* are the rule of thumb in many advanced democracies. Caldwell (2005) showed entrepreneurs 'invest' in political campaigns and are later rewarded by contracts, purchasing commitments or seats in the House of Lords. Syal and Ball (2011) discovered that nearly one in five staff pass-holders in the House of Lords is involved in lobbying. These arguments found support in the work of Bourdieu (1997)—'Principles of Economic Anthropology'—who conceptualised market as part of a field which in turn influenced its dynamics. His starting point was that economic life resulted from the encounter between actors with special dispositions (*habitus*) in the economic field. The structure of the field consisted of power relations maintained through various forms of capital (e.g., financial, technological, social and symbolic). The economic field was dominated by struggles but also influenced by what happened outside the field, especially at the state level.

States influence the workings of human activity in the economic and social arenas through laws and regulations. Sociological inquiries in this area have tried to establish to what extent legality constitutes "actual determinants of human behaviour" (Weber [1922] 1968: 312). From this perspective, law is connected to the notion of *order*, which in turn is essential for a society and the well-functioning of any economic activity. "An order will be called…*law* if it is externally guaranteed by the probability that physical or psychological coercion will be applied by a *staff* of people in order to bring about compliance or avenge violation" (Weber [1922] 1968: 34). Weber takes his argument further in the theory of legitimation showing that duration in time is crucial for the concept of order and that political order is more likely to last if people find it legitimate. However, the "legal order of legal theory has nothing directly to do with the world of real economic conduct, since both exist on different levels. One exists in the realm of the *ought*, while the other deals with the world of the *is*" (Weber [1922] 1968: 312).

In this way, *the analysis of economic initiative in relationship to law intersects with the sociology of deviance* (Merton 1938; Hobbs 2013). The strain theory (Merton 1938) argues that anomie and deviance are the result of a disjuncture between cultural goals and institutionalised means to achieve them. In order to adapt, people face five options: innovation, conformity, ritualism, retreatism and rebellion. Innovation, in the economic initiative as well as in deviance, starts with accepting the cultural goals irrespective of the drastic or illegitimate means that it might require. In the face of difficulties and uncertainties prompted by the economic environment, actors experiment by developing alternative, sometimes illicit strategies that through habituation and custom come to be morally approved by their close environment (Roth 1978). Gouldner (1964) talked about a form of institutionalised deviance through the concept of 'mock bureaucracies' in which the governing rules are generally known and ignored. In these settings deviation from the rules is status enhancing. The tensions between 'normative order' and 'factual order' (Parsons 1982) can lead to operative crime (Ruggiero 2007), but this is not necessarily bad, as it can promote the change of official rules that have been proven unsatisfactory. Dalton's study of organisations (1959) describes a very fluid environment based on shifting alliances, pursuit of narrow interests, a climate of struggle and antagonism for the regular organisational activities. The cliques and conflicts that surround the organisational life are hidden from outsiders, "scrupulously and skilfully camouflaged so that the resulting policies appear to be in harmony with the official ideology of the organisation" (Mouzelis 1967: 59). Instrumental use of policies is used to legitimise the organisation in the eyes of the surroundings through "legalisation of the workplace" (Edelman 1992) while accommodating managerial interests.

An interesting development of this line of argument is the case of whistle-blowing, or what happens when an employee decides to expose the employer for unlawful/unethical behaviour (Alford 2001; Rothschild and Miethe 1999). Loyalty to the organisation and camouflaging conflicts could be turned around against the whistle-blower. For example, most former communist countries have institutionalised whistle-blowing as part of their international commitments to 'fight corruption' and incentivised it through financial rewards. In practice, money is rarely cashed, because the prize is conditioned by a definite conviction for corruption (Bratu 2013). By creating the whistle-blowing institution, states promote the anti-corruption legislation and "mediate the impact of law on society by helping to construct the meaning of compliance" (Edelman 1992: 1557).

Transnational Regulations: Development Aid and Crime Narratives

So far, the discussion has focused on the role of law and state and their impact on the economic process. However, EU funding as an economic process is not only a product of the national and micro-level interactions but also the result of transnational governance. Designed in Brussels through direct negotiations with individual states, taking into account international interests and corporate assessments, EU funding fuses together different traditions of civil service under the notion of 'supranationalism' (Tsebelis and Garrett 2001). This section looks at new technologies of governing promoted in relationship to development, Europeanisation and international aid. It shows that in governing aid flows, the theme of development through foreign funding has metamorphosed into the theme of crime through corruption and violence narratives.

The current debates about foreign aid essentially boil down to one question: has the developed world provided enough financial support to help others out of poverty? The answer is crucially linked to the role that corruption and violence play in the impoverishment of nations. Sachs (2005), as a tireless campaigner for more international development assistance, argues that corruption and violence are symptoms of poverty that could be cured through financial aid, thus ensuring the countries in need to jump-start economic growth. "The wealth of the rich world...makes the end of poverty a realistic probability by the year 2025" (Sachs 2005 in Fisman and Miguel 2010: 11). Easterly (2006) holds the opposing view: he contends that advanced states are spending too much on foreign aid already. The trillions of US dollars spent so far have not helped the poor, but have been spent on grandiose, centrally planned projects (e.g., hydroelectric dams, four-lane highways) in countries that lacked the capacity to oversee them. The countries receiving aid should be well governed (e.g., strong institutions, powerful civil society, free media) *and* supervised by other agencies in order to ensure that the money reaches the poor. Meanwhile, Easterly argued, aid initiatives should focus on small-scale entrepreneurs, who are the capable 'Searchers', to find solutions for local problems (Easterly 2006).

Recently, international development has widened its scope to incorporate not only quantified development (poverty reduction) but also donors' ideas about social and cultural intervention (Easterly 2006). The modern concept of good governance includes political pluralism and prudent fiscal policies as *sine qua non* pre-requirements of poverty reduction. Thus, foreign aid is conditioned by institutional redesign at central and local levels, driving the implementation of new technologies of government as part of a 'modernisation' process. In this context, the anti-corruption agenda plays a major role, aiming at restraining bureaucratic discretion and strengthening external oversight, through a credible, apolitical monitoring system (Rose-Ackerman 1999; Klitgaard 1988). The new agencies created (e.g., auditing agencies and integrity organisations) as part of an anti-corruption movement are embedded in a broader system of checks and balances where effectiveness depends on the separation of political powers. Thus the *dynamics of corruption rhetoric and anti-corruption practices are part of a wider political economic context whose relevance is critical for the understanding of EU funding.*

Anthropology and sociology of social change see development aid as a vehicle of change (Hart 2000; Blundo and De Sardan 2006) despite the lack of congruence between development policies and their effects (de Sardan 2005). These accounts offer grass-roots knowledge about the impact and internalisation of development agents and institutions and point to their (in)effectiveness. In discussing the (un)anticipated consequences of the 'development and growth' process, anthropologists analyse multicultural encounters between developers and developees, deployed in the language of sociocultural logics, brokerage and 'popular technical knowledge' (Hart 2000; de Sardan 2005; Blundo and De Sardan 2006). Even though the bulk of the research relies on African studies, the implications go beyond this continent.

A critical stand suggests that development models are doomed to fail given the gap between the nature of the intervention (which is usually disconnected from the history and inadequate to local social needs) and everyday realities (Escobar 1991; Scott 1998). In this sense, development models are a form of colonialism with institutional and ideological effects that impose social hierarchies (developer over the 'to be developed') and rankings of knowledge (scientific over indigenous). Ethnographic literature (Harrison 2010) shows that corruption is potentially the outcome of development in postcolonial Africa leading to the spread of an 'assistentialist' culture (de Sardan 1999; Blundo and De Sardan 2006). High levels of perception are not associated with real practices of corruption (Parry 2000), but excessive concern for this topic becomes a pessimistic reflection of development policies. Eastern Europe displays similar trends (Torsello

2012), but here anti-corruption organisations have flourished through foreign aid and funding, leading to an anti-corruption industry (Bryane and Bowser 2009). Ethnographic work focusing on India shows how excessive anti-corruption rhetoric can mask real needs for local and national interventions, including non-governmental organisation (NGO) activities to counter 'corruption flagella' (Tanzi 1998). It is no accident that several political careers were made and broken by the use of (anti)corruption narratives (Bratu 2013; Torsello 2012).

A development project always claims to be coherent and makes use of specific rhetoric devices to portray it. Coherence can be found at four different levels: compliance with the technical model, compatibility with the national policy, conformity with the donors' norms and internal coherence of the project (de Sardan 2005). The 'language of the project' is a constant work of translation which is within the job description of skilled consultants (who have to transpose policy goals into practical interventions and vice versa).

In relation to the practices of mediation and intermediation, development literature brings forward the concept of corruption. In Africa, corruption was discussed in terms of the patron-client model and network analysis (Boissevain 1974; Medard 1986; Bayart 1993; Medard 1997) and was traditionally entangled in the neo-patrimonialism and 'the politics of the belly' (Medard 1997). Given the blurred boundaries between public and private spheres and the positive value attached to this practice, scholars emphasised public office as a source of constant legal and illegal income (Hart 2000). Postcolonial and post-communist societies present 'striking similarities' (Sajo 1998) in the sense that in both systems corruption is portrayed as a structural problem deriving from clientelist practices which are not incidental and isolated happenings, but a social phenomenon (Mungiu-Pippidi 2013). Given the importance attached to corruption by transnational organisations and locals, the next section gives a wide theoretical framework for understanding corruption.

Through the Lens of Corruption

The definition of corruption reflects its ambiguity, the lack of consensus among academics, policy-makers, civil society, control and enforcement actors. Heidenheimer (1970) argued that three key concepts organise the debates: public opinion, public interest or public office. Public opinion-centred definitions focus on the public's understanding of corruption (Scott 1972), thus turning public opinion into both the source and the judge of corruption. Public interest definitions suggest that through corruption, the public's interest is violated in favour of a small group (Friedrich 1972). Criticised for their vagueness (Rose-Ackerman 1999), the concepts of public interest and public opinion were found unsuitable for policy purposes, rendering corruption 'unmeasurable'. Definitions centred on public office (Myrdal 1968; Nye 1967) focus on the distinction between public and private and the misuse of public power. This view was quickly adopted by international organisations, that is, the World Bank (WB), International Monetary Fund (IMF) and Transparency International (TI), who define corruption as the abuse of public power for private gain. This view was widely legitimised by TI through its Corruption Perception Index (Galtung 1998). The idea that corruption could be measured—countries could be ranked according to an index—was so appealing to the international community that this index became a powerful advocacy tool, despite its methodological shortcomings. In this way, the conventional paradigm of corruption started to dominate international debates at the end of the 1990s on the basis of three main assumptions: corruption could be defined, measured and changed (Ledeneva 2013a). Recent scholarship (Bryane and Bowser 2009; Krastev 2004; Ledeneva 2013a) describes a massive failure of the conventional paradigm showing that:

1. The present definition of corruption assumes a clear distinction between public and private spheres which is difficult to document empirically (Ledeneva 1998; Torsello 2012);
2. Contemporary measurement tools account only for the perception of corruption, providing little evidence about experiences;
3. Anti-corruption policies implemented on the basis of current research methodologies have either failed, or the present research instruments are incapable of capturing the nature and scope of reforms.

Sociological and anthropological studies (Blundo and De Sardan 2006; Haller and Shore 2005; Ledeneva 1998; de Sardan 1999, 2005; Wedel 1986; Yang 1994) have traditionally focused on the deep structure of corruption, emphasising that it is a mechanism that conceptualises the state in everyday encounters by humanising bureaucracy (Gupta 1995). They show that cultural specificity is essential for understanding the sociocultural logics of action, especially gift giving and the workings of solidarity networks

(Yang 1994; Ledeneva 1998; de Sardan 1999). Research on gift exchange (Malinowski 1922; Mauss 1925; Bourdieu 1977; Yang 1994; Ledeneva 1998) has shown that the practice of gift giving is a compulsory pattern of response in certain contexts, both an art and a necessity of everyday activities, encompassing both gift and favour exchanges (Wedel 1986; Yang 1994; Ledeneva 1998). The logic of solidarity networks reflects a web of mutual assistance entangled in social relations and obligations. The role of the networks is to provide support and act as a safety nets or buffers between the individual and the state, offering information and translation of bureaucratic practices (Wedel 1986). An expanded network is also a sign of increased social capital (Wedel 1986). The existence of networks and favours exchange is acknowledged in language—*guanxi*, China (Yang 1994), and *blat*, Russia (Ledeneva 1998), but any exchange is disguised in the 'language of help', thus making these transactions morally superior to corruption. However it is a too fine line between *blat* and corruption, impossible to detect empirically and embedded in the narratives of justification. In the context of transition to the market economy, it is argued that these traditional practices have been transformed in corruption, and this transformation is read as a moral decay of the society (Ledeneva 1998).

Recent contributions from the anthropology of corruption document a departure from the Weberian model of bureaucracy (Anders and Nuijten 2009; Pardo and Prato 2004). In *Corruption and the Secret of Law*, Anders and Nuijten (2009) stress that in order to understand corruption researchers should move away from the Western dichotomist view of public-private/state-society that leaves no room for positive ethnographic contributions. Similarly, Pardo and Prato (2004) argues that the legal conceptualisation of corruption is marked by inherent ambiguities due to cultural particularism. He recommends analysing morality as a space in which ideas of legality and illegality collide with universal values. Alternatively, he suggests focusing on the role of state who "through institutional blindness can allow the interests of the elites" (Pardo and Prato 2004: 6). In this case, the state is an active agent rendering more opaque the borders of legality, exploited by power elites who, through law, give significance to and legitimise corruption. A key anthropological finding is the discursive power of corruption. Haller and Shore (2005) focused on practices that make corruption a semantic of governance, thus suggesting that it is a common way to make sense of politics. Torsello (2012) described how environmental movements used corruption talk (allegations or facts) to frame their protests and communicate with the wider public. This strategy builds on the generalised public talk sustained by media reports and locals' high levels of perceived corruption.

Such an approach turns the gaze to a classical sociological concept—the *definition of the situation*, which in this case is conducted through discursive means. W.I. Thomas (1967) stated that a social situation *is* what the participants define it to be. In other words, reality is a matter of definition. Social situations are not only defined in the present but also shaped by past experiences. The past can be made malleable through biographical reinterpretation and dialogue, as in the communist countries that continually rewrote their history books to create a heroic past (Zajda 2003). Through language, new meanings are assigned to old facts, which in turn become 'institutions' (Berger and Luckmann 1966), thus gaining the social recognition of 'permanent' solutions to 'permanent' problems.

This constructionist view further developed into a full theory by Berger and Luckmann (1966) has been instrumentally employed to shed light on contemporary anxieties typically portrayed using vocabularies of crime (e.g., mugging [Hall et al. [1978]/2013). In discussing organised crime, Hobbs (2013) argues that this is a socially constructed phenomenon, "exported [from North America] like a criminal justice version of Starbucks" (2013: 12), while its perception is highly influenced by a particular understanding of globalisation linked with "the expansion of illegal economic activities and its cosmopolitan associations" (2013: 12). Hobbs goes further to show that contemporary understandings of organised crime are based on stereotypes, recollections and reinterpretations of the past. This book employs a critical approach view of corruption defining it as a rebranding mechanism—it creates new labels for vernacular ways of doing things, changing the meanings associated with contemporary entrepreneurial practices or reporting the present in a language compatible with global anxieties.

Entrepreneurship as Work

Entrepreneurship is a key concept in understanding what drives *change* in the modern economy (Krizner 1997; Schumpeter 1942). Coined by Schumpeter (1942), the concept of entrepreneur was subsequently invested with different meanings according to disciplinary needs. Political scientists (Schneider and Teske 1992) use it to denote an individual who changes the direction of politics; anthropologists (Wong 1998) working on migration describe entrepreneurship as a response to blocked opportunities; criminologists (Ruggiero 1996) employ it to explain the particular dispositions that take people into criminality; and sociologists (Hobbs 2013) uncover it as a key characteristic of the modern urban environment linked to consumerism and hedonism. From a network analysis perspective (Burt 1992), entrepreneurship involves linking together various points from different networks that are in need of each other. The conventional sociological view refers to entrepreneurs as individuals who take the risk to found new organisations "which occurs as a context-dependent, social and economic process" (Thornton 1999: 20).

For Schumpeter (1942) entrepreneurship was the engine of economic growth as it was based on a new combination of existing materials and forces resulting in introducing new goods and production methods, opening new markets and finding new sources of raw materials. Investing entrepreneurs with almost superpowers of charisma and leadership, he argued that entrepreneurship must be placed in its social and historical context, showing that "no one is an entrepreneur forever, only when he or she is actually doing the innovative activity" (Schumpeter 1942 in Swedberg 2000: 18). The innovative capacity is the key element that distinguishes between entrepreneurs and other actors more inclined to follow tradition, because it "incessantly revolutionizes the economic structure from *within*, incessantly destroying the old one, incessantly creating a new one. This process of 'creative destruction' is the essential fact about capitalism" (Schumpeter 1942: 83). Disruptions generated by creative destruction are exploited by individuals well equipped to notice the emerging opportunities (Krizner 1997; Shane and Venkataraman 2000).

As opposed to Schumpeter, the neo-Austrian school describes entrepreneurs as constant searchers for low buys and high sells who establish equilibrium in the society through arbitrage (Krizner 1997). Baumol (1993) argued that depending on the social structure and context, entrepreneurship can be destructive as well as constructive. If Weber's ([1930] 1976) entrepreneurs were innovative but also self-restrained, in Schumpeter's view innovation and deviance go hand in hand in the economic process. As Ruggiero (1996) noticed, this view of entrepreneurship need not be applied only to law-abiding individuals linking Merton's theory of deviance (1957) to Schumpeterian concepts underpinning innovation. Deviants *ab initio* because of the very innovative practices employed through deviations from the norm, entrepreneurs force or bend the societal rules pushing the boundaries of acceptable behaviour.

In doing so, they take risks—another key concept in the entrepreneurship theory—of loss due to the unpredictability of the environment. Risk and uncertainty define their social role of promoting work and the circulation of goods, which becomes functional for the entire society (Ruggiero 1996). The risks of the enterprise justify the unorthodox practices and redeem actors in the eyes of the community. If in Schumpeter's view, risk and uncertainty formed the basic conditions of individual entrepreneurial affairs, contemporary scholarship redefines risk as a potential social loss (Ruggiero 1996).

Sociological concern with entrepreneurship can be linked with three broad themes (Aldrich 2005): first, entrepreneurs both reproduce and challenge the existing social order by constructing organisations that are embedded in the social and cultural environments reflecting societal conditions under particular historical circumstances (Stinchcombe 1965); second, entrepreneurship ensures the reproduction of the existing population through incremental additions to the organisational landscape (Carroll and Hannan 2000) and generates new populations by carving out niches for new organisations (Aldrich and Fiol 1994); and third, entrepreneurship impacts on the levels of stratifications and inequality by generating high levels of employment volatility through job creation and destruction. For example, between 1992 and 1996, in the USA, 11.2 million net new jobs were created of which 70% were by new organisations (Birch 1997).

The literature distinguishes between several types of entrepreneurs, but of particular sociological interest in the past decade and also for this book have been start-ups (Alrdirch 1999; Kim and Alrdirch 2005). The start-ups capture the chaotic and disordered flavour of the business-founding process or what Stinchcombe (1965) referred to as *the liability of newness. Nascent entrepreneurs* are individuals who initiate serious activities likely to culminate in a start-up or are giving 'serious thought to a new business' (Reynolds and White 1997) while engaged in at least one possible entrepreneurial activity (e.g., writing a business plan, looking for facilities and acquiring know-how). Research on life course and entrepreneurship (Boeker 1988; Freeman 1983; Romanelli 1989) shows that first founding attempts are made in their late 30s or early 40s, as by then individuals would have accumulated enough work experience, financial resources (even though this variable does not seem to deter people) and the capacity to capitalise on knowledge and contacts gained in previous jobs (Becker 1993). Existing social networks provide the new entrepreneur with ideas about opportunities and sources of funding (Burton et al. 2002). In some cases, new owners can establish themselves in the same line of business, serving the same customers that they previously had while employed (Cooper 1986; Johannisson 1988). In other cases, the practices, identities and vocabularies promoted by an occupational subculture can be transferred to other settings (Van Maanen and Barley 1984) as in the case of former police officers who find employment in security agencies. Nascent entrepreneurs can capitalise on their ethnic belongings and social position as migrants, thus becoming *transnational entrepreneurs* (Portes et al. 2002). The traditional niche of ethnic migrants has been small shopkeeping, but recent research (Saxenian 2000) pointed out that highly skilled Chinese and Indian engineers from Silicon Valley have built transnational social and economic networks in their original countries. Actors with an interest in "particular institutional arrangements and ... leverage resources to create new institutions or to transform existing ones" (Maguire et al. 2004: 657) are denoted by the concept of *institutional entrepreneurs*. DiMaggio (1988: 14) argued that "new institutions arise when organised actors with sufficient resources see in them an opportunity to realise interests that they value highly," thus creating a "whole new system of meaning that ties the functioning of disparate sets of institutions together" (Garud et al. 2002: 196).

In order to build up new business ventures, entrepreneurs rely on various forms of capital (Bourdieu 1997). Contrary to any expectations, *financial capital* is not a *sine qua non* requirement for entrepreneurs. In Germany, higher capitalisation was required presumably due to tighter regulations (Kim and Aldrich 2005). Formal sources of financial capital encompass private funding and bank loans. Generally, banks are reluctant to lend money to start-ups due to their loss history. By categorising new businesses as 'high risk', bankers demand higher interests while conducting extensive background checks on the founders and thorough assessments of financial viability. Most entrepreneurs find such practices oppressive (De Meza and Southey 1996) and thus tend to rely on informal sources of capital. Unsure of how the market would react, they choose to start small, avoid borrowing and rely on their own savings and personal assets (Aldrich 2005). For nascent entrepreneurs who are not already in advantageous positions, high-status brokers, with more social or financial resources, power, or prestige, can facilitate access to opportunities (Aldrich 2005).

Cultural capital (Bourdieu 1997) is directly linked to entrepreneurs' capacity to secure cooperation, which in turn seems to be an essential feature for framing issues and communicating goals. Ruef et al. (2003) showed that half of new enterprises were set in partnerships, most likely in an attempt to share the risk and pool financial and social resources. Drawing outsiders into a project is based on entrepreneurial capacity to frame issues in a psychologically powerful manner (Gartner et al. 1992) which encourages other people to believe in their competence and trustworthiness. The rhetoric of 'charisma' from the classical literature (Schumpeter 1942) returns in the theoretical discussions of leadership—for example, Czarniawska-Joerges (1989: 7) talks about how leaders have a "capacity to confer a convincing interpretation of reality, an attractive vision of possible future, and a prescription of how to reach that vision." Cultural capital can be connected with *social capital* for skilful individuals, enhancing their reputation, which then becomes a form of *symbolic capital.*

Cultural capital is a key variable in explaining which entrepreneurs mobilise the resources needed, directing the argument into issues related to gender. Research has shown that women own disproportionately small shares of business and are less likely to become nascent entrepreneurs (Reynolds and White 1997). Women's enterprises tend to be small, concentrated in retails and service sectors (Baker et al. 1998). Historical explanations for this state of affairs invoke women's underrepresentation in ownership, their exclusion from the business discussion networks (Carter et al. 1996) and restricted access to government contacts and information (Lerner et al. 1997). If women are not likely to occupy key positions in the financial business sectors, they are unlikely to have equal opportunities with men in becoming entrepreneurs (Rytina and Morgan 1982). However, recent research has shown that women are on the verge of breaking the 'glass ceiling' in employment relations, despite their overrepresentation in junior jobs.

New Industries

While Schumpeter raises the possibility that entrepreneurs could use their resources to create entirely new industries, it was Stinchcombe (1965) who offered a detailed sociological study of entrepreneurship in this area. He observes that "organisational forms and types have a history" (Stinchcombe 1965: 153) being influenced by the social and historical context. The emergence of new organisational forms depends on three factors, he argues: technological innovation and social structural support for new developments, entrepreneurs' access to power and wealth and the changing structure of labour markets. Thus, in establishing new industries' workforce characteristics (e.g., level of skill and literacy), market forces (e.g., barriers to entry, density in a particular sector) and legal constraints (whether public or private/corporate) shape entrepreneurial outcomes (Suchman et al. 2001).

Neo-institutionalists (Aldrich and Fiol 1994; Fligstein 2001) develop this argument by showing that institutional factors also affect new industries. Organisational population growth depends on acquiring cognitive and sociopolitical legitimacy. In the first instance, entrepreneurs need to create effective routines and competencies under conditions of ignorance, risk and uncertainty. Knowledge can be acquired through experimentation or creative recombination of existing models, thus leading to *cognitive legitimacy* (Aldrich and Fiol 1994). The concept refers to the situation in which an activity/product becomes so familiar that people take it for granted and other participants on the market tend to reproduce it. In the second stage, entrepreneurs need to establish links with external environment which might not acknowledge their existence or utility. Gaining *sociopolitical legitimacy* involves *moral acceptance* by conforming to cultural norms and values and *regulatory acceptance* indicated by new laws passed to oversee an industry. Even though these processes start at organisational level, eventually they involve the wider community, the state and in some cases international agencies. If heterogeneous interests are involved, diverse social groups can be affected and mobilised and entrepreneurial efforts to gain legitimacy made more difficult (Lounsbury 2001). Institutional theory reintroduces agency, interests and power into the study of entrepreneurship showing that the emergence of novelty is not an easy and predictable process, but the result of struggles, conflict and political negotiations.

In an analysis of contemporary entrepreneurship in Romania, the importance of socialist heritage is undeniable (Mandel and Humphrey 2002; Kaneff 2002; Verdery 2004). However, it is also important to acknowledge the impact of globalisation and contemporary capitalist processes as a counterbalance to path-dependent theories (Burawoy 1998). The absence of business infrastructure, little private enterprise tradition and the hostile economic environment imposed the reorganisation of work.

Work as Entrepreneurship

Sociology of work owes a great deal of its insights to Chicago School contributions. According to Everett C. Hughes (1971) modern people's identity is shaped by work, so what happens in the workplace has a strong impact on their lives and is a reflection of wider societal influences. The richness of ethnographic material produced by the American sociologists influenced three main areas: work and professions (Whyte 1943), informal relations at the workplace (Roy 1959) and work-related conflicts (Dalton 1959; Crozier 1964). Many of the findings and insights are still relevant. Godard (2004) analysed the relationship between workplace practices and performance, concluding that there were no general 'best practices', only elements contingent upon the environment of the workplace (e.g., process of production, product and labour markets). Donald Roy's 'Banana Time' (1959) uncovered many of the everyday dramas at work. Thirty years later, following on Roy's steps, Burawoy (1977) conducted his ethnography in the same Chicagoan factory showing that workers devised various ways to make the time pass. 'Making out' had two aspects: being paid and finding something interesting to do.

Subsequent research in the Marxist tradition spanned the area of industrial sociology focusing on conflict at work (Beynon 1985), the political economy of industrial relations and the 'labour process' (employees' behaviour, employment relations and issues related to work design and organisation). The pursuit of capitalist interests was considered to shape deep conflicts between employees and employers, but the relationship has not proven straightforward. For example, accumulation of profit requires a certain degree of alignment between employer and worker interests in the workplace (Burawoy 1985), without directly determining patterns of control and resistance. One of the most famous contributions in this tradition is Braverman's deskilling argument (1974); he stated that capitalism was associated with a trend towards deskilling, through routinising and mechanising of work tasks. The increasing specialisation of tasks on which the division of labour was based (Durkheim 1892) thus became disintegrative under the influence of technical and social factors.

Technology is a key dependent variable for explaining the process of accessing EU funding. A wide understanding of technology involves the tools, machines, control devices as well as the principles, techniques and reasoning involved in carrying out the work tasks. It is no surprise that a range of social theorists have endowed technology with causal power (McLoughlin 1999), talking about the 'iron hand of technology' (Kerr et al. 1973) or the 'remorseless working of things' (Hill 1988). The tragedy of technology completely absorbs individuals into the technical properties of the system, leaving no alternative to the apparently intrinsic evolution of the industrial society. Conversely, technology was seen just as a necessary, but not sufficient condition for social change. Hobsbawm (1985) pointed out that in its early days, the Industrial Revolution was rather primitive; hence the motor of change was individual motivation rather than new knowledge. Following this line of argument, MacKenzie and Wajcman (1999) speak about the 'social shaping of technology' showing that a wide range of social factors and interests influence the emergence of any given technology.

Badham (2005) treats workplaces as 'socio-technical configurations' defining them as "complex webs of human and non-human elements that are locally configured in context in the pursuit of formal and informal, explicit and implicit purposes and goals" (123). The proponents of actor-network theory (Latour 1987, 2005) abolish completely the division between human and non-human actors, arguing that the distinction between the natural and social world is a myth of modernisation; hence, machines, principles and people can be analysed as equivalent actors in a network of activities. Castells (1996) coined the term 'information society' to describe the globalised dimension of change driven by the 'networking logic' of information and communication technologies (ICTs), which makes global flows of capital more significant than local production of goods. The informational capitalism is a networked social order, challenged not by the working classes as traditional capitalism, but by a variety of social movements concerned to protect their identities instead of their material interests. This position was criticised for the lack of empirical evidence and inadequate theoretical grounding to show causal mechanisms (Watson 2008).

Technological advancements shaped the work process and organisations through *flexible specialisation* (Piore and Sabel 1984; Sabel and Zeitlin 1997). Microelectronics increased the speed of communication, leading to a breakdown of the mass markets associated with Fordism by providing customised products to specialised market niches, building trusting and cooperative relations with employees. These trends changed workers' competences as they had to be able to use advanced technologies, be proficient across a range of tasks and be ready to switch among them as demand required, thus leading to upskilling. However, when looking at *marginal workers* from the informal, underground economic sectors, it is difficult to support this argument. Individuals populating these marginal productive areas are low-paid, flexible workers, involved in precarious regular or irregular employment (Portes 1994). It is debatable whether the inhabitants of these worlds are increasing their skill levels enough to allow for upward mobility or remain trapped in poverty. The flexible specialisation theory was criticised because it underestimated the costs of computer-led production and oversimplified the mass production process (Williams et al. 1992).

Contemporary work practices are affected not only by skill level, technology and flexible specialisation but also by the blurring of the manufacturing-service distinction. Hybrid forms of work practices have been brought together in the fast food business. In these restaurants, labour is "highly rationalised and the goal is the discovery of the best, most efficient way of grilling a hamburger, frying chicken or serving a meal" (Ritzer 1998: 178). 'McDonaldisation' is based on a mix of principles of mechanisation, rationalisation and routinisation (Ritzer 1998) leading to a new form of work organisation through *standardisation*, recognisable in other service sectors like banking or retailing. Bryman (2004) argues that the contemporary economic world moves towards Disneyisation of culture and society with the use of brands and themes of shops, hotels and restaurants. This adds a new dimension to work demands, as workers are increasingly expected to give theatre-like performances. Du Gay (1996) shows that new work settings involve a 'hybrid' type of activity that combines economic with cultural functions. The service sector, he argued, develops its own technologies of work relating to interpersonal and emotion management, thus enhancing particular skills aimed at 'winning over the hearts and minds of the customers'.

The Firm

The arguments discussed so far shape the organisational form in which entrepreneurship takes place—*the firm*. Jensen and Meckling see the firm as a collection of contracts among employees, customers, creditors and so on, concluding that the firm is a "legal fiction," consisting of "a nexus of contracting relationships" (1976: 311). Burns (1963) proposed a two-type schema of firms: *mechanistic*, adapted to relatively stable conditions, and *organismic*, suitable for conditions of change and uncertainty, with a fluid structure and no clear division of labour. The latter inherits from Schumpeter's conception of entrepreneurship in which innovation played a crucial role.

In post-socialist countries, entrepreneurship takes place in small- and medium-sized enterprises (SMEs), as these are more flexible entities that offer learning opportunities (Aidis and Sauka 2005). Despite their short lifespan due to the lack of finance (EBRD 1994–2004; Pissarides 2004), SMEs provide alternative employment opportunities. Many people who were left unemployed as a result of the mass privatisation programme chose to start a small business. For some, this was the beginning of a new career, stimulated by the fact that even rudimentary business methods obtained profit. This would explain the lack of match between previous formal training and the type of business—for example, a teacher who sells apples. The transfer of previous illegal entrepreneurship experience proved successful for the new business sector. However, the SME sector in transition faced enormous challenges which ran from low purchasing power (Aidis 2006), lack of qualified workers, the complex issue of taxation (e.g., high level of taxes, the frequent changes to tax policies, the ambiguity of tax policies) (Aidis 2006; EBRD 1994–2004), bureaucracy, corruption and unfair competition from a large informal economy. Small businesses were more likely to be vulnerable in highly risky environments than their larger counterparts, as they lacked the finance and the lobbying power to exercise influence in more complex situations. Furthermore, EU market changes favoured large enterprises as opposed to SMEs and put extra burdens on SMEs' budgets, as they had to comply with new technical standards and invest in skill development.

From 'Disorganised Capitalism' (Lash and Urry 1987) to 'Unlicensed Capitalism' (Hobbs 2013)

After discussing the modes of coordination of economic and social life emphasising the role of state and transnational regulations, the concept of entrepreneurship and work-related elements, the last section turns to analysing the blurred boundaries of economic activities. This section frames theoretically the fluidity of the economic and social process drawing on sociological, anthropological and criminological insights into informality, crime and post-socialism. The purpose is to explore the intersections between social structures, policies and enforcement practices in order to uncover the opportunities provided or created by entrepreneurs acting in the informal, illegal, illicit arenas.

Disorganised Capitalism (Lash and Urry 1987)

The fragmentation of modern life is associated with "heterogeneity, plurality, constant innovation and pragmatic construction of local rules and prescriptives agreed upon by participants" (Watson 2008) and increasing movements of capital across the world that limits the nation state's capacity of reaction. Such trends lead to "disorganised capitalism" (Lash and Urry 1987) which entails a cultural addition to its economic dimension by fetishising cultural images that fragment traditional cultural and class identities. Globalisation is "a process of increased density and frequency of international or global social interactions relative to local or national ones" (Walby 2003: 32) and 'an empirical condition of the modern world' characterised by complex connectivity.

The effects of this pool of interdependence created by money flows, cultural transmissions or socio-technological connectivity are discussed by two opposing arguments: convergence and divergence. Convergence proponents argue that societies which are industrialised tend to become more alike in their societal characteristics and work arrangements (Bryman 2004). Divergence proponents oppose, arguing that despite globalisation, societies and work places retain their local flavour, even though they respond to certain globalising pressures. A third explanation recently emerged argues that increasing connections and similarities around the world tend to coexist with local and national differences, showing that *societalisation* (Walby 2006) is a matter of degree. The implications of these debates for economic sociology and the work process in particular are enormous as they uncover important assumptions about work relationships; work patterns; linkages between work, economy and society; and identity construction by and through work.

Post-socialist Capitalism

The global trends of capitalism are shaped by the context of this research. Post-socialism literature is convergent in stating that the former communist countries from Southern Eastern Europe have undergone profound changes in the last 20 years (Ledeneva 1998). Such changes were driven by the more or less sudden switch in the political system (from communism to democracy), in the economy (from planned economy to the 'free market') and in the general social arrangements. Recent trends in post-socialism scholarship have moved away from the overgeneralised view of a coherent post-communist space, thus introducing the concept of 'varieties of socialism' (Frieden 2006), which draws on Hall and Soskice's 'varieties of capitalism' (2001).

Studies of socialist regimes show that these 'varieties' have been characterised by scarcity of consumer goods, the emphasis put on production rather than consumption, the marginal role of the markets, the centrally planned economy and the ambiguous character of property rights (Alexander 2004; Eyal et al. 1998; Mandel and Humphrey 2002; Kornai 1992; Ledeneva 1998; Szlelenyi et al. 1994; Verdery 2004; Yang 1994). In Romania, where the communist regime completely abolished private property, the issue regarding property rights was especially difficult. The introduction of private property, which followed the process of 'de-collectivisation' (1991), modified Romanian property rights and created 'mutant' forms of property—fuzzy property (Verdery et al. 1996) or recombinant property (Stark 1996). According to Verdery this process took two main forms: *property restitution*, which meant giving back the houses and land that have been nationalised or collectivised during communism, and *property creation*, which involved "dissolving state ownership over goods and objects that have been created during the socialist period, by socialist means" (Verdery 2004: 5). The latter had dramatic effects, as privatisation meant the dissolution of the state-owned factories by giving shares of the company to the employees. With little training in the market transactions, people failed to seize this economic opportunity, the context favouring the ones who already occupied management positions. This situation was coupled with the breakdown of the communist party as the unique ruling body, which, according to Eyal et al. (1998), encouraged a change in the elites. In this context, it is interesting to note that the path-dependent theory suggest that no change in elites accompanied this new political environment (Kornai 1992). According to others, this new political situation created 'greedy elites' or robber barons (Josephson 1962) that use different forms of capital to make profit by unorthodox means.

Rather than focusing on elites' behaviours, this book puts the emphasis on the experiences and practices of people in everyday encounters. At the ground level, research shows that the development of informal networks of support to acquire goods in short supply (Wedel 1986; Yang 1994) led to the privatisation of public life through the practice of *blat/guanxi* which enhanced horizontal solidarity (Ledeneva 1998), which ultimately eroded the system from inside (Kotkin 2002). Moreover, the informal exchange supported the development of the second informal (but not necessarily illegal) economy, where trust played an important role in the etiquette of private arrangements (Wedel 1986). The vertical solidarity was developed through patronage (Ledeneva 1998; Wedel 1986; Yang 1994). These practices perpetuated a low degree of confidence in bureaucracy and high trust in acquaintances. The socialist systems introduced the 'ideology of equality and practice of difference' (Ledeneva 1998) through the creative practices of bureaucratic avoidances. In the socialist regimes the social capital, enhanced by the belonging to multiple networks, was the most important form of capital, followed by the cultural capital. Economic capital played only a marginal role due to the paucity of consumer goods (Eyal et al. 1998).

Unlicensed Capitalism (Hobbs 2013)

The modern trends that organise the social and economic life around the work environment determined the "formation of a community of practice structured around various levels of entrepreneurial performance that are played out within the context of an unlicensed form of capitalism whose fluid parameters are defined by the chaos and fragmentation of deindustrialisation" (Hobbs 2013: 232). This community of practice is based on fluid networks of ad hoc coalitions that perform their entrepreneurial work routines competently in illegal as well as legal markets.

Sociological research has long documented that formal organisations not only provide opportunities for engaging in illegal/informal activities but sometimes incentivise it. In *Men Who Manage*, Dalton (1959) argued that running a business involved more than the officially recognised resources. Most employees responded affirmatively when asked secretly if willing to help out the organisation if paid thus overriding issues of morality or illegality. Ditton's (1977a) ethnography of fiddling showed that the organisational setting and culture of the bread factory effectively encouraged and socialised employees into fiddling. More recent work on tax heavens (Shaxon 2011) emphasised that banks and other financial services are the main users of these jurisdictions, despite the common stereotype which placed professional criminals at the top. Ruggiero (2013) argued that offshore networks enable global financial crime by creating the appropriate secretive and stable environment, which has barely been reformed in the recent years.

The 'disorganised capitalism' that characterises modern societies provided further opportunities for the engagement in 'unlicensed capitalism', especially for people or corporations in positions of power. For example, in 2012 the 'London interbank offered rate' (Libor) was at the core of criminal activity conducted by several banks which had gained illicit profits by moving the exchange benchmarks. Barclays Bank agreed to pay £290 million to redress (Ruggiero 2013) outraged customers. One of the paradoxes of modernity is that an economic activity and its opposite are typically adopted and 'marketised' at the same time. Commenting on several cases of illegal waste dumping in Germany, Ruggiero noticed that "the development of illegal dumping services runs in parallel with the very increase in environmental awareness, the latter forcing governments to raise costs for industrial dumping, which indirectly encourages industrialists to opt for cheaper, if illicit solutions" (2013: 43). The 'dirty collar crime' against the environment was the result of successful cooperation between industry (to avoid taxation), officials (who provided false certifications) and criminals who innovatively adapted their conduct to change the rules and become market leaders. For example, HSBC agreed to pay a record of £1.2 billion to settle allegations that it allowed terrorist organisations to move their financial resources through the system. Such unruly coalitions (Verdery et al. 1996) produce financial gains that may eventually re-enter the mainstream economy, due to the instability of illegal markets.

In this way, actors move competently between various registers of legality, sometimes within the frame of a working day, paying little attention to theoretical and legal boundaries. The same act can make one to be both a crook and a benefactor. As Carolyn Nordstrom (2007: 99) put it, "some profit by acting outside the law. And while they clearly profit personally, their actions often bring development to their communities." In a twisted way, they "act as agents for development because they rebuild regional industry, donate to health and education, and bring in critical resources for the citizenry" (Nordstrom 2007: 100).

The work environment can be exploited for criminal purposes just as much as the business environment, giving rise to crime at work. White-collar crime (Sutherland 1983) is particularly apt to reflect the fluidity of profit-driven activities due to its invisibility (both of the perpetrator and of the victim), highly skilled practitioners that mimic the legality of legitimate transactions, and the far-reaching social damage (Ruggiero 2013). White-collar crime refers to "a person of respectability and high social status" who commits crime "in the course of his occupation" (Sutherland 1983: 7). Sutherland's aim was to draw attention to the fact that crime is not committed only by the poor, uneducated, working class members of the society. Regardless of the definitional ambiguities (what does it mean 'high social status' and how is one to measure 'respectability'?), this account opened up an entire strand of sociological and criminological inquiry. Later on, Cressey (1953: 12) showed that "some people in the position of financial trust violate that trust"; Clinard and Yeager (1980) showed that 582 corporations were responsible for 1554 crimes; however, corporate violations were more difficult to uncover, due to their complexity (cf. Punch 1996: 52). Maurice Punch used the concept of ***organisational deviance*** to denote "influential people who utilize their resources for ends which some other people define as illicit, and then, not infrequently, employ that power or those resources to protect themselves from the consequences of social control" (Punch 1996: 57). As my research is not focused on the study of organisations, I prefer Ditton's (1977a, Henry 1978) concept of 'occupational deviance', which is more connected to entrepreneurial innovative capacity, informal rewards, the manipulation of work situations and employee deviance for and against organisations.

Deviant careers within the business area are possible because "the norms of commerce are really qualified guidelines for a zone of acceptable activity, rather than categorical imperatives demanding particular courses of action" (Ditton 1977a: 174). The structure and values of the society thus make the necessary references for analysing this matter. Romania's recent history and sociocultural logics of action in an unpredictable economy normalises deviant behaviours and promotes favourable definitions to bypassing the law. Armed with "large portions of justifying rhetoric from cultural interpretation of business" (Ditton 1977a: 176), the new entrepreneurs do not consider themselves to be criminals, even though they admit their conduct "might have been related to an unusual business trend" (Cressey 1953: 112). Irrespective of the definitional issue, success is a direct consequence of entrepreneurs' social capacity for creating win-win situations. In order to be successful, one must be able to exploit the environment by both creating and using opportunities. "Knowing one's business environment is crucial for the development of the business. In this sense, it is necessary not only to have a detailed knowledge of the market, but also of the criminal law in one's operating area" (Klockars 1975: 186).

Consequently, the criminal law becomes business law, as it can open or close business opportunities.

The use of creative skills in handling both the formal and informal norms makes the job of control difficult for various reasons. The first difficulty is related to the complex nature of the business and the intricate arrangements concealed by the work of professionals who know well the weaknesses of business regulations. Professional lawyers, accountants, computer specialists have the job to hide any dubious transactions. Secondly, as Hobbs (1988) has shown in the case of East London, the police and the entrepreneurs are intertwined in the same culture and have the same cultural codes about what is admissible and not, thus making it difficult not to sympathise/empathise with the businessmen. Thirdly, the state institutions responsible for control face legal deficiencies and administrative complexities, which make it hard to detect and punish dubious business arrangements.

Throughout this section, I tried to provide some theoretical avenues suitable for analysing the way in which Romanian entrepreneurs access EU funding. My main objective was to put forward a dynamic understanding of reality and show that concepts like legal and illegal, formal and informal were imagined arenas of coherent behaviours. In practice, however, there were no shifting borders between formal/informal/illegal, as deviant behaviours relied on the same norms and values as the non-deviant. The process of accessing EU funding brings in contact different types of entrepreneurs who interact according to the guiding principles of profitability. In a highly unpredictable environment, they reduce the risks by relying on solidarity networks and old patterns of behaviour. In this environment, the face value changes for the value of one's face, due to the netiquette of social arrangements. However, the social protocols of honouring are complemented by economic shrewdness, as the entrepreneurs "juggle numerous currencies, multiple businesses and complex commodity flows" (Nordstrom 2007: 98).

Conclusion

This chapter provided a theoretical framework for analysing the process of accessing EU funding in Romania. It argued that as an economic process, EU funding is a hybrid arena, situated at the intersection of three modes of coordination: hierarchies, markets and networks. The design of EU funding is regulated and monitored by transnational institutions and the national government. The second section looked at the impact of state on the economy and the role of development aid for economic development, showing that development funding is embedded in crime and corruption narratives. In this context, corruption becomes a rebranding mechanism that labels vernacular practices using transnational vocabularies of crime. The third section turned to analyse entrepreneurship and work-related literature, showing that entrepreneurs are the major vehicle of change, leading to the setup of new industries, which in turn change the work routines. Finally, section four connected economic sociology with criminology and sociology of deviance by looking at the blurring boundaries between legal and illegal arenas. The next chapter will work with this framework to explain the *process* of accessing EU funding on the ground.

Bibliography

Agnew, J. 1986. *Worlds Apart: The Market and the Theatre in the Anglo-American Thought 1550–1750*. New York: Cambridge University Press.

Aidis, R. 2006. Laws and Customs: Entrepreneurship, Institutions and Gender During Transition. In *SSEES Occasional Series*. London: University College London.

Aidis, R., and S. Sauka. 2005. *Entrepreneurship in a Changing Environment: Analyzing the Impact of Transition Stages on SME Development*. Turku: European Council for Small Businesses.

Aldrich, H.E. 2005. Entrepreneurship. In *Handbook of Economic Sociology*, ed. N. Smelser and R. Swedberg, 451–477. Princeton, NJ: Princeton University Press.

Aldrich, H.E., and M.C. Fiol. 1994. Fools Rush In? The Institutional Context of Industry Creation. *Academy of Management Review* 19: 645–670.

Alrdirch Howard, E. 1999. *Organizations Evolving*. London: Sage.

Alexander, C. 2004. Value, Rights, and Changing Bodies: Privatization and Property Rights in Kazakhstan. In *Property in Question. Value Transformation in the Global Economy*, ed. Katherine Verdery and Caroline Humphrey, 251–273. Oxford: Berg.

Alford, F.C. 2001. *Whistle-Blowers: Broken Lives and Organizational Power*. New York: Cornell University Press.

Aligica, D.P., and V. Tarko. 2012. State Capitalism and the Rent-Seeking Conjecture. *Constitutional Political Economy* 23 (4): 357–379.

Alvesson, M., and P. Thompson. 2005. Post-bureaucracy? In *The Oxford Handbook of Work and Organization*, ed. R. Batt Ackroyd, P. Thompson, and P. Tolbert. Oxford: Oxford University Press.

Anders, G., and M. Nuijten, eds. 2009. *Corruption and the Secret of Law: A Legal Anthropological Perspective*. London: Ashgate.

Axelrod, R. 1984. *The Evolution of Cooperation*. New York: Basic Books.

Badham, R. 2005. Technology and the Transformation of Work. In *Handbook of Work and Organization*, ed. S. Ackroyd, R. Batt, and P. Thompson, 115–137. Oxford: Oxford University Press.

Baker, W. 1981. Markets as Networks: A Multimethod Study of Trading Networks in a Securities Market. PhD diss., Department of Sociology, Northwestern University.

Baker, W.E., R.R. Faulkner, and G.A. Fisher. 1998. Hazards of the Market: The Continuity and Dissolution of Interorganizational Market Relationships. *American Sociological Review* 63: 147–177.

Baumol, William J. 1993. Formal Entrepreneurship Theory in Economics: Existence and Bounds. *Journal of Business Venturing* 8 (3): 181–294.

Bayart, J.-F. 1993. *The State in Africa: The Politics of the Belly*. London: Longman.

Becker, G. 1993. *Human Capital*. Chicago, IL: University of Chicago Press.

Benveniste, G. 1977. *Bureaucracy*. San Francisco: Boyd and Fraser Publishing.

Berger, P., and T. Luckmann. 1966. *The Social Construction of Reality*. New York, USA: Doubleday, Allen Lane, The Penguin Press.

Beynon, H. 1985. *Working for Ford*. 2nd ed. New York: Penguin.

Birch, D., L. 1997. Small Business Research Summary. In *RS*. Washington DC: United States Small Business Administration.

Birch, David L. 1997. *Small Business Research Summary. In RS Number 183*. Washington, DC: United States Small Business Administration.

Bjelopera, J.P., and K.M. Finklea. 2010. *Organized Crime: An Evolving Challenge of US Law Enforcement*. Washington, DC: Congressional Research Service.

Blundo, G., and O. De Sardan. 2006. *Everyday Corruption and the State. Citizens and Public Officials in Africa*. London and New York: Zed Books.

Boeker, W. 1988. Organizational Origins: Entrepreneurial and Environmental Imprinting at the Time of Founding. In *Ecological Models of Organization*, ed. Glenn R. Carroll, 33–51. Cambridge, MA: Ballinger.

Boissevain, J. 1974. *Friends of Friends: Networks, Manipulators and Coalitions*. New York: St. Martin's Press.

Bourdieu, P. 1977. *Outline of A Theory of Practice*. Cambridge: Cambridge University Press.

———. 1997. Le champ économique. *Actes de la recherche en sciences sociales* 119: 48–66.

Bratu, R. 2013. The Former Soviet Union. In *Controlling Corruption in Europe. The Anticorruption Report*, ed. Alina Mungiu-Pippidi, 55–67. Berlin: Barbara Budrich Publisher.

Braudel, F. 1982. *The Wheels of Commerce*. New York: Harper and Row.

Braverman, H. 1974. *Labor and Monopoly Capital: The Degradation of Work in the Twentieth Century*. New York: Monthly Review Press.

Bremmer, I. 2010. *The End of the Free Market: Who Wins the War Between States and Corporations*. New York: Portfolio.

Bryane, M., and Bowser, D. 2009. The Evolution of the Anti-corruption Industry in the Third Wave of Anti-corruption Work. http://works.bepress.com/bryane_michael/50

Bryman, A. 2004. *The Disneyization of Society*. London: Sage.

Burawoy, M. 1977. *Manufacturing Consent: Changes in the Labor Process under Monopoly Capitalism*. Chicago: University of Chicago Press.

———. 1985. *The Politics of Production: Factory Regimes Under Capitalism and Socialism*. London: Verso.

———. 1998. The Extended Case Method. *Sociological Theory* 16 (1): 4–33.

Burns, T. 1963. Industry in a New Age. *New Society* 18: 17–20.

Burt, R. 1992. *Structural Holes: The Social Structure of Competition*. Cambridge: Harvard University Press.

Burton, M.D., J. Sorenson, and C. Beckman. 2002. Coming from Good Stock: Career Histories and New Venture Formation. In *Social Structure and Organizations Revisited*, ed. M. Lounsbury and M. Ventresca, 229–262. Amsterdam: JAI/Elsevier.

Caldwell, G. 2005. Corruption at the Core of Congress. *The Financial Times*, December 3.

Callon, M. 1998. Introduction: The Embeddedness of Economic Markets in Economics. In *Laws of the Market*, ed. Michel Callon. Oxford: OUP.

Carroll, G.R., and M.T. Hannan. 2000. *The Demography of Corporations and Industries*. Princeton, NJ: Princeton University Press.

Carter, N.M., W.M. Gartner, and P.D. Reynolds. 1996. Exploring Start-Up Sequences. *Journal of Business Venturing* 11: 151–166.

Cascio, W.F. 2000. Managing a Virtual Workplace. *Academy of Management Executive* 14: 81–90.

Castells, M. 1996. *The Rise of the Network Society: The Information Age: Economy, Society, and Culture*. Oxford: Blackwell.

Clinard, Marshall B., and Peter C. Yeager. 1980. *Corporate Crime*. New York: Free Press.

Coase, R. 1937. The Nature of the Firm. *Economica* 4: 386–405.

Cooper, A.C. 1986. Entrepreneurship and High Technology. In *The Art and Science of Entrepreneurship*, ed. D. Sexton and R.W. Smilor, 153–168. Cambridge, Mass: Ballinger.

Courpasson, D., and S. Clegg. 2006. Dissolving the Iron Cages? Tocqueville, Michels, Bureaucracy and the Perpetuation of Elite Power. *Organization* 13 (3): 319–343.

Cressey, D.R. 1953. *Other People's Money: A Study in the Social Psychology of Embezzlement*. Glencoe, IL: The Free Press.

Crozier, Michel. 1964. *The Bureaucratic Phenomenon*. Chicago, IL: University of Chicago Press.

Czarniawska-Joerges, B. 1989. *Economic Decline and Organizational Control*. New York: Praeger.

Dalton, M. 1959. *Men Who Manage*. New York: John Wiley and Sons.
De Meza, D., and C. Southey. 1996. The Borrower's Curse: Optimism, Finance, and Entrepreneurship. *Economic Journal* 106: 375–386.
De Sardan, J.P. Olivier. 1999. A Moral Economy of Corruption in Africa? *The Journal of Modern African Studies* 37 (1): 25–52.
———. 2005. *Anthropology and Development. Understanding Contemporary Social Change*. London and New York: Zed Books.
DiMaggio, P. 1988. Interest and Agency in Institutional Theory. In *Institutional patterns and culture*, ed. L. Zucker, 3–22. Cambridge, MA: Ballinger Publishing Company.
Ditton, J. 1977a. *Part-Time Crime: An Ethnography of Fiddling and Pilferage*. London: Macmillan Press.
Drucker, P.F. 1992. The New Society of Organizations. *Harvard Business Review* 70: 95–104.
Du Gay, P. 1996. *Consumption and Identity at Work*. London: Sage.
———. 2000. *In Praise of Bureaucracy: Weber, Organization, Ethics*. London: Sage.
Durkheim, E. 1892. The Rules of the Sociological Method. New York: Free Press.
Easterly, W. 2006. *The White Man's Burden: Why the West's Efforts to Aid the Rest Have Done So Much Ill and So Little Good*. New York: The Penguin Press.
EBRD. 1994–2004. Transition Report. London.
Eccles, Robert G. 1985. *The Transfer Pricing Problem: A Theory for Practice*. New York: Lexington Books.
Edelman, L.B. 1992. Legal Ambiguity and Symbolic Structures: Organizational Mediation of Civil Rights Law. *American Journal of Sociology* 97: 1531–1576.
Escobar, A. 1991. Anthropology and the Development Encounter: The Making and Marketing of Development Anthropology. *American Ethnologist* 18 (4): 658–682.
Eyal, G., I. Szelenyi, and E. Townlsey. 1998. *Making Capitalism Without Capitalists: Class Formation and Elite Struggles in Post-Communist Central Europe*. London and New York: Verso.
Farrell, C.M., and J. Morris. 2003. The Neo-Bureaucratic State: Professionals and Managers and Professional Managers in Schools, General Practices and Social Work. *Organisation* 10 (1): 129–157.
Finley, M. 1973. *The Ancient Economy*. Berkeley: University of California Press.
Fisman, R., and E. Miguel. 2010. *Economic Gangsters: Corruption, Violence, and the Poverty of Nations*. Princeton, NJ: Princeton University Press.
Fligstein, N. 1996. Markets as Politics: A Political-Cultural Approach to Market Institutions. *American Sociological Review* 61: 656–673.
———. 2001. *The Architecture of Markets: An Economic Sociology of Twenty-First-Century Capitalist Societies*. Princeton, NJ: Princeton University Press.
Freeman, J.H. 1983. Entrepreneurs as Organizational Products: Semiconductor Firms and Venture Capital Firms. In *Advances in the Study of Entrepreneurship,*

Innovation, and Economic Growth, ed. G. Libecap, 33–52. Greenwich, CT: JAI Press.

Frieden, J. 2006. *Global Capitalism: Its Fall and Rise in the Twentieth Century.* New York: W.W. Norton.

Friedrich, Carl J. 1972. Corruption Concepts in Historical Perspective. In *Political Corruption. A Handbook*, ed. A. Heidenheimer, J. Johnston, M. LeVine, and V. Tanzi, 15–24. London: Transaction Publishers.

Galtung, F. 1998. Criteria for Sustainable Corruption Control. *The European Journal of Development Research* 10 (1): 105–128.

Gartner, W.B., B. Bird, and J. Starr. 1992. Act as If: Differentiating Entrepreneurial from Organizational Behavior. *Entrepreneurship: Theory and Practice* 16: 13–32.

Garud, R., S. Jain, and A. Kumaraswamy. 2002. Institutional Entrepreneurship in the Sponsorship of Common Technological Standards: The Case of Sun Microsystems and Java. *Academy of Management Journal* 45: 196–214.

Godard, J. 2004. A Critical Assessment of the High-Performance Paradigm. *British Journal of Industrial Relations* 42 (2): 349–378.

Gouldner, A. 1964. *Patterns of Industrial Bureaucracy.* New York: Free Press.

Granovetter, M. 1973. The Strengths of Weak Ties. *American Journal of Sociology* 78 (6): 1360–1380.

———. 1974. *Getting a Job: A Study of Contacts and Careers.* Cambridge: Harvard University Press.

Gupta, A. 1995. Blurred Boundaries: The Discourse of Corruption, the Culture of Politics, and the Imagined State. *American Ethnologist* 22 (2): 375–402.

Hall, P.A., and D. Soskice. 2001. *Varieties of Capitalism. The Institutional Foundations of Comparative Advantage.* Oxford: OUP.

Hall, S., C. Crittcher, T. Jefferson, J. Clarke, and B. Roberts. 2013. *Policing the Crisis. Mugging, the State and Law & Order.* 2nd ed. London: Palgrave Macmillan.

Haller, D., and C. Shore, eds. 2005. *Corruption. Anthropological Perspectives.* London: Pluto Press.

Harrison, E. 2010. Unpacking the Anticorruption Agenda: Dilemmas for Anthropologists. *Oxford Development Studies* 34 (1): 15–29.

Hart, K. 2000. *Money in an Unequal World.* London: Texere Publishing Limited.

Heidenheimer, A.J. 1970. Perspectives on the Perception of Corruption. In *Political Corruption. A Handbook*, ed. A. Heidenheimer, J.M. Johnston, M. LeVine, and V. Tanzi, 149–163. London: Transaction Publishers.

Henry, S. 1978. *The Hidden Economy: The Context and Control of Borderline Crime.* Oxford: Martin Robertson.

Hill, Stephen. 1988. *The Tragedy of Technology: Human Liberation Versus Domination in the Late Twentieth Century. Responsibility: Stephen Hill.* London: Pluto Press. Imprint.

Hobbs, D. 1988. *Doing the Business : Entrepreneurship, the Working Class and Detectives in the East End of London.* Oxford: Clarendon Press.

———. 2013. *Lush Life. Constructing Organized Crime in the UK*. Oxford: Oxford University Press.

Hobsbawm, E.J. 1985. *Bandits*. Harmondsworth: Penguin.

Hughes, E.C. 1971. *The Sociological Eye. Selected Papers on Institutions and Race*. Vol. 1. Chicago: Aldine.

Jaques, E. 1990. In Praise of Hierarchy. *Harvard Business Review* (January–February): 127–133.

Jensen, M.C., and W.H. Meckling. 1976. Theory of the Firm: Managerial Behavior, Agency Costs, and Ownership Structure. *Journal of Financial Economics* 3: 305–340.

Johannisson, B. 1988. Business Formation: A Network Approach. *Scandinavian Journal of Management* 3: 83–99.

Josephson, M. 1962. *The Robber Barons*. New York: Harcourt, Brace and World.

Kaneff, D. 2002. The Shame and Pride of Market Activity: Morality, Identity and Trading in Postsocialist Rural Bulgaria. In *Markets and Moralities*, ed. R. Mandel and C. Humphrey, 33–51. New York: Berg.

Keohane, R. 1986. Reciprocity in International relations. *International Organizations* 40 (1): 1–27.

Kerr, C., J.T. Dunlop, F.H. Harbison, and C. Myers. 1973. *Industrialism and Industrial Man*. Harmondsworth, Middlesex: Penguin.

Kim, Phillip H., and E. Alrdirch Howard. 2005. Entrepreneurship and Social Capital. *Foundations and Trends in Entrepreneurship* 1 (2): 1–52.

Klitgaard, R. 1988. *Controlling Corruption*. Berkeley: University of California Press.

Klockars, C.B. 1975. *The Professional Fence*. London: Tavistock Publications.

Kornai, J. 1992. *The Socialist System: The Political Economy of Communism*. Oxford: Clarendon Press.

Krastev, I. 2004. *Shifting Obsession. Three Essays on The Politics of Anticorruption*. Budapest: CEU.

Krizner, I.M. 1973. *Competition and Entrepreneurship*. Chicago and London: University of Chicago Press.

———. 1997. Entrepreneurial Discovery and the Competitive Market Process: An Austrian Approach. *Journal of Economic Literature* 35 (1): 60–85.

Lash, S., and J. Urry. 1987. *The End of Organised Capitalism*. Cambridge: Polity Press.

Latour, Bruno. 1987. Vizualisation and Cognition: Thinking with Eyes and Hands. *Knowledge and Society: Studies in the Sociology of Knowledge, Past and Present* 6: 1–40.

———. 2005. *Reassembling the Social: An Introduction to Actor-Network-Theory*. Oxford and New York: Oxford University Press.

Ledeneva, A.V. 1998. *Russia's Economy of Favours. Blat, Networking and Informal Exchange*. Cambridge: Cambridge University Press.

Ledeneva, A. 2013a. A Critique of the Global Corruption "Paradigm". In *Postcommunism from Within. Social Justice, Mobilization and Hegemony*, ed. Jan Kubik and Amy Linch, 297–332. New York and London: New York University Press.
Lerner, Miri, Candida Brush, and Robert Hisrich. 1997. Israeli Women Entrepreneurs: An Examination of Factors Affecting Performance. *Journal of Business Venturing* 12 (4): 315–339.
Lorenz, E.H. 1989. Neither Friends, nor Strangers: Informal Networks of Subcontracting in French Industry. In *Trust: Making and Breaking of Cooperative Relations*, ed. D. Gambetta, 194–210. Oxford: Basil Blackwell.
Lounsbury, M. 2001. Institutional Sources of Practice Variation: Staffing College and University Recycling Programs. *Administrative Science Quarterly* 46: 29–56.
Mackenzie, D., and J. Wajcman, eds. 1999. *The Social Shaping of Technology*. 2nd ed. Buckingham: Open University Press.
Maguire, S., C. Hardy, and T.B. Lawrence. 2004. Institutional Entrepreneurship In Emerging Fields: HIV/AIDS Treatment Advocacy in Canada. *Academy of Management Journal* 47: 657–679.
Malinowski, B. 1922. *Argonauts of the Western Pacific*. London: Routledge.
Mandel, R., and C. Humphrey, eds. 2002. *Markets and Moralities. Ethnographies of Postsocialism*. Oxford: Berg.
Marshall, A. 1936. *Principles of Economics*. London: Macmillan.
Mauss, M. 1925. *The Gift*. London: Routledge.
McLoughlin, C. 1999. Culturally Responsive Technology Use: Developing an Online Community of Learners. *British Journal of Educational Technology* 30 (3): 231–245.
Medard, J.-F. 1986. Public Corruption in Africa: A Comparative Perspective. *Corruption and Reform* 1 (2): 115–131.
———. 1997. La Corruption Internationale Et l'Afrique. *Revue Internationale De Politique Comparee* 4: 413–440.
Merton, R. 1938. Social Structure and Anomie. *American Sociological Review* 3 (5): 672–682.
———. 1957. *Social Theory and Social Structure*. New York: The Free Press.
Mouzelis, N.P. 1967. *Organisation and Bureaucracy: An Analysis of Modern Theories*. Chicago, IL: Aldine Publishing.
Mullen, P. 1990. Which Internal Market? The NHS White Paper and International Markets. *Financial Accountability and Management* 6 (1): 33–50.
Mungiu-Pippidi, Alina, ed. 2013. *Controlling Corruption in Europe. The Anticorruption Report*. Berlin: Barbara Budrich Publisher.
Myrdal, G. 1968. *Asian Drama: An Enquiry into the Poverty of Nations*. Vol. 2. New York: The Twentieth Century Fund.
Nordstrom, C. 2007. *Global Outlaws*. In *Crime, Money and Power in the Contemporary World*. Berkeley, Los Angeles and London: University of California Press.

North, D. 1981. *Structure and Change in Economic History.* New York: W. W. Norton.

Nye, J.S. 1967. Corruption and Political Development: A Cost-Benefit Analysis. *The American Political Science Review* 61 (2): 417–427.

Pardo, I., and G. Prato, eds. 2004. *Between Morality and the Law. Corruption, Anthropology and Comparative Society.* London: Ashgate.

Parry, J. 2000. The Crisis of Corruption and the Idea of India—A Worm's Eye View. In *Morals of Legitimacy: Between Agency and System*, ed. I. Pardo, 27–56. Oxford: Berghahn Books.

Parsons, T. 1982. *On Institutions and Social Evolution.* Chicago, IL: University of Chicago Press.

Piore, M.J., and C.F. Sabel. 1984. *The Second Industrial Divide.* New York: Basic Books.

Pissarides, F. 2004. Financial Structures and Private Sector Development in the New Europe. In *Financial Intermediation in the New Europe: Banks, Markets and Regulation in the Accession Countries*, ed. D. Masciandoro. Northampton, MA: Edward Elgar.

Polanyi, M. 1954. *The Great Transformation.* Boston, MA: Beacon Press.

Portes, A. 1994. The Informal Economy and Its Paradoxes. In *The Handbook of Economic Sociology*, ed. R. Swedberg and N.J. Smelser, 426–453. New York: Russell Sage Foundation.

Portes, A., W.J. Haller, and L.E. Guarnizo. 2002. Transnational Entrepreneurs: An Alternative Form of Immigrant Economic Adaptation. *American Sociological Review* 67: 278–298.

Powell, W. 1990. Neither Market nor Hierarchy: Network Forms of Organisation. *Research in Organizational Behaviour* 12: 295–336.

Punch, Maurice. 1996a. *Dirty Business: Exploring Corporate Misconduct: Analysis and Cases.* Thousand Oaks, CA: Sage Publications.

Reed, M. 2005. Beyond the Iron Cage? Bureaucracy and Democracy in the Knowledge Economy and Society. In *The Values of Bureaucracy*, ed. P. Du Gay. Oxford: Oxford University Press.

Reynolds, P.D., and S.B. White. 1997. *The Entrepreneurial Process: Economic Growth, Men, Women, and Minorities.* Westport, CT: Quorum Books.

Richardson, G.B. 1972. The Organization of Industry. *Economic Journal* 82: 883–896.

Ritzer, G. 1998. *The McDonaldization Thesis: Explorations and Extensions.* London: Sage.

Romanelli, E. 1989. Organization Birth and Population Variety: A Community Perspective on Origins. In *Research in Organizational Behavior*, ed. M. Staw and L. Cummings. Greenwich, CT: JAI Press.

Rose-Ackerman, S. 1999. *Corruption and Government. Causes, Consequences and Reform.* Cambridge: Cambridge University Press.

Roth, G. 1978. Introduction. In *Economy and Society: An Outline of Interpretative Sociology*, ed. M. Weber. Berkeley: University of California Press.

Rothschild, J., and T.D. Miethe. 1999. Whistle-Blower Disclosures and Management Retaliation: The Battle to Control Information about Organization Corruption. *Work and Occupations* 26 (1): 107–128.
Roy, D.F. 1959. 'Banana Time' Job Satisfaction and Informal Interaction. *Human Organization* 18 (4): 158–168.
Ruef, M., H.E. Aldrich, and N.M. Carter. 2003. The Structure of Organizational Founding Teams: Homophily, Strong Ties, and Isolation among U.S. Entrepreneurs. *American Sociological Review* 68: 195–222.
Ruggiero, V. 1996. *Organized and Corporate Crime in Europe. Offers that Can't Be Refused*. Aldershot: Dartmouth Publishing.
———. 2007. It's the Economy Stupid! Classifying Power Crime. *International Journal of the Sociology of Law* 35 (4): 163–177.
———. 2013. *The Crimes of the Economy. A Criminological Analysis of Economic Thought*. New York: Routledge.
Rytina, S., and D. Morgan. 1982. The Arithmetic of Social Relations: The Interplay of Category and Network. *American Journal of Sociology* 88: 88–113.
Sabel, C.F., and J. Zeitlin, eds. 1997. *World of Possibilities. Flexibility and Mass Production in Western Industrialization*. Cambridge: Cambridge University Press.
Sachs, J. 2005. *The End of Poverty: Economic Possibilities for Our Time*. New York Penguin Press.
Sahlins, M. 1972. *Stone Age Economics*. Chicago: Aldine.
Sajo, A. 1998. Corruption, Clientelism and the Future of the Constitutional State in Eastern Europe. *East European Constitutional Review* 7 (2): 37.
Sartori, G. 1987. *The Theory of Democracy Revisited. Part 2*. Chatham NJ: Chatham House Publishers.
Saxenian, A.L. 2000. Networks of Immigrant Entrepreneurs. In *The Silicon Valley Edge: A Habitat for Innovation and Entrepreneurship*, ed. Chong-Moon L. Miller, G.M. Hancock, and H.S. Rowen, 248–268. Stanford, CA: Stanford University Press.
Schneider, M., and P. Teske. 1992. Towards a Theory of the Political Entrepreneur. *American Political Science Review* 86: 737–747.
Schumpeter, J.A. 1942. *Capitalism Socialism and Democracy*. London: Allen and Unwin.
Scott, J.C. 1972. Handling Historical Comparisons Cross-Nationally. In *Political Corruption. A Handbook*, ed. A. Heidenheimer, M. Johnston, J. LeVine, and V. Tanzi, 129–145. London: Transaction Publishers.
———. 1998. *Seeing Like a State. How Certain Schemes to Improve the Human Condition Have Failed*. New Haven and London: Yale University Press.
Selznick, P. 1949. *TVA and the Grass Roots*. Berkeley and Los Angeles: University of California Press.
Shane, S., and S. Venkataraman. 2000. The Promise of Entrepreneurship as a Field of Research. *The Academy of Management Review* 25 (1): 217–226.

Shaxon, N. 2011. *Treasure Islands. Uncovering the Damage of Offshore Banking and Tax Heavens*. New York: Palgrave Macmillan.

Smelser, N.J., and R. Swedberg, eds. 2005. *The Handbook of Economic Sociology*. 2nd ed. Princeton, NJ: Princeton University Press.

Smith, A. 1826. *An Inquiry into the Nature and Causes of the Wealth of Nations*. 4th ed. London: W. Strahan and T. Cadell.

Stark, David. 1996. Recombinant Property in East European Capitalism. *American Journal of Sociology* 101 (4): 993–1027.

Stinchcombe, A.L. 1965. Social Structure and Organizations. In *Handbook of Organizations*, ed. James G. March, 142–193. Chicago, IL: Rand McNally.

Stinchcombe, Arthur I. 1985. Contracts as Hierarchical Documents. In *Organization Theory and Project Management*, ed. A.L. Stinchcombe and C. Heimer, 121–171. Oslo: Norwegian University Press.

Suchman, M.C., D.J. Steward, and C.A. Westfall. 2001. The Legal Environment of Entrepreneurship: Observations on the Legitimation of Venture Finance in Silicon Valley. In *The Entrepreneurship Dynamic*, ed. B. Schoonhoven and E. Romanelli, 349–382. Stanford, CA: Stanford University Press.

Sutherland, Edwin H. 1983. *White-Collar Crime: The Uncut Version*. Yale: Yale University Press.

Swedberg, R. 2000. The Social Science View of Entrepreneurship: Introduction and Practical Applications. In *Entrepreneurship: The Social Science View*, ed. R. Swedberg, 7–44. Oxford: Oxford University Press.

Syal, R. and Ball, A. 2011. One in Five Pass-Holders in Lords Linked to Lobbying. *The Guardian*, November 9.

Szlelenyi, I., K. Beckett, and L.P. Likng. 1994. The Socialist Economic System. In *The Handbook of Economic Sociology*, ed. R. Swedberg and N.J. Smelser, 234–255. New York: Russell Sage Foundation.

Tanzi, V. 1998. *Corruption Around the World: Causes, Consequences, Scope and Cures*. Washington, DC: International Monetary Fund.

Thomas, William Isaac. 1967. *The Unadjusted Girl. With Cases and Standpoint for Behavioral Analysis*. New York; Evanston; London: Harper & Row.

Thompson, E.P. 1971. The Moral Economy of the English Crowd in the Eighteenth Century. *Past and Present* 50: 78–98.

Thompson, G., J. Frances, R. Levacic, and Jeremy Mitchell, eds. 1991. *Markets, Hierarchies and Networks. The Coordination of Social Life*. London, Thousand Oaks, and New Dehli: Sage.

Thornton, P.H. 1999. The Sociology of Entrepreneurship. *Annual Review of Sociology* 25 (1): 19–46.

Thrift, N. 2001. 'It's the Romance, Not the Finance, That makes the Business Worth Pursuing': Disclosing A New Market Culture. *Economy and Society* 30: 412–432.

Torsello, D. 2012. The New Environmentalism? Civil Society and Corruption in the Enlarged EU. *Urban Anthropology*, ed., G. Prato and I. Pardo. Surrey: Ashgate.

Tsebelis, G., and G. Garrett. 2001. The Institutional Foundations of Intergovernmentalism and Supranationalism in the European Union. *International Organization* 55 (2): 357–390.
Uzzi, B. 1997. Social Structure and Competition in Interfirm Networks: The Paradox of Embeddedness. *Administrative Science Quarterly* 42: 35–67.
Van Maanen, J., and S. Barley. 1984. Occupational Communities: Culture and Control in Organizations. In *Research in Organizational Behavior*, ed. M. Staw and L. Cummings, 287–365. Greenwich, CT: JAI Press.
Verdery, K. 2004. The Obligations of Ownership: Restoring Rights to Land in Postsocialist Transylvania. In *Property in Question. Value Transformation in the Global Economy*, ed. K. Verdery and C. Humphrey, 139–159. Oxford: Berg.
Verdery, K., J.C. Chesnais, H. David, C. Karnoouh, S. Nancy Leys, and V. Tismaneanu. 1996. Post-1989 Intellectual Cooperation and Intellectual Property Rights: A Romanian Case. *East European Politics and Societies* 10 (2): 328–332.
Von Hayek, F. 1989. Spontaneous ('Grown') Order and Organized ('Made') Order. In *Order—With or Without Design?* ed. N. Modlovky, 101–123. London: Centre for Research in Communist Economies.
Walby, S. 2003. *Modernities, Globalisation and Complexity*. Vol. 1. London: Sage.
———. 2006. *Complex Social Systems in a Global Era*. London: Sage.
Watson, T.J., ed. 2008. *Sociology, Work and Industry*. 5th ed. London: Routledge.
Weber, M. 1968. *Economy and society*. Vol. 1. New York: Bedminster.
Weber, M. 1976. *Protestant Ethic and the Spirit of Capitalism*. London: Allen & Unwin.
Wedel, J. 1986. *The Private Poland*. New York: Facts on File Publications.
White, H. 1970. *Chains of Opportunity: System Models of Mobility in Organizations*. Cambridge, MA: Harvard University Press.
Whyte, W. 1943/1955. Street Corner Society: The Social Organisation of a Chicago Slum. Chicago, IL: University of Chicago Press.
Williamson, O.E. 1975. *Markets and Hierarchies: Analysis and Antitrust Implications*. New York: Free Press.
Williams, Karel, Colin Haslam, and John Williams. 1992. Ford Versus 'Fordism': The Beginning of Mass Production? *Work, Employment and Society* 6 (4): 517–555.
Wong, B. 1998. *Ethnicity and Entrepreneurship: The New Chinese Immigrants in the San Francisco Bay Area*. Boston, MA: Allyn and Bacon.
Yang, M. 1994. *Gifts, Favours and Banquets. The Art of Social Relations in China*. London: Cornell University Press.
Zajda, Joseph. 2003. The Politics of Rewriting History: New History Textbooks and Curriculum Materials in Russia. *Internationa Review of Education* 49 (3): 363–382.

CHAPTER 3

Transnational Constructions of Development and Control

This chapter contextualises the research by looking at the history of EU funding and the incorporation of the EU provisions into Romania's domestic legal framework. It argues that EU funding, as an ideal type of economic activity, was shaped by EU anti-corruption policies, practices and assumptions that were incorporated into a new institutional establishment which systematically associated EU funding with corruption. High levels of control generated by suspicion coupled with a particular cultural entrepreneurial ethos that essentially shunned state interventionism led to a 33.4% absorption rate in December 2013.[1] The first part of this chapter provides a historical overview of EU funding at the transnational level showing that concern with corruption was rooted in the need to protect the financial interests of the EU. Conversely, as the second part of the chapter shows, in Romania anxieties about corruption have taken precedence over preoccupation with safeguarding the financial interests of the EU.

EU Cohesion Tools

Designed with the aim of reducing the income disparities between EU member states, the common budget has always been an arena dominated by political fights and anxieties. In 1979, Margaret Thatcher, the British prime minister, expressed her concerns about the fair distribution of EU budget in rather harsh terms. Her famous injunction 'I want my money

R. Bratu, *Corruption, Informality and Entrepreneurship in Romania*, Political Corruption and Governance,
https://doi.org/10.1007/978-3-319-66667-9_3

back!' pointed to the fact that the common European budget was based on a redistributive mechanism that designated some EU members as net contributors and others as net receivers. Such concerns have survived and grown despite the fact that (or maybe, *precisely because*) the context has changed. Historically, EU regional policy was reflected in the European Regional Development Fund established in 1975.[2] This was a modestly funded institution, heavily controlled by the member states that were in the EC at the time, which offered assistance for investments, industrial and service sector schemes. In the following three decades, the EU has undergone a process of enlargement (27 member states presently), fashioned a unique financial unit—the euro—created transnational institutions of governance to regulate the social behaviour within member states and encouraged the free movement of labour within the Schengen Area by abolishing internal borders. A few major geopolitical events have altered the European social order dramatically: the fall of the Iron Curtain, 9/11 and the 2008 financial crisis had effective symbolic implications for European social identity and regulations. After bailing out Greece for the second time, the EU set up a permanent crisis mechanism to shore up the euro.

Regional policy has also undergone major changes after 1979, through the addition of new structural funds (e.g., the Cohesion Fund established in 1993) and budgetary expansion (in 2011 the voted budget was €141.9bn). After the landmark reform in 1988 which introduced the idea of multi-annual financial framework, structural funds have increased their profile in the region. Based on the experience of the states that were in the EU 15, it was hoped that the countries from Central and Eastern Europe would become efficient multilevel governance structures impacting on the regional governance structures and policy practices, thus reducing regional economic disparities. The ratification of the Lisbon Treaty (which came into force on 1 December 2009) had a major impact on the EU budget in three ways: it gave equal powers to the European Parliament and the Council of the European Union in approving the EU budget, it simplified the budget control procedure and it introduced the multi-annual financial framework as part of the EU law (Milio 2010). The budgetary expansion and EU enlargement were accompanied by increased anxiety about the possibility of fraud in the new EU member states. Such fears were expressed institutionally through the enforcement of strict regulations governing European funds.

The preoccupation with safeguarding the financial interests of the EU started in the 1970s at the EU level. Up until that moment, regulating fraud against the EU was not considered a priority despite the great impact on the credibility of the European project that might have been anticipated probably due to the fact that the community budget was entirely dependent on member contributions and thus each state bore the responsibility for controlling fraud. However, after 1976, the community developed its own resources (Szarek-Mason 2010), and nearly 20 years later, the EU managed to develop an anti-fraud policy. As Simone White remarked (1999), before the 1990s, the EU approach to fraud control was rather 'fragmentary', as there was no common definition of what constituted fraud and it was left to the member states to define and sanction crime in relationship to the financial interests of the EU.

Thus, at the European level, safeguarding the financial interests of the EU preceded the preoccupation with corruption (Szarek-Mason 2010). Corruption itself became an issue precisely because it was prone to facilitate fraud against the EU. The conventions and protocols adopted later strengthened this logic reflected institutionally in the activity of OLAF (Office Européen de Lutte Antifraud), which has gained more powers and has become more active in the area of corruption since 2007. The Commission started to tackle the matter systematically after 2000, which coincided with the first Eastern Enlargement (2004) and reached new peaks around 2007, when Romania and Bulgaria joined the EU. For example, immediately after the second Eastern Enlargement in 2008, the European Commission decided to withhold EU funding payments for Bulgaria. Reuters[3] reported that: "The two reports on Bulgaria—one on [EU] funds and the other on judicial reform—were the harshest criticism ever levelled by Brussels at a member state. A report on fellow newcomer Romania, which also joined in January 2007, pointed to political and judicial obstruction of corruption trials but avoided sanctions."

The EU Budget and Rules of Funding

The main sources of income for the EU budget are custom duties, a proportion of the VAT (value-added tax) and a percentage of each country's GNI (gross national income). As such, I contend that an analysis of the EU's budget mirrors the political influence and monetary participation of member countries. In 2010, the EU budget showed €141bn in commitments and €122.9bn in revenues.[4] The EU has six main areas of expenditure: sustainable growth; agriculture, environment and rural development; EU as a global player and citizenship; freedom; and justice. However,

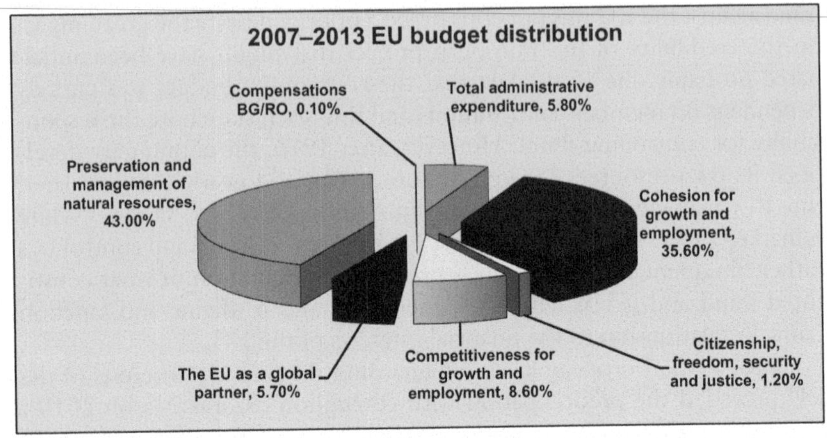

Fig. 3.1 The EU budget distribution for 2007–2013. Source: http:\\www.2007-2013.eu

agriculture absorbs the biggest proportion of funds being allotted 43% of the EU budget (Fig. 3.1).

The EU budget allocation for a specific member state does not mean that funds are transferred directly to the member state in a particular year. The budget for a member state is included in multi-annual funds which aim to fulfil EU's policies or objectives, such as the European Fund for Regional Development, Cohesion Fund, Social European Fund and the European Agricultural Guarantee Fund. These funds contain several operational programmes, measures and projects separately contracted. There are three types of payment made by the European Commission to the national authorities: pre-funding (advance funds which are paid automatically in the first three years of the financial timeline 2007–2013), intermediate payments (the Commission refunds payments made by the state to the beneficiaries) and final payments. Accordingly, the financial allocation follows the n+3 communitarian rule, which means that the funding has to be spent in three years from allocation.

Romania: Two EU-Funded Agricultures

In 2009, Romania's contribution to the EU budget was approximately €1bn, which represents an average of €45 per person. After redistribution, Romania received €2.6bn from the EU, which was mostly spent on agricultural development. At a first glance, it would appear that being part of the EU is a profitable state of affairs for Romania. However, things are more complicated than this and hide deeper inequalities. For example, the financial support given to Romanian farmers is 30% less than what their Western counterparts receive (but this unequal financial contribution should have been adjusted by 2017). The main reason is that Romania has a bigger but less developed agricultural sector than the older members of the EU and bigger financial commitments would have put too much strain on the EU budget.[5]

In Romania roughly 30% of the population has agriculture as its main occupation—this is five times more than the EU average (INS 2013).[6] Even though the trend is declining, this is still the biggest concentration in the EU member states. At the same time, the size of Romanian family farms is very small, with an average of 3 hectares per family unit and 2.6 million households with less than 1 hectare. Consequently, the biggest rural population in Europe is working in small uneconomical farms, producing only for their own consumption, thus maintaining subsistence agriculture.

This subsistence agriculture encapsulates the social structure and problems of the Romanian rural environment such as hidden unemployment and poverty. In 2007 the average income from agricultural activities contributed only 20% of the total income of the average household whose members had agriculture as their main occupation. These statistics point to the fact that one in two people lives below the poverty line (Luca 2009).

Agriculture absorbed the economic shocks of the 1990s. The enforced deindustrialisation was reflected by high levels of unemployment in urban areas. Concomitantly the process of property restitution which started in 1991 [after the communist period] re-established the old property rights. These two factors explain patterns of urban-rural migration which translated into an increase of the proportion of population working in agriculture from 28.5% in 1989 to 43.5% in 2001 and 30% in 2005 (see Luca 2009). The former urban population that migrated to the rural areas had survived by cultivating small lots of land and producing for their own consumption.

EU support for agriculture is manifested in subventions proportional to the size of the property. The Romanian policy regulating agricultural subsidies aims to support farmers who own over one hectare. Luca (2009) show that this policy left out the 2.6 million households with lots smaller than 1 hectare. Furthermore, small farms (between 1 and 5 hectares) have received approximately 25% of the EU subventions. At the same time, less than 1% of farms with over 100 hectares have received over 50% of the subventions. The middle sector is underdeveloped using about 12% of the land. Consequently, the context facilitated the emergence of "two different agricultures: once characterised by subsistence (fragmentation of land and small lots, produce for own consumption, receive little or no support from the EU funding) and another one, highly competitive, based on big farms—hundreds of hectares and technologically developed" (Luca 2009).

Despite the need for investment, by December 2013, Romania managed to use only a small share—roughly 33%[7] of its available funding. The absorption rates (June 2013) within the 27 EU member states show that Romania is at the very bottom of the list. Poland, for example, which has an agricultural sector comparable to Romania managed to access nearly 60% of the funding. Bulgaria, which also joined the EU in 2007, has a 40% rate, which is quite extraordinary considering that the European Commission had suspended payments in 2008 amidst allegations of corruption and fraud.[8] The situation was worse in 2011, when Romania managed to access only 9% of the EU allocation (SAR 2011). Such low absorption rates are perceived as a public loss because the EU will automatically withdraw any funds unspent by the end of the financial period. The availability of these funds (which are perceived as 'God's gift'), the time pressure and the Romanians' incapacity to make use of this opportunity have acquired an inevitably pathetic tone, expressed in the rhetoric of 'now or never'. Political analysts talk about 'an absurd drama' (SAR 2011), government officials complain about the scarcity of good projects, while potential beneficiaries criticise the harsh economic conditions and the difficulty of the EU rules for structural funding. Instead of being a tool to achieve European cohesion, structural funding has become a symptom of disjunction through systematic associations with corruption.

This first section has focused on the process of EU funding and showed how is this process designed and managed at European level. After establishing the link between corruption and EU funding, the following section turns to providing a short social history of Romania through the lens of corruption and entrepreneurship. The socialist shortage economy and the lack of private property had placed money and consumerism very low on the scale of social values. Social status and prestige were thus constructed on different criteria, like education, political affiliation or professional competency. The 1989 Revolution upset this stability and promoted new values. Money became a measure of success and introduced inequality into a world that had been traditionally constructed on the principles of egalitarianism. In a short time, everybody wanted to be a *patron* (boss/manager), have their own business, make money and never again work for the State. The new culture favoured independence, entrepreneurship, material wealth, innovation and consumerism.

'The Same People': Socialism and Post-socialism

Socialist Entrepreneurs

Before the end of the 1980s, Romania had established itself as a socialist country with a centrally planned economy emphasising production rather than consumption. In December 1989, Romania had a gross national product of approximately US$162bn (an exchange rate of US$14,440 per leu[9]). The main sources of income for the state budget were industry (58%) and agriculture (15%). Politically, the country was ruled by a Communist Party which was proportionally the largest in Central and Eastern Europe with over 3.7 million members (Stoica 2006).

The socialist economy was inextricably linked with *nationalisation*, *collectivisation* and *industrialisation*. The first two phenomena transferred property rights from the individual to the state, so by the end of the regime, the state was the main resource holder. Industrialisation was the chosen long-term solution for increasing standards of living and reducing disparities between Romania and other European countries. Economic development was based on five-year plans—an imitation of the Soviet *gosplans*—which encompassed a series of centralised planned actions that were designed to bring quick development (Verdery 2004).

After the Second World War, Romania was in a very difficult economic situation, with a massive war debt and almost entirely subordinated economically to the Soviet Union. The Romanian Communist Party (established first as a branch of the Soviet Communist Party and then an independent entity) started an accelerated process of industrialisation, which had ecological implications for the population as it changed the composition of the workforce from mainly agricultural to industrial workers. As the main industrial plants were situated in cities, the process of industrialisation led to rural-urban migration. In turn, this created a housing problem, which was solved by a rapid development of the construction sector. The industrialisation process was anything but smooth, and this fact coupled with a severe energy crisis and the communist leaders' ambition to pay the foreign debt in full (over US$10bn in mid-1980s) worsened the standards of living (Verdery 2004) and prepared the ground for the 'economy of shortages' (Wedel 2003; Ledeneva 1998).

The first decade after the Second World War was dominated by the setup of communism regime. This process entailed the systematic destruction of former political, social and economic elites. By a twist of fate, the contemporary attempt to convict the regime symbolically was led by Vladimir Tismaneanu, presently Professor at the University of Maryland as head of the *Presidential Commission for the Study of Dictatorship in Romania*. He is the son of Leonte Tismaneanu, a high-profile *nomenklatura* member who was sent from Moscow in 1948 to build up communism in Romania. His nomination for the Commission stirred numerous polemics, with Paul Goma—a former political prisoner—openly expressing his mistrust of the 'Bolshevik offspring'[10] in his private journal, publicly available on the internet. The final report does mention Leonte Tismaneanu as a prominent party member responsible for indoctrination.[11]

The area where I conducted my research hosted the *Pitești Experiment* which is considered the most intensive brainwashing torture programme in Eastern Europe (Ierunca 1990). Pitești was the prison facility that aimed to 're-educate' political prisoners in order to alter their personalities, discard their political or religious convictions to become fully obedient to the newly established regime. Nicolae Purcarea, who at the age of 17 was sentenced to 15 years imprisonment on political grounds, recounted the harshness of the Pitești regime:

> The main protagonist of re-education was Eugen Turcanu, himself a political prisoner. "He was Satan himself. He had a phenomenal, visceral hatred that you could read in his eyes […] He was athletic with a big jaw […]. There were two awful things: sole beating and testicle beating … and after they beat you up, if you faint they pour some water over you to recover and keep beating you up. Eventually they sent you by the shit bucket, throw down a wet rag and tell you to run on it. It's like walking bare feet on broken glass … What a horrible invention! […] The main problem was they wanted you to turn from victim into executioner. This is what drove me crazy. I could not hit anyone, just couldn't. " There were two categories of prisoners: 'bandits' and 're-educated' or 'human and non-human' … Our comforts were pearl barley soup, poetry and praying. 'Whoever shared the cell with a priest was lucky because that one understood God. *Nicolae Purcarea, political prisoner*[12]

In the same geographical area, political imprisonment was offset by anti-communist resistance groups that hid in the nearby mountains. Led by Toma Arnautoiu, the Nucsoara group formed in 1949 and the last members were arrested roughly ten years later.[13] In this case the entire village was a collateral collective victim of the communist regime because it suffered the numerous raids and repeated tortures carried out to discover the location of the resisters. During the early 1990s there was not much sympathy for the surviving members of the anti-communist group who were blamed for bringing the attentions of the *Securitate* down on the village (Mungiu-Pippidi and Althabe 2002).

The socialist state had slowly turned into a totalitarian state by the end of the 1980s and was trying to regulate as many areas of people's lives as possible: from establishing one's residence (either through job, or forced residence), regulating migration (both within the borders of the state and outside) to imposing pronatalist policies (through the 1966 Decree that prohibited abortion). Private property was virtually non-existent, and the second economy was also strongly discouraged, especially after the 1970s. The 'family background' expressed by father's occupation had a strong impact on children's future, and so, being part of the second economy had far-reaching effects. For example, the children of self-employed individuals had lower chances of joining the Romanian Communist Party than peasants' offspring who had 'healthy origins'. They also had lower chances of entering universities and/or entering employment in urban areas. Without a university degree they had fewer chances for upward mobility in the Party hierarchy, as towards the end of the 1980s the leaders had come to favour educational credentials (Stoica 2006).

> *CB: I worked in this area for 30 years. Before joining the militia forces, I was county head of the Party. I grew up here. When I was your age or younger, I worked in a factory on a lathe ... you know what that is? ... it's metal work. Eight hours a day, I mean eight hours per night. I used to do night shifts because I played football and did boxing day-time. After sports I would go to evening classes because I wanted to finish high school. My parents did not have the money to keep me in high school, so they sent me to do vocational training. When I got my job, I decided to do it on my own. After nearly fifty years in this area, I know pretty much everyone that matters ... criminals, politicians, doctors, professors ... you name it. And they know me. You know, people have not changed. It's the same people that I played football with, or worked night shifts or met while a policeman. It's the same people, I am telling you! Some are richer, some are in prison, some are dead, but their children are here [...]*

> Maybe the sources of income are legitimate and I don't mean **legal**, but **legitimate**. For example, it once happened around 1986 or 1987, don't really remember … there was this guy, nice, smiley, good football player, he just liked drinking a bit too much. His wife shows up with a fur coat—now that's expensive stuff. I sniffed around … nothing. I went and talked to him. The man was honest, I could see it. His in-laws sold three pigs and gave their daughter/his wife the money to buy a fur coat. It was not legal to raise pigs and sell them without paying taxes, but people from the country … what could I have done? My own parents were doing the same! I let him go but told him to keep the wife and the fur at home because people talk!" (CB, retired police officer)

As the above quote shows, by 1989, Romania was an egalitarian society which did not allow for significant differences of material wealth between its members. However, the economy of shortages had polished the entrepreneurial skills of the locals. Goods in short supply were acquired through networks of friends and family and informal economy thrived—cognac, coffee and Kent cigarettes were typical products exchanged on the favour market that was essentially a non-monetised economy. A three-digit car number was a sign of status reserved for members of the middle or high political echelons. The principle of common property ownership created a particular work ethic guided by the relationship with the product of work. On the one hand employees might have been less interested in producing good quality work, and on the other hand they were more inclined to fiddle, steal or appropriate components of the 'common good'. In this context, the boundaries between the legal, licit and moral (and their antonyms) were blurred. People had a pragmatic approach to the concept of legality, considering first the morality and the necessity of an action and only later its legality. The entrepreneurial skills developed in this period related more to survival instinct, dissimulation, negotiating acceptable boundaries with authorities and developing strong networks of support.

An essential point is that even though socialism has officially died on Christmas Day 1989 when Ceausescu and his wife were executed, people and practices have continued in the same ways, ensuring stability over the transition period. 'The same people'—the expression used by CB in the above quote—points to the reproduction of elites (Szelenyi and Szelenyi 1995) *and* cultural practices that form the contemporary habitus (Bourdieu 1977). The next section turns to the transition period showing the ways in which such cultural practices and forms of capital have been altered by the social and political context which eventually linked entrepreneurship with corruption.

Entrepreneurs of Transition

The Revolution created an 'open historical situation' (Wittfogel 1981 in Wedel 2003) because the breakdown of the former communist structure was replaced by a fluid state of affairs that created almost infinite possibilities. In this moment of massive transformation, when the political, economic, administrative spheres were undergoing irreversible changes, the most reliable entities proved to be the 'old solidarity networks'. The networks of support that had acted as a safety net during communism now helped to ensure stability and provided access to various opportunities. And the most entrepreneurial individuals took advantage to make money, win influence and become successful. The savvy Romanian entrepreneur was reinvented in December 1989.

Gigi Becali's Story[14]

> ...With the jeans it's true ... I brought a truck load of jeans [from Turkey]. Back then, for every $1 invested in Turkey, you got $15 return in Romania. I brought $40,000-$50,000 merchandise simply because I could not bring $150,000 merchandise. I brought a load of pens and ten truck-loads of soap. And those walkmans ... just because they were in a warehouse and nobody was doing anything with them. Did I steal? Did I force anyone to buy? Back then there were no taxes. The money that I got from trading, I invested in real estate. I bought a CAP [former state-owned farm] with $1500 and sold it in a few months with $25,000 ... I took it for animals, wanted to do agriculture ... I was investing in agriculture, not real estates. But then when some Greeks told me to sell for $25,000 and they gave me the money ... I kept this a secret and invested all my money in real estate."[15] (Gigi Becali)

The story of Gigi Becali—entrepreneur, philanthropist, owner of Steaua Football Club, former member of the European Parliament, former deputy in the Romanian Parliament, party leader for The New Generation Party, later imprisoned for corruption and fraud serving a three and a half year sentence—is an extraordinary recount of upward mobility that resembles Schumpeter's ideal entrepreneur (1942). A Macedo-Romanian, like Gica Hagi, the great football player, and his godfather, he was a shepherd before the Revolution, inheriting the family business from his father who had established a flourishing trade with cheese, meat and wool under the protection of the communist elites. His family had moved from Albania to Pipera, near Bucharest in the 1950s. The communist regime required everybody to have a job, so Gigi Becali was employed in state factories as stoker and locksmith, despite having more than sufficient means to survive. One of his cousins, Victor Becali, worked in car repair, while the other one—Giovani Becali—was scalping cinema tickets during high school. After several attempts to leave the country, Giovani eventually managed to reach Germany in the 1980s. Without a stable income, he confessed to having tricked tourists into buying counterfeit Rolex watches.[16] Through his family connection with Gica Hagi, by 1989 Gigi Becali was already close to the national football team, providing players with milk, cheese and yogurt during their intensive training sessions. After the Revolution, he started importing jeans, soap and pens from Turkey, selling them in Romania. During the early 1990s he worked on fulfilling his father's dream of having a big animal farm, with pigs, sheep, cows, thus investing extensively in parcels of land. Subsequently, these investments have proved a gold mine promoting him to the Forbes Romania Rich List (in 2012 he held the 22nd position, but after his 2013 conviction he dropped to the 85th position).[17]

Around the late 1990s, Gigi Becali exchanged some of his land parcels with the Ministry of Defence, resulting in $892,758 damage to the state for which he was convicted in May 2013. In parallel he continued to fund Steaua Football Club and took it over in 2003, after an alleged discussion with another high-profile Romanian Premier League figure—Mitica Dragomir—who told him that "being the president of Steaua is cooler than being the president of Romania."[18] Around the same period, Gigi Becali obtained control of several key former communist companies—for example, munitions, farming and metal factories. An outspoken figure with Orthodox beliefs, he donated large sums for church renovation and for Romanian monks at Mount Athos and also built over 300 houses for flood victims. He ran for president of Romanian in 2004 with his own party—The New Generation—but obtained only 1.77% of the votes. In 2006, after reaching the semi-finals in UEFA (Union of European Football Associations) with Steaua, he celebrated the success along with President Traian Basescu, in Golden Blitz—a restaurant where only the presidential inner circle was allowed. The location was owned by Dorin Cocos, a major donor to presidential campaigns, whose wife Elena Udrea subsequently held various ministerial portfolios—ranging from Minister of Tourism to Minister of European Integration.

In 2009 Gigi Becali was an elected member of the European Parliament, but in 2012 he resigned in order to stand as a candidate for deputy in the Romanian Parliament and was elected with about 70% of the votes. In 2013 Gigi Becali was convicted and imprisoned for fraud and corruption.

In the 'Suitcase affair' he was accused of trying to bribe the players from U Cluj football team to 'correctly defend their chances to the title' against CFR Cluj, offering to reward them with 100,000 euro per player if they won. This was the last match from Romanian Premier League—if CFR Cluj lost, Becali's team, Steaua București, would have won the title and gone on to play in the European League. The suitcase containing 1.7 M euro was confiscated by the Anti-Corruption Directorate prosecutors in a restaurant in Cluj while the Steaua officials were watching the game and waiting to see if the reward was necessary or not. CFR won 1–0 so there was no reason to pay the rewards. Nevertheless, the prosecutors opened the file against Gigi Becali in 2008, and five years later he has convicted to three years of imprisonment by the High Court of Cassation and Justice after having previously acquitted him in 2012.

Gigi Becali's story shows how he used to his advantage the 'openness' of Romania's post-communist situation which was partly an outcome of the breakdown of the legal system. Typically for this period, even though involved in illegal activities, he did not define himself as a criminal. On the one hand this relates to the practice acquired during communism of divorcing morality from legality. In those days actions such as coming late to work, performing an abortion, acquiring goods in short supply through informal means were not considered crimes. On the other hand, immediately after the Revolution, there was a general feeling that everything was permitted—expressed by Becali as "back then, there were no taxes." This sense of legal pluralism was preserved long after the formal re-establishment of a regular legal system and represented a fertile terrain to build the new entrepreneurial spirit. Another example from my fieldwork exemplifies the sense of legal pluralism and typical moneymaking routines. After the Revolution, the new leadership in Bucharest decided to reward the people who made "a remarkable contribution" to overthrowing Ceaușescu by awarding them 'Revolutionary Certificates'. The criteria for awarding such certificates were not clear, but there were clear benefits to possessing one. The person who was awarded such a certificate was, for example, exempted from paying taxes. In no time, the certificates could be bought or received as a reward, to the point that some who fought against the demonstrators to preserve the communist regime and the Ceaușescu family obtained one.

The story of Gigi Becali, as extraordinary as it may seem, is the story of entrepreneurship shaped by the context of social and economic transition, luck, intuition and egomania. Despite his phenomenal upward mobility, Becali's ways of doing business are typical for the context. Entrepreneurship was also striving at the lower levels. Some people chose technical unemployment[19] before migrating to Western countries for work or setting up small firms. In other cases, people engaged in barter using the products of the enterprise they worked in. They stole or bought cheap products from their workplace (e.g., porcelain, screws, tyres, textiles), transported them abroad in their cars and exchanged them for whatever the local market demanded. The preferred destinations were Turkey (for jeans[20] and gold), Hungary (for coffee and food) and former Yugoslavia (for cognac). Everything was for sale and everything could be bought. The demand side of the market was hungry for products, no matter what the products were: music cassettes, stereos, colour TVs, blankets, jewels, houses, cars, parcels of land to build houses, and so on. For example, at the beginning of the 1990s it was common to import merchandise from Turkey and sell it in Romania; later, it became unprofitable because, following the global trends, cheaper consumer goods had started to be imported from the Asian markets. For example, Geta, one of my respondents, recounts her experience with Turkish imports:

> I was very brave … you know … I went to Turkey and imported stuff from there. Andrei [her husband] was busy at work; he did not want to join. But I went there by myself … sometimes with Dana [her sister]. We did not speak Turkish or anything but there were so many Romanians that you did not need to. We had this old Dacia Break … we would fill it with China porcelain or whatever worked on the market … sold it there and bought jeans and gold to re-sell in Romania. It depended what we were asked for […] I never left my job, no! I could not know what would happen … you know some transports were good, some were bad … I was left with merchandise … you could not count on that. Besides, I used to sell most of the stuff at work. Why would I have left my job?" (Geta, entrepreneur)

Geta further explained that as a low-level entrepreneur she was more vulnerable to market forces than Gigi Becali. She did small-scale trades using her private car, as opposed to the large enterprise described in the previous example. Furthermore, while Becali chose to diversify his business endeavours in order to counteract contextual uncertainty (by investing in real estate or football), Geta maintained her job in a state enterprise. The logic of practice (Bourdieu 1977) is similar referring to diversification of income sources, but the actual practices are very different, one emphasising complete change and attention to the market and the other one pointing to mixed strategies that combine the stability of a state job with the entrepreneurial endeavours required on the market.

International affairs opened up further economic opportunities. During the Yugoslav war, illegal trade over the Danube flourished. Oil products such as petrol and diesel fuel were in high demand, but other products like detergents could be smuggled as well. Between 1992 and 1995 and in 1999, while Romania maintained an embargo with Yugoslavia, illegal commerce flourished in the areas around the border between the two countries. During that period there was a common expression: *a face embargoul* (doing the embargo) which referred to breaking the embargo. Fortunes were made quickly (some were also spent quickly) with the help of the border guards who were willing to turn a blind eye for a small fee. The embargo had negative economic effects of the national economy (Romania lost over US$2bn), but it created a market for smuggling and helped the local economy and daring entrepreneurs, who were not afraid to risk their freedom for money.

The Macroeconomic Reading of Gigi Becali Story

The macroeconomic version of Gigi Becali's story is rather bleak. The recession that started in 1991 was undoubtedly prolonged by high rates of inflation. As shown in Fig. 3.2, in the first few years after the Revolution, the inflation rate increased over 30 times from 5.1 in 1990 to 170.2 in 1991. The trend continued until 1994, when the economy registered the first significant decrease from 256.1% in 1993 to 136.7% in 1994. The economy was not stable enough to sustain such a decrease, though, and in 1994 the inflation increased five times compared with the previous year. After that peak it constantly decreased, which shows that the economy slowly became more stable and displayed signs of sustainable growth. The UN Economic Commission for Europe argued that the main source of inflation in the first years after the Revolution was the financial loss caused

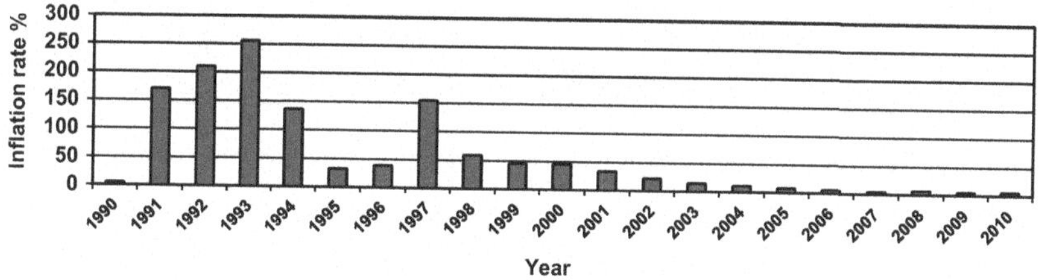

Fig. 3.2 Inflation rate in Romania 1990–2010. Source of data: Institutul Naţional de Statistică (National Institute of Statistics) http://www.insse.ro/cms/rw/pages/ipc.ro.do

by the state-owned enterprises that had not been privatised (*Tinerama*, no. 146, September, 1993).

This economic evolution is also reflected in the changes in the gross national product (Fig. 3.3). Similar with inflation rate, the gross national product (GNP) had negative changes until 1993, switched to positive values until 1996 and then only reverted to negative until 2000. The 2008 crisis impacted Romania in 2009, when the GNP had a negative value of 7.1 as compared to the previous year.

As shown in Fig. 3.4, the GNP and the inflation rate displayed similar patterns throughout the 20-year period from 1990 to 2010. The high and low values occur at about the same time and most likely connected to the process of privatisation.

Another important indication of the economic state of the country is the exchange rate between Romanian Leu (ROL) and US dollar. Historical trends show constant depreciation of the Romanian currency from 1990 till 2003. Immediately after the Revolution, the value of US dollars increased dramatically as compared to the Romanian currency—from 21.56 in 1991 it reached a value of 33,200 in 2003. This represents an increase of over 15,000 times in the value of the dollar (Fig. 3.5). During this period the Romanian currency was depreciating so fast that most people preferred to keep their savings in US dollars and conduct market transactions in foreign currency. A side effect of the depreciation was the proliferation of exchange and mortgage houses during the early 1990s. Exchange houses offered better prices for foreign currency than the banks and had the advantage of never being short of cash. The figures below show the evolution of the ROL-US dollar exchange rate

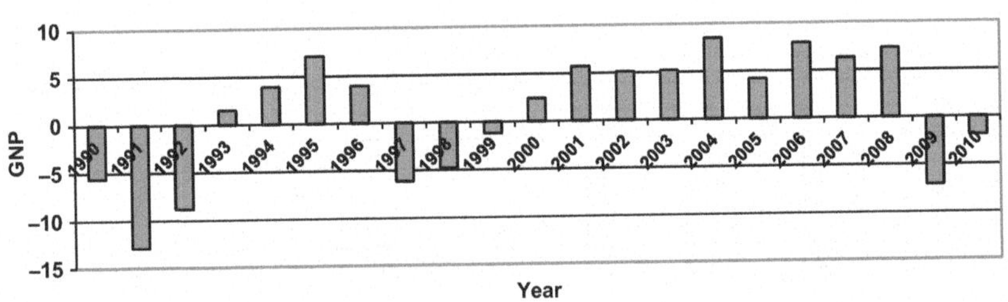

Fig. 3.3 The evolution of the gross national product in Romania 1990–2010. Source of data: UNECE and businessday.ro http://www.unece.org/fileadmin/DAM/stats/publications/Countries_InFigures2011.pdf; www.businessday.ro

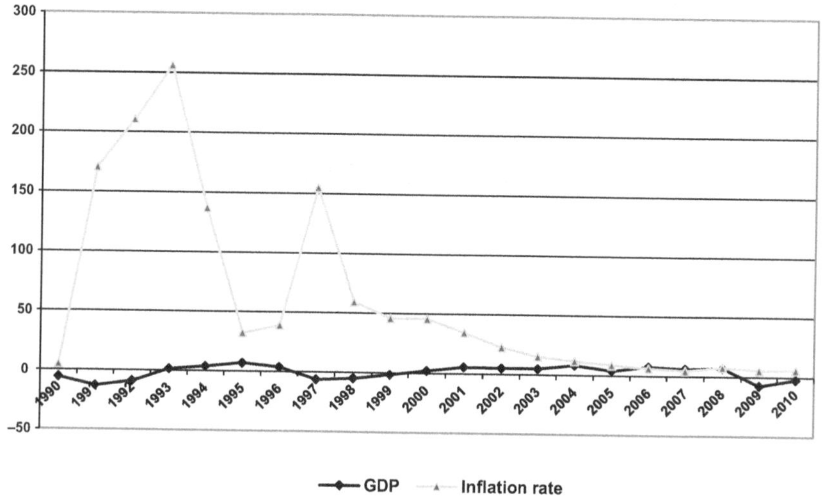

Fig. 3.4 The evolution of GDP and inflation rate between 1990 and 2010

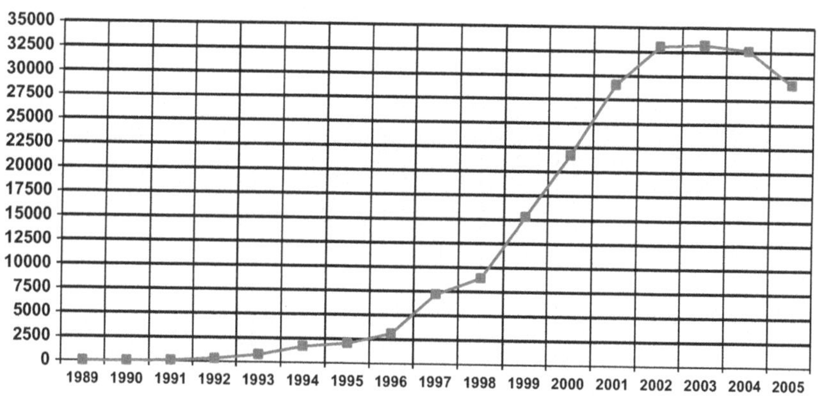

Fig. 3.5 Yearly average official exchange rates: Romanian Leu per US dollar 1989–2005 before denomination. Source: Banca Naţională a României (National Bank of Romania) http://www.bnr.ro/Raport-statistic-606.aspx

from 1989 to 2010. In 2005, the government decided to denominate the Romanian currency, by four digits. The ROL became RON (Fig. 3.6). Figure 3.5 shows the evolution of the RON-US dollar exchange rate between 2005 and 2010.

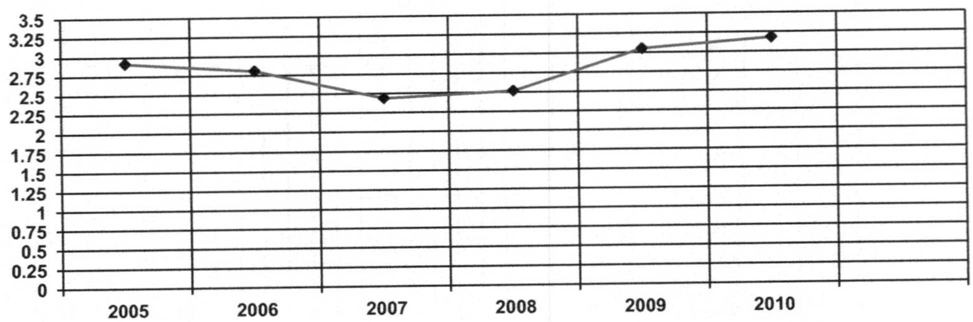

Fig. 3.6 Yearly average exchange rates: Romanian Leu per US dollar 2005–2010 after denomination. Source of data: Banca Națională a României (National Bank of Romania) http://www.bnr.ro/Raport-statistic-606.aspx

The economic recession had serious social effects, especially because privatisation raised the rate of unemployment. As shown in Fig. 3.5, tipping points occurred in the years 1994 and 1999 (around 11%). In only three years, the unemployment rate increased from 1.8 in 1991 to 11 in 1994. These periods coincide with the successful privatisation of various state enterprises and with the closing down of the former socialist industrial plants. In a more stable economy, former workers in these organisations would have been absorbed by other sectors, but in the Romanian context this was not the case. The state offered little protection for this category of people who were particularly vulnerable as they were not psychologically ready to become jobless (since the communist regime required everyone to have a job) and had few skills to face the market economy, especially in such volatile conditions. Some have argued (Popescu-Birlan 1994) that it was the slow pace of privatisation that led to the gradual increase in poverty. However, this seems unlikely, as other countries (e.g., Poland) who have adopted a faster pace, sometimes known as 'the shock therapy' displayed similar patterns. Even though Romania's progress has been slow, it has improved somewhat in the last years (until 2008 when the financial crisis hit Romania too) as shown in the figures above. The unemployment rate started to decrease from 10.2 in 2002 reaching a minimum of 4.3 in 2007; the GNP had small but positive values for eight years between 2000 and 2008, while the inflation rate decreased constantly (Fig. 3.7).

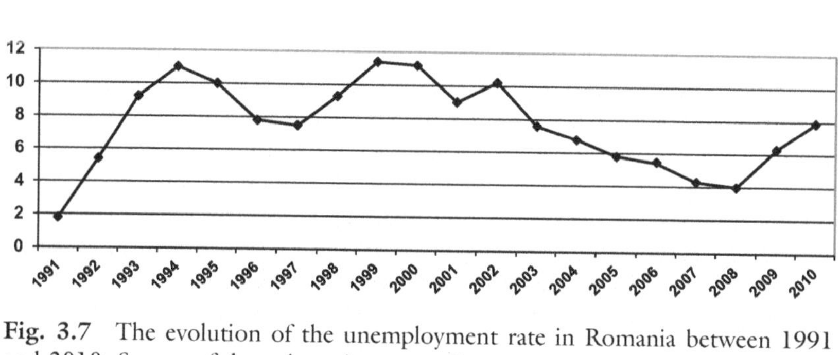

Fig. 3.7 The evolution of the unemployment rate in Romania between 1991 and 2010. Source of data: Agenţia pentru Ocuparea Forţei de Muncă (National Agency for Employment) http://www.anofm.ro/evolutia-ratei-somajului-in-perioada-1991-2010

Trading the State's Wealth: Privatisation

The unique environment of Romania in transition was marked by the creation of property rights. As Katherine Verdery remarks (2004), this occurred through two distinct processes: property creation and property restitution. The first involved the transfer of goods from state property to private property and the second giving back property to its former owners (or their offspring).

The right to private property was established by the 1991 Constitution (Article 44 from the fundamental law guarantees the right to private property). In an attempt to avoid the abuses of the previous regime, the new Constitution introduced a unique feature unique among European states, by stating that in Romania, the licit character of wealth was presumed (Art. 44 (8)). This constitutional article creates great confusion presently and makes the prosecutors' job more difficult in the cases of inexplicable wealth. It basically makes the confiscation of wealth impossible unless there is proof of a crime beyond reasonable doubt. The recent discussions about revising Art. 44 (8) were not able to amend or replace it, which shows that the memories of the communist regime are still fresh and the anxiety of experiencing past abuses is too strong. Ironically, my fieldwork shows that a direct consequence for EU funding accession is that applicants could launder money under the protection of this article. In order to obtain EU funding, an applicant is required only to prove the co-funding capacity for a project, but not to prove that the sources of income are legitimate. This aspect allowed, for example, several former migrants who have worked abroad illegally to successfully access EU funding.

One of the most important laws regarding privatisation, Law 58, was passed in August 1991. It stipulated that the newly created Fund of State Property was the main body in charge of the complete privatisation of the state-owned commercial companies. The Fund of State Property was granted 70% of the companies' capital and was required to privatise them within seven years. The rate of inflation made this task impossible, and the privatisation process was inevitably prolonged. By the end of 1993 an OECD report indicated that only 2% of the industrial sector was privatised (Romania Libera 28 August 1993 in Popescu-Birlan 1994).

Privatisation offered opportunities for quick enrichment for those entrepreneurial enough, who had some financial means or were in key hierarchical positions, like Gigi Becali. A typical mechanism was to set up a private company and then transfer funds from the state company to the private firm. Another common route to enrichment was to consistently manage a state company so badly that it went bankrupt (some examples are further discussed in Chap. 8). Eventually the company would be sold (usually to the former manager) at a very low price. Both cases rely on bribing the departmental directors and the officials in order to turn a blind eye. By the end of 1993, the investigators had uncovered 1200 serious illegal acts committed by the managers of several state-owned companies (Adevarul, 1 December 1993). Various Romanian officials and managers took advantage of the lucrative opportunities offered by privatisation (Mungiu-Pippidi 2006).

The Agricultural Sector: Rural Entrepreneurs

RB: *What do you say about getting your land back?*

NB: *It's horrible! I resent it! What am I going to do with it now? I am old, don't have the strength to work hard anymore. My children have left for the city ... they don't care about land, they have good jobs there. Here, in the country, the living conditions are not good [...] It's very expensive to have my land back. Since I can't work, I need to hire people, but now everybody is busy with their own land, and those who don't have are ripping me off. I pay 50 Romanian Lei per day for hoeing plus food and* ***tuica*** [Romanian brandy]. *I need three people for five days. My pension is a little over 200 Lei. You do the calculations. Oh, and it's not only hoeing ... it's also planting, picking, putting fertiliser ... These people in government know nothing about our work, otherwise they would not have given the land back [...]. Besides, I don't need so much corn or flour or plums for* ***tuica*** *... This old one [points to her husband] is already drinking too much!*

RB: *But then, why do you keep working the land? I mean ... if you don't need all these products...*

NB: *[rather shocked by the idea] Oh, but that is impossible! What would people say? We would be the laugh of the village! No way!*

RB: *But aren't you a bit glad to get your land back ... you are* ***proprietar*** *[an owner] now!*

SB: *Yeah, yeah ...* ***proprietar*** *with no means to work what I own...*

(NB and SB, peasants)

Re-establishing property rights through reinstating former owners was received with mixed feelings in rural areas. As the above quote shows, the direct beneficiaries of this political move found themselves in the rather awkward position of 'owners with no means of production'. This results in hybrid economic relations that are based on both monetary and non-monetary arrangements—in this case money and food are part of the payment. The land encompasses various forms of capital—much less financial (as it is not a profitable business) and much more historical and symbolic (because any work is done with reference to the entire community). If the purpose of household economy was producing for its own consumption (Polanyi 1954), the above quote shows that in an attempt to maintain their symbolic capital people produce more than they need. The surplus is sold to intermediaries who travel the villages in old 4x4 cars shouting that they buy corn, plums or wheat. Intermediaries prefer to buy the raw products because they are cheaper, can be sold fast and the buyer can control the quality of the final products.

Law 18/1991 re-established the property rights of the former owners or their offspring. Rural areas were greatly impacted as the law dismantled the former state-owned farms (the Agricultural Cooperative of Production, or CAP). The new owners wanted to work their parcels but lacked the technological resources that were the property of the former CAPs and the workforce (as everyone had their own lot, it was very difficult to find people to work the land, especially in the absence of technology). A side effect of restitution was the fragmentation of rural space, which is even now characterised by a small farm structure where work is performed with traditional tools due to the lack of access to machinery, buildings, financial capital and low income levels. This phenomenon has had long-term impacts, especially for accessing EU funding, as described in the previous section.

In rural areas, the level of unemployment and poverty has been consistently higher than in the cities. Dismantling the industry has left the residents of rural areas with agriculture as their main source of income. However, agriculture is a highly volatile business in Romania, as it is dependent on weather, performed with rudimentary tools and thus the productivity is very low. People produce for their own consumption that creates the 'subsistence agriculture'. According to the UN Economic Commission for Europe in 2009, agriculture contributed 7% to the GNP and employed almost one third of the Romanian population (29%).[21]

Creating an agricultural sector based on individual farming was more a political move than an economically wise decision. The goal of the new leadership at the beginning of the 1990s was not to make the production system more efficient, but to change the social paradigm and introduce variations in the ownership structure. In this process of paradigmatic change (from socialism to neoliberalism), little attention was paid to the social costs of such policies.

Closely linked to the privatisation process, the agricultural changes were interpreted by theorists as an attempt to revitalise entrepreneurship in rural areas (Repassy and Symes 2008), a strategy to transform agriculture (Gomez y Paloma and Segre 1993), a post-communist way to divide common property (Oberschall 1996), or even a new religion (Luckmann 1967). Irrespective of the theoretical explanation provided, most scholars agree on the fact that generally the privatisation and the transformation of agriculture in Southern Eastern Europe led to a gradual economic recession.

Political Changes

> How could a kid born in the Soviet Union know that he would die in the EU? Not even the Kremlinologists knew this. Only my grandma knew it. She used to say: my family lived in three (meanwhile four) countries without ever having left the village. (Vasile Ernu, Moldavian writer[22])

The Romanian transition entailed first and foremost a shift from Eastern-Russian political influence to Western-EU political affiliation. The political spectrum did not offer a wide array of options, as most parties had similar agendas which were developed top-down, from the parliamentary debates, and not from grass-roots constituencies. These agendas have been heavily shaped by the international constraints regarding the supremacy of the neoliberal market and EU accession. Consequently, political parties had few policy options but to keep the substantive policy commitments related to the EU entry, without destroying their own popularity (Miroiu and Cerkez 2013).

> The successful competitive strategies have been those of technocracy, populism, and nationalism—the last two tending to be combined. These political discourses dominate because they offer politicians maximum flexibility to look as though they are competing, even if all governments face remarkably similar state policy pressures. (Grzymala-Busse and Abby Innes 2003: 68)

In most cases, competing politicians chose populism as the preferred tactic for winning elections. This resulted in a highly personalised debate about "corruption, personal competence, property restitution, relatively trivial disputes within political parties or with neighbouring states, and disputes over who was on which side of the barricades in the communist period" (Grzymala-Busse and Abby Innes 2003: 67).

These harsh economic conditions created a sense of dissatisfaction among the population who blamed the political class for the lack of improvement in the standard of living. This was augmented by the fact that second-echelon communist leaders had become the democratically elected representatives of Romanians. Some argued that nothing had changed, that it was like a Romanian saying went: "Aceeaşi Mărie cu altă pălărie" ("The same Marie [personal name] with a different hat"). A well-known journalist, Ilie Serbanescu, wrote at the time: "The restoration is total. All the [leading] positions are occupied by people of the past who cannot help thinking like they used to think in the past … The reform process is completely blocked…" *(22,* no. 35 (137)). Furthermore, certain elites, largely from the former *nomenklatura*, had gained access to resources by combining financial capital with political influence. These "unruly coalitions" are "loose clustering of elites, neither institutionalised nor otherwise formally recognised" (Verdery 1996: 193), "less institutionalised, less visible, less legitimate" than political parties (1996: 194). A good example is the energy sector which is dominated by a small group of individuals who buy cheap energy from the state and sell it at increased prices to the public (Ionita et al. 2011).

Romania initiated the formalities to join EU in the early 1990s and put forward its candidacy in 1995[23] under the social democrat governance (Social Democratic Party—PSD). The European Commission had monitored Romania since 1997 and published an annual Regular Report since 1998. In 2002, the EU had announced that Romania and Bulgaria had not managed to advance rapidly enough in fulfilling the Copenhagen criteria and would not join EU in 2004. However, it was decided to support both countries in joining EU in 2007 if they fulfilled all the criteria for accession.

The European Commission set up special mechanisms for Romania and Bulgaria to ensure that they both internalised the *acquis communautaire*. For Romanian governments faced with shrinking budgets, this was an enormous task, and the costs for setting up the state administration and its capacity to implement these laws were huge. Before joining the EU,

Romania had to harmonise its national legislation with EU standards on every possible front from banking regulations to victims' protection. All these had to be integrated into the legislative framework and implemented with the highest priority. The European Commission has acknowledged since 1999 that Romania had fulfilled all the political criteria for accession. However, the Regular Reports pointed to problems on Chap. 24—Justice and Home Affairs, especially in regards to corruption. The Commission described corruption as 'widespread and systemic', stating in strong terms that it impeded on the country's capacity to develop and fulfil the *acquis communautaire* (See Romania country reports for 2005, 2006).

Corruption

The past decade was characterised by the globalisation of anti-corruption policies in the form of international conventions. These conventions provided the international community with a standardised set of anti-corruption instruments. Romania has also become part of the global anti-corruption movement by signing the United Nations Convention Against Corruption (UNCAC), the Stability Pact Anti-corruption Initiative (2000), the OECD's cooperation framework on the fight against corruption[24,25] and adopting the Council of Europe Civil and Criminal Law Conventions on Corruption. The expansion of the anti-corruption domain was accompanied by the multiplication of international/regional partnerships that monitored and incentivised the implementation of anti-corruption reforms. For example, in 1999 Romania became part of GRECO (Group of States Against Corruption), took an active role in the Council of Europe's Programme of Action against Corruption and is under European Commission's close supervision through the Mechanism of Cooperation and Verification.

The anti-corruption reforms followed a generic pattern based on a set of tools and ideas provided by the international community. The 'one size fits all' approach (Kpundeh 2004: 127) prescribed a 'holistic anti-corruption strategy' (Galtung 1998; Langseth et al. 1999) which involved, among others, institutional redesign to increase accountability, legal reforms, an independent media, public awareness, an active civil society, economic liberalisation and deregulation (World Bank 2000; Transparency International 2000; UN 2004; UNDP 2004). The semantic expansion of corruption was doubled by the development of the anti-corruption market. By 2003, a rough estimation of the global market size for anti-corruption was around

$100 M, "making anti-corruption an industry in itself—an industry in which Central and Eastern Europe was a valuable market niche" (Bryane and Bowser 2009: 17). By 2009, the fight against corruption, particularly in Eastern Europe and Former Soviet Union, had become a multibillion dollar industry (Bryane and Bowser 2009). But while governments and donors spent more and more to fight corruption, only a tiny fraction of the police cases dealt with this crime. For example, the EU has spent millions of euro on cross-border anti-corruption programmes, but Europol was involved in only a few cases of corruption (Bryane and Bowser 2009).

However, the Brussels-driven Europeanisation did not always have the expected results. Despite the complete institutional redesign and the substantive changes of legislation, analysts duly noticed that the laws were not implemented and the newly set up institutions were not used (EC 2002, 2003, 2004, 2005, 2006; Freedom House 2005; SAR 2011). In other words, Europeanisation lacked substance. The resistance to change doubled by the pressure put on the government to over perform reform perverted the democratic mechanisms of governance. For example, the 2003 EC country report for Romania noticed an abuse of emergency ordinances, while the 2006 EC country report mentioned 105 emergency ordinances approved between February and July 2006. More recently the government has employed the vote of confidence and had assumed responsibility for passing particular items of legislation; in 2009 the government wanted to assume responsibility for the adoption of the new Criminal and Civil Codes, invoking the urgency of the matter (eventually, the codes were adopted through ordinary procedure in September 2010) (TI 2011). Even though these are extraordinary measures, they have been normalised by overuse. This situation creates not only a perpetual sense of urgency, but at a more subtle level, subverts the democratic process because these are all mechanisms to *bypass* parliamentary debates.

Over the past few years (2005–2012), the anti-corruption ethos that aimed to reform the entire society was translated in awareness campaigns, emergency lines, opinion polls, workshops, meetings and training sessions. Using PHARE (Poland and Hungary: Assistance for Restructuring their Economies) funding, the Ministry of Justice conducted an €1.8 M anti-corruption campaign between 16 October 2007 and 27 February 2008. The Ministry of European Integration ran an anti-corruption campaign with the slogan 'I do not give bribes—I do not take bribes' (*E.U. nu dau spaga—E.U. nu iau spaga*)—based on wordplay—the message was that EU members have nothing in common with corruption. The General Anti-Corruption Directorate (DGA) and the National Integrity Agency (ANI) popularised the telephone 'green line' (TelVerde) that citizens can use free of charge to report corruption crimes committed by ministry employees, while the Fight Against Fraud Department (DLAF) focused on preventing fraud to the EU budget. Partnerships and strategic alliances between civil society and state institutions were established. For example, DGA conducted several such exercises: "Let's get it over with the envelopes!" ("Gata cu plicurile!") in cooperation with Romanian Postal Service (on the basis of a protocol between the two institutions, all envelopes and receipts issued for the public use will be stamped with anti-corruption messages and information about the green line), 'Travel the anti-corruption route' (in cooperation with RATB, the Bucharest Public Transport Network), 'I am financing slavery' (in cooperation with a local branch of Asociatia Pro Democratia).

These campaigns, the international pressures expressing the necessity of adopting the *acquis communautaire* and the demands of the international financial institutions and business community had transformed corruption into a catastrophe. Thus, the 'fight against corruption' had become a complex endeavour, with moral entrepreneurs (Becker 1963) and policy entrepreneurs (Zahariades 2014) making use of various strategic approaches. So far, Romania has had four anti-corruption strategies, all of them reflecting a change in the 'fight against corruption'. The first anti-corruption (SNA I: 2001–2004) strategy aimed to align the political and penal semiotics by making the legislative framework in relationship to corruption as comprehensive as possible. The second strategy (SNA II 2005–2007) aimed to establish the institutional architecture dedicated to corruption control and prevention. The third anti-corruption strategy (SNA III 2008–2011) was mainly focused on the vulnerable sectors and local administration. The fourth anticorruption strategy (2012–2015) introduced clearer mechanisms for evaluating previous achievements, while empahsising the importance of preventive measures.

Did We Have Corruption Before [the Revolution]?

> What corruption before 1989? Don't even think about it! There was the [Communist] Party! **Securitatea** was following your every move! Forget it! Maybe some low-level train 'godfathers', nothing more… (CB, police officer, retired)

> Of course we had corruption! It was the Communist Party that was most corrupt! You really don't know anything about this area? About our history? In these mountains, we had the resistance movement. Fifty kilometres down the road was the Pitești experiment… (AB, former political prisoner, retired)

> Yeah, there was corruption, but it wasn't a priority for law enforcement. As prosecutors, we did not care about it ... it was a work-related thing ... nothing fancy... (IA, prosecutor, judicial inspector, retired)

> What does corruption mean? I do not understand it. We did not use this word when I was younger. (NB, peasant, agricultural worker)

The above quotes display a wide range of opinions regarding corruption that effectively contextualise its meaning through association with the state apparatus and its priorities. A more detailed law enforcement perspective is offered by CB below.

> Well, it was a bit different ... I mean ... we did not have as it is today ... The thing is we had it in the Criminal Code, but it was not our main thing, as it is now. You know, we work on performance indicators, always have ... always will ... So for me, as an economic police inspector there are some targets I needed to achieve. For example ... a certain number of frauds, embezzlements things like that. I did heavy stuff, not corruption ... back then that was for pussies ... you know beginners. They would usually realise towards the end of the month that they did not do much work and would go on train raids ... everyone travelled **cu nasul** ['with the godfather'—the common denomination for train ticket inspectors]. Get some of those, make a criminal file and move on ... easy, no? As for me ... no! I had to deal with very complex cases, with high profile individuals. The trick was that everything was state property back then and everyone was in the [Communist] Party, so you had to be careful. Nobody got to be an accountant or a director of a major factory if they were not quite high up not only in the Party hierarchy, but also in the Securitate. (CB police officer, retired)

Formal attempts to define corruption in Romanian legislation are rather recent. Before the Revolution, the 1969 Criminal Code mentioned corruption only in two distinct cases: corruption of a minor for sexual purposes and corrupting a witness to commit perjury (Banciu et al. 2005). None of these cases had much in common with the present understanding of the concept, which generally referred to 'the abuse of public power for private gain'. The crimes that incorporated the modern meaning of corruption were instead grouped under chapter 'Crimes in relation to work' and were decoded as bribe giving, bribe taking, trade in influence and receiving of undue goods (Articles 254–257, Criminal Code 1969). However, the concept of corruption was never used in relation to these crimes (Banciu et al. 2005).

CB explained that, as a work-related offence, corruption was not a priority for law enforcement. He elaborated this point by saying that in order to achieve the performance indicators law enforcement would 'raid the trains'. This point relates to a typical practice of cultural travelling routines—when I was a student, my friends and I rarely bought train tickets as we considered it an unnecessary expense. When travelling in large groups, we would all contribute with small amounts leaving a male friend to stay on the train corridor smoking and wait for 'the godfather' [train ticket inspector]. The corridor was full of contributors. When the 'godfather' arrived, the person would give the money and point to the group. With an expert eye, the conductor would count the money and quickly assess if the amount correlated to the size of the group. This cultural practice was transformed by law enforcement into a crime category the effects of which could still be traced in the early 2000s. Research conducted by the Romanian Institute of Criminology (Banciu et al. 2005) analysed the sentencing patterns for corruption cases and the socio-demographic characteristics of the offenders (covering all the definitive sentences for this crime between 1998 and 2002). The results profiled train conductors as a high-risk category for corruption offences, further noticing that 77% of convictions were directed at offenders with no previous record, approximately one quarter of the offenders convicted for corruption were unemployed (23.8%), about 10% were low-level security staff and 5% were retired.

These patterns of crime did not match the perceived levels of corruption (which portrayed corruption in Romania as 'systemic' according to Transparency International local reports [2002, 2003]), and in 2000, the Parliament adopted "Law 78/2000 on preventing, discovering and sanctioning of corruption acts." Apart from establishing in penal language the modern understanding of corruption, this law effectively linked it to EU funding. Four major types of crime were included under the umbrella of corruption: offences mentioned by the 1969 Criminal Code (bribe giving, bribe taking, trade in influence and receiving of undue goods); crimes associated with corruption (a rather heterogeneous category including crimes as diverse as fraudulent privatisations, bending the rules of crediting, commercial operations incompatible with professional status, the abuse of confidential information, blackmail if committed by certain categories of civil servants); other categories of crimes regulated by the Criminal Code or special laws that were in direct relation or assimilated to corruption (such as the abuse of power against the public interest); and crimes against the financial interests of the EU (this last category was included to respect the 1995 PIF Convention).[26]

By 2003, anti-corruption was delivered in packages. For example, Law 161/2003 (along with Law 52/2003, branded as the Anti-corruption Pack) criminalises conflict of interest; institutes prohibitions for high public servants (members of government, state secretaries and sub-secretaries, prefects and sub-prefects) to issue administrative or judicial acts that would produce a benefit for themselves, their partners or any relative to the first degree; defines new categories of incompatibilities for public servants; modifies and brings clarifications to other laws regarding corruption (e.g., Law 78/2000, Law 188/1999).

Despite the multiplication of legal provisions, the justice system was not achieving the desired effects, because it continued to target 'petty corruption' as proven by conviction patterns (Banciu et al. 2005). Corruption's insidious nature demanded an even more comprehensive approach to eradicate not only low-level offences but also high-level corruption committed by high-status officials that heavily affected the public budget. This need for expressive justice (Garland 2002) was encapsulated in the setting up of the National Anti-corruption Prosecutor's Office (NAPO) in 2000. Since then, anti-corruption institutions have proliferated—for example, the DGA, ANI and, in connection to it, National Council of Integrity (CNI) set up in 2007, individual anti-corruption units within various ministries—showing that this crime had become too important and its control demanded a *specialisation of the justice circuits*.

The NAPO was set up in 2002 at the request of EU and with €2 M funding through a PHARE programme. As the aim of NAPO was to target high-level corruption, it focused on cases involving sums higher than €100,000 or high-ranking officials. As a distinguishing feature, NAPO's institutional complement included not only prosecutors but also experts and its own judiciary police. To reflect the importance attached to this institution, NAPO prosecutors were paid 40% more than their counterparts in the General Prosecutor's Office on the grounds that they were dealing with high-level corruption (Freedom House 2005). This, coupled with the lack of transparency in the selection procedure, created a lot of resentment in the prosecutorial body (Freedom House, 2005: 82). Ironically, the main anti-corruption institution was suspected of corruption.

The new codification of corruption was accompanied by the reform of the justice system in order to ensure a rigorous application of the legislation. The disturbance in the traditional economy of illegalities required a system that would administer force differently in order to maintain the new adjustments. In line with the orthodoxy of transparency, the justice establishment had to be made independent, predictable and impartial, which was a rather surprising turn to Jeremy Bentham's classical criminology. In a 2010 report, the Superior Council of Magistracy admitted that its programmes were designed to take into account the funding opportunities and the international reports about the Romanian justice system. This short-term political calculation was bound to affect the long-term development of the Romanian justice system by overspecialising a significant body of magistrates in particular areas.

'Moral Entrepreneurs' (Becker 1964): Anti-corruption as an Electoral Tool

The 2004 elections were won by a liberal-democratic coalition, and the new government decided that fighting corruption was its main priority (EC 2005). Monica Macovei, a former prosecutor during communism and a former member of civil society during the transition, was appointed the new Minister of Justice. She emerged as the leader of anti-corruption movement. Her efforts were highly appreciated by the European officials, and on 1 January 2007, Romania joined the EU. Romanian officials were less appreciative of Mrs Macovei's efforts and the Senate voted a motion against her which led to her dismissal. Her successor, Mr Tudor Chiuariu, spent less than a year in office and was dismissed by President Basescu when charged in a corruption case.

Due to the EC's close monitoring, the institutional architecture continued to change according less to the needs of the system and more to the international recommendations. However, as opposed to the previous stage, the new government was more focused on developing preventive partnerships between public institutions and the civil society. For the first time after the Revolution, NGOs were regularly invited to participate in public decisions. Furthermore, there was a marked change in the style of management of the public institutions. Ministers started to behave like managers of private companies, and a new economic ethos was brought to the justice system. Public institutions were governed according to strategies and action plans, which designed clear lines of action and strict deadlines. Independent audits were conducted and matters of cost-effectiveness were considered of utmost importance. And all these changes were somehow determined, reported, explained or justified through corruption or, to be more precise, through anti-corruption.

Monitoring Corruption in an EU Member State

When admitted into the EU in 2007, Romania was not considered fully prepared, with corruption being flagged as the main problem. Consequently, the European Commission set up the Cooperation and Verification Mechanism (MCV) to ensure further close monitoring in this area. This Mechanism does not have a particular deadline and is designed to stay in place until all the benchmarks are considered achieved. The third anti-corruption strategy (SNA III 2008–2010) focused on the fourth benchmark established by MCV (which advised the government to adopt further measures to prevent and control corruption in the local administration), but it also took into account other national and international evaluations (e.g., GRECO, TI). Aiming at building the institutional capacity of the anti-corruption establishment, the strategy used the language of risk to define the vulnerabilities of specific sectors while emphasising the need to conduct further research to identify additional dangers and organise anti-corruption awareness campaigns.

Subsequent country reports started to praise the law enforcement agencies. For example, the 2010 EC country report noticed the effectiveness of institutional cooperation between DGA and prosecutors in tackling complex cases of corruption, which was partially attributed to the high level of expertise displayed by the DGA police officers and a positive reflection of DGA's specialisation and its exclusive focus on corruption. In 2011, DGA played a major role in a spectacular investigation conducted by the DNA which targeted border police and customs officers. This success pointed to a 'new level of institutional capability' (EC country report 2011), which justified the hopes that this institution could become involved in more complex cases involving public procurement or organised crime.

After Romania had joined the EU without having solved its problems regarding corruption, the European community expressed anxiety that the new member state would use corrupt means to affect the financial interests of the EU. The sense of discomfort was related to the fact that the pre-accession funds were interpreted as training for the local elites, who would later use corrupt means to commit fraud on the common budget. For this reason Brussels officials expressed their dissatisfaction with the volatility of the institutions dealing with the investigation of EU funds, even considering the activation of the safeguard clause. The main problem derived from the fact that the local counterpart of European Anti-fraud Office (OLAF), the Department for the Fight against Fraud (DLAF), has been shaken by a decision of the Romanian Constitutional Court (CC) in November 2009, which declared the legal basis of DLAF unconstitutional. The legislation was later amended, but in 2011, the EC noticed that DLAF's administrative capacity and the quality of administrative action remained weak.

The international anxieties related to the enhanced possibility of fraud to the common budget are mirrored by the national anxieties regarding the possibility of losing the funds. In order to attract more funding, a new institution was set up in September 2011—the Ministry of European Affairs. Apart from that, there were also shifts in other bodies that dealt with structural funds. The Authority coordinating the structural instruments was moved under the direct supervision of the Prime Minister in February 2011 (to give an impulse to EU funding), while the PHARE Office (OPCP—the Office for PHARE Payments and Contracts) was transformed in a directorate within the Ministry of Public Finances, losing some of its responsibilities in favour of the Schengen and the Post-accession Programme Directorate.

Conclusion

The transition from socialism to capitalism represented a massive change for Romanian society with short-term high social costs and long-term negative consequences for the economic development. Romania entered late modernity under the close supervision of international organisations (EU, IMF, World Bank) which designed and monitored this change in an attempt to align Romanian society with the international standards ('integration from above'). This capitalism-by-design impacted the society through price liberalisation, opening up of the market and massive privatisation. These aspects shaped people's economic behaviour and determined the adoption of various strategies of coping with uncertainty. As active and creative actors of European integration, Romanian entrepreneurs learned to adapt their old patterns of behaviour to the new economic opportunities in order to improve their life trajectories. This process of behavioural adjustment, or 'integration from below', was shaped by the necessity to adopt the EU *acquis communautaire*. In the case of Romania, the EU conditionality was fashioned using narratives of corruption.

The process of accessing EU funding has been shaped by anxieties regarding corruption. The official fears regarding the possibility of fraud to the European budget translated in high levels of control and numerous bureaucratic delays. In short, the negotiations regarding structural funds were encapsulated by over-regulation which contained a set of rules that were to guide the access of funds while shaping a new entrepreneurial spirit. However, few Romanian entrepreneurs had the financial capacity to co-fund the EU projects (Chap. 8) and the patience to understand all the rules involved in this process as detailed in the next chapter. Predictably, this led to a small absorption rate, which was interpreted as a failure of the authorities and debated in inevitably pathetic tones. Unpredictably, it reinforced the segregation of agriculture by creating a small, profitable and productive sector that attracted high levels of funding and a large subsistence sector that could not attract funding. Thus, over-regulating structural funding has made accessing EU funding more a political than an economic process.

Notes

1. http://www.fonduri-ue.ro.
2. Unless stated differently, this section is based on the information provided by the EU official website: http://europa.eu/policies-activities/funding-grants/index_en.htm.
3. http://www.reuters.com/article/2008/07/23/eu-bulgaria-idUSL2310252272008O723.
4. According to the EU official website: http://ec.europa.eu/budget/budget_detail/next_year_en.htm.
5. http://ec.europa.eu/budget/budget_detail/next_year_en.htm.
6. http://www.insse.ro/cms/files/statistici/comunicate/com_anuale/ocup-somaj/somaj_2012r.pdf.
7. http://www.fonduri-ue.ro/.
8. http://www.reuters.com/article/2008/07/23/eu-bulgaria-idUSL23102522720080723.
9. http://intl.econ.cuhk.edu.hk/exchange_rate_regime/index.php?cid=27.
10. http://paulgoma.free.fr/includes/Despre_Tismaneanu_11_puncte_HTML.php.
11. http://www.presidency.ro/static/ordine/RAPORT_FINAL_CPADCR.pdf.
12. http://adevarul.ro/cultura/istorie/video-nicolae-purcareasupravietuitor-fenomenului-pitesti-victima-refuzat-devina-calau-marturii-despre-reeducarea-printortura-1_5145820900f5182b851a2806/index.html.
13. http://www.rfi.ro/articol/stiri/cultura/rezistenta-anticomunista-munti-povestea-familiei-arnautoiu.
14. This story is partially based on media review, partially on informal interviews.
15. http://adevarul.ro/news/societate/becali-recunoscut-facut-avere-vandut-blugi-adusi-turcia-1_50acb4bd7c42d5a6638898e8/index.html.

16. http://m.romanialibera.ro/exclusiv-rl/documentar/doua-decenii-de-rafuieli-cu-justitia-ale-clanului-becali-bisnita-evaziune-fiscala-spalare-de-bani-violenta-254728.html.
17. http://www.gsp.ro/gsp-special/diverse/averea-i-a-scazut-dramatic-gigi-becali-a-picat-pe-locul-85-in-topul-forbes-pe-primele-doua-pozitii-doi-patroni-din-fotbal-411773.html.
18. http://adevarul.ro/news/eveniment/ascensiunea-decaderea-gigi-becali-bisnita-blugi-laparlamentul-european-apoi-celula-1_519b9d95c7b855ff56131d97/index.html.
19. Technical unemployment was an intermediate step between employment and unemployment at the beginning of the 1990s when there was no demand for the products of a particular state enterprise. Basically, people were sent home and paid 70% of wages in order to be available on call. A subsequent move was to encourage people to choose unemployment by offering them to give up their jobs in exchange for a sum of money. Thus in the case of big socialist factories, the layoffs were done gradually.
20. Before the Revolution it was semi-forbidden to wear jeans as this iconic item of American apparel was a symbol of capitalism and decadence.
21. http://www.unece.org/fileadmin/DAM/stats/publications/Countries_InFigures2011.pdf.
22. http://adevarul.ro/news/politica/amintirile-unui-kominternist-intelesul-politrucilor-1_52ebb486c7b855ff56f66a07/index.html.
23. Romania submitted its application for EU membership on 22 June 1995 and started negotiations for accession on 15 February 2000, following the Helsinki European Council in December 1999.
24. http://www.unodc.org/documents/treaties/UNCAC/WorkingGroups/workinggroup4/2011-August-22-.
25. Available at http://rai-see.org/wp-content/uploads/2015/05/SPAI_for_SEE-Compact_and_action_plan.pdf.
26. This law was revised and completed several times (by Law 161/2003, Law 521/2004, emergency ordinance 124/2005 issued by the government, etc.), only to include more offences under the heading of corruption.

Bibliography

Banciu, D., S. Radulescu, and D. Ioan. 2005. *Coruptia in Romania. Realitate Si Perceptie Sociala*. Bucuresti: Lumina Lex.

Becker, H. 1963. *Outsiders Studies in the Sociology of Deviance*. New York: Free Press.

———. 1964. *The Other Side*. New York: Macmillan.

Bourdieu, P. 1977. *Outline of A Theory of Practice*. Cambridge: Cambridge University Press.

Bryane, M., and Bowser, D. 2009. The Evolution of the Anti-corruption Industry in the Third Wave of Anti-corruption Work. http://works.bepress.com/bryane_michael/50

EC. 2002–2006. *Regular Reports on Romania's Progress Towards Accession*. Brussels: European Commission.

Freedom House. 2005. *Politicile Anticoruptie ale Guvernului Romaniei*. Bucuresti: Raport de Evaluare.

Galtung, F. 1998. Criteria for Sustainable Corruption Control. *The European Journal of Development Research* 10 (1): 105–128.

Garland, D. 2002. *The Culture of Control: Crime and Social Order in Contemporary Society*. Oxford: OUP.

Gomez y Paloma, Sergio, and Segrè Andrea. 1993. Agriculture in the Transition from a Command to a Market Economy: The Case of Latvia. *Agriculture and Human Values* 10 (1): 60–69.

Grzymala-Busse, A., and I. Abby. 2003. Great Expectations: The EU and Domestic Political Competition in East Central Europe. *East European Politics and Societies* 17 (1): 64–73.

Ierunca, Virgil. 1990. *Fenomenul Pitesti*. Bucuresti: Humanitas.

Institutul Naţional De Statistică. 2013. Ocuparea Si Somajul in Anul 2012. Cercetarea statistică asupra forţei de muncă în gospodării (AMIGO). Comunicat de Presa no 92, April 17. http://www.insse.ro/cms/files/statistici/comunicate/com_anuale/ocup-somaj/somaj_2012r.pdf

Ionita, S., O. Nutu, L. Stefan, and A. Mungiu-Pippidi. 2011. Beyond Perception. Has Romania's Governance Improved After 2004? *Governance and Corruption: Romanian Journal of Political Science* 11 (1): 23–56.

Kpundeh, S.J. 2004. *Building State Capacity in Africa*. Washington: World Bank Publications.

Langseth, P., R. Stapenhurst, and J. Pope. 1999. National Integrity Systems. In *Curbing Corruption: Toward a Model for Building National Integrity*, ed. R. Stapenhurst and J. Kpundeh Sahr, 127–150. Washington: World Bank.

Ledeneva, A.V. 1998. *Russia's Economy of Favours. Blat, Networking and Informal Exchange*. Cambridge: Cambridge University Press.

Luca, Lucian. 2009. *O Ţară Şi Două Agriculturi:România Şi Reforma Politicii Agricole Comune A UE*, ed. Cristian Ghinea. Bucharest: Centrul Roman de Politici Europene.

Luckmann, T. 1967. *The Invisible Religion: The Problem of Religion in Modern Society*. London: Macmillan.

Milio, S. 2010. Twenty Years of European Funding: Italy Still Struggling with Implementation. In *Italy Today: The Sick Man of Europe*. Oxford: Routledge.

Miroiu, Adrian, and Şerban Cerkez. 2013. *Competitia Politica in Romania*. Iaşi: Polirom.

Mungiu-Pippidi, A., and G. Althabe. 2002. *Secera şi Buldozerul: Scorniceşti şi Nucşoara. Mecanisme de Aservire a Ţăranului Român*. Iasi: Polirom.

Mungiu-Pippidi, A. 2006. Corruption: Diagnosis and Treatment. *Journal of Democracy* 17 (3): 86–99.

Oberschall, Anthony. 1996. Opportunities and Framing in the Eastern European Revolts of 1989. In *Comparative Perspectives on Social Movements: Political Opportunities, Mobilizing Structure and Cultural Framings*, ed. D. McAdam, J. McCarthy, and M. Zald, 93–121. Cambridge: Cambridge University Press.

Polanyi, M. 1954. *The Great Transformation*. Boston, MA: Beacon Press.

Popescu-Birlan, L. 1994. Privatisation and Corruption in Romania. *Crime, Law and Social Change* 21 (4): 375–379.

Répássy, Helga, and David Symes. 2008. Perspectives on Agrarian Reform in East-Central Europe. *Sociologia Ruralis* 33: 81–91.

SAR. 2011. *Raport Anual. Romania in 2011*. Bucuresti: SAR.

Schumpeter, J.A. 1942. *Capitalism Socialism and Democracy*. London: Allen and Unwin.

Stoica, C. A. 2006. Once upon a Time There Was a Big Party: The Social Bases of the Romanian Communist Party. Part II. *East European Politics & Societies August* 20 (3):447-482.

Szarek-Mason, P. 2010. *The European Union's Fight Against Corruption : The Evolving Policy Towards Member States and Candidate Countries*. Cambridge: Cambridge University Press.

Transparency International. 2000. *TI Sourcebook. Confronting Corruption: The Elements of a National Integrity System*. Berlin: Transparency International.

———. 2011. *Raportul Național asupra Corupției Octombrie 2009—Februarie 2011*. Bucuresti: Transparency International.

United Nations. 2004. *Anti-corruption Toolkit*. New York: UN.

United Nations Development Programme. 2004. *Anti-corruption Practice Note*. New York: UNDP.

Verdery, Katherine. 1996. *What Was Socialism, and What Comes Next?* Princeton, NJ: Princeton University Press.

Verdery, K. 2004. The Obligations of Ownership: Restoring Rights to Land in Postsocialist Transylvania. In *Property in Question. Value Transformation in the Global Economy*, ed. K. Verdery and C. Humphrey, 139–159. Oxford: Berg.

Wedel, J. 2003. Clans, Cliques and Captured States: Rethinking 'Transition' In Central and Eastern Europe and the Former Soviet Union. *Journal of International Development* 15: 427–440.

White, S. 1999. Investigating EC Fraud: The Metamorphosis of UCLAF. *Journal of Financial Crime* 6 (3): 255–260.

World Bank. 2000. *Anti-corruption in Transition*. World Bank: A Contribution to the Policy Debate. Washington.

Zahariadis, Nikolaos. 2014. The Shield of Heracles: Multiple Streams and the Emotional Endowment Effect. *European Journal of Political Research* 54 (3): 466–481.

CHAPTER 4

Bottom-Up European Integration: EU Ideal Types Versus Romanian Innovations

Building on the previous chapter that describes the context of this research as characterised by striving entrepreneurship and shaped by transnational anxieties regarding the possibility of defrauding EU citizens' money, this chapter aims to analyse the process of accessing EU funds in Romania. It follows both the logic of the *process* and the actors involved, showing the dynamics and interactions between them. Throughout the chapter I argue that the actors are influenced by multiple frames of meaning (regulatory, political, economic); act at the intersection of different markets (e.g., market for consultancy, market for tourism, market for construction); move between registers of eligibility, compliance and profitability; and, in doing so, they use a wide range of practices (formal, informal, legal, extralegal and sometimes illegal). The chapter has three main parts. I begin with the 'official story' and show how the process of EU funding is presented by the official guides. The second section is a case study focusing on a public actor who had accessed EU funding. The main reason for putting this case forward is to show the entire process through an applicant's eyes. The last part of the chapter builds on the theoretical framework and puts forward the model that will guide the analysis of EU funding throughout the thesis.

R. Bratu, *Corruption, Informality and Entrepreneurship in Romania*, Political Corruption and Governance,
https://doi.org/10.1007/978-3-319-66667-9_4

Structural Funding for Rural Development

How to Access Structural Funding for Rural Development?

Ah, but it's very easy! Prepare your funding application, submit it and if it is good you get the money. If not … you make it better! (D, bureaucrat)

M: I heard that the EU gives money … free money … for young farmers. I submitted two funding applications because the first one was not good. The second was awarded the maximum grade in June. The Agency sent me a letter sayin' that I was eligible for 40,000 euros. Now … what to do? I set up a firm to be able to get the money. When I got back to the Agency they told me it was a mistake. The file was still perfect, they said, but I was not a 'young' farmer anymore. That knocked me out! I was 35, ready to start my business and … now that. After everything that happened to me I think that if you don't have **o pila** [connections] you can kiss EU funding goodbye. My file stayed in a drawer for months until I was not a young farmer anymore.

R.B: *How did the Agency explain this?*

M: *They blamed it on the system* [software] *saying that it makes the selections at the national level, not really checking the age thing. That could only be done when I got there to sign the contract. As for the delay … lack of workforce.*

(M, applicant)

There is a wide gap between the two stories and this gap will be explored in the rest of the chapter. According to the official guide, there are seven main steps involved in receiving this type of funding, as shown in Fig. 4.1. The first stage involves filling in the funding application and bringing in the required documents to prove the necessity and the viability of the project. Once the funding is approved, the applicant signs the contract with the Agency and may start the procedures for public procurement (if a public actor) or acquisition of materials/provider of services (if a private actor). Assuming a private actor does not need funds, he/she may proceed with the work and prepare a file to be reimbursed.

Official narratives are usually not adequate for portraying the complexity of human endeavours. In the case of EU funding though, they are particularly apt to hide complexity, justifying the bureaucratic behaviour

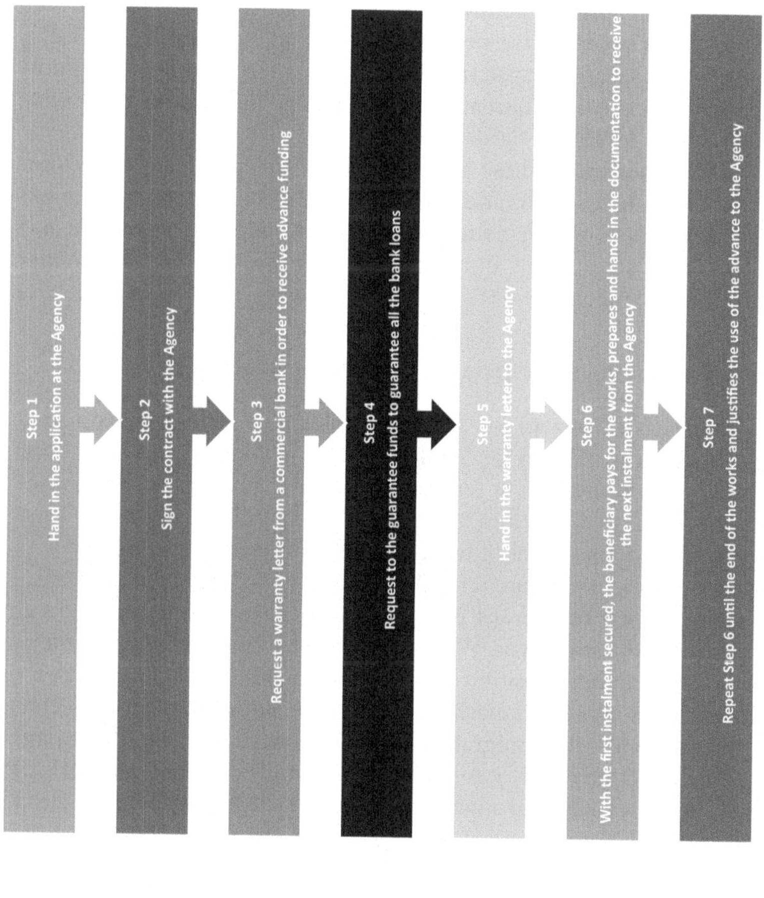

Fig. 4.1 The application process as described by the EU agency in Romania. Source: APDRP (Agenția de Plăți pentru Dezvoltare Rurală și Pescuit), Application Guide for Measure 313, 2010

in a language based on EU idioms. The 'iron hand of technology' (Kerr et al. 1973) encapsulated in 'the software', the lack of human resources and the irreversibility of rules effectively construct the machinery of bureaucracy along the lines described by Weber ([1922] 1968). Even the 'mistake' is thought of as an outcome of the 'system' whose rules nobody can really understand (Latour 2005). M decoded this situation through narratives of corruption, pointing to *pile* [connections]. He further explained that he would have needed someone to 'take care' of his file, informing him earlier about the situation. In his interpretation corruption meant breaking down the bureaucratic machinery into warm social relationships (Gupta 1995; De Sardan 2005).

The next section takes these points further through a case study of a public actor who had sought and secured funds to build a road in a small village. This example uncovers the dynamics of the application process and shows that each step entails numerous actions that will be further discussed in the third section.

Cornelia's Road: The Public Actor

Mrs Cornelia is the mayor of a Romanian village with approximately 15,000 inhabitants. She is a cheerful, large woman in her late 50s. Cornelia's husband died about ten years ago, leaving her with a big household to run and two children to raise. Nowadays, she splits her time between the activities typical of her two roles (landowner and mayor).

Cornelia represents the archetypal progressive woman. Her job trajectory is characterised by upward mobility, moving from contract teaching to accountant and then mayor. Within the universe of the village, Cornelia has reached the highest position and has maintained it for 20 years. Her attachment to the place is remarkable, as she has not even been subjected to the typical rural-urban migration which characterised the 1970s and 1980s. This is materialised occupationally through the physical work of the land and socially through everyday practices, behaviours and symbols.

Madame Mayor has 'healthy origins'[1] and displays both signs of stability and flexibility. Cornelia was offered to run for a position 'closer to the centre', which she refused:

C: *I need to be near my home. If I leave who is going to take care of the potatoes and grapes? [...]*

R.B: *Maybe if you have more money, you could hire someone to do that.*
C: *No, I have to be here myself. There are no people to hire. Everybody is abroad, working to make money. They went to Spain to pick strawberries, while their crops back home were not taken care of. The village is mostly left with old people, because youth left.*

Her enduring logic and principles were contextualised behaviourally. For example, in order to maintain her position, she has changed her party affiliation frequently. "I did not want to go to Vadim [extreme right] as I don't like him. Let's hope it won't be necessary! [...] It's a bit ridiculous as I am the same person, but I had to be careful. If the party in power changes, the mayors have to change too, otherwise we don't get any support from the **judet** [county]. **Centrul** [the centre] does not like people who don't have the same political colour. And we all know that the light comes from the centre, don't we?"

Cornelia's frequent allusions to 'the Centre' indicate her recognition of a specific kind of authority and decision-making mechanism. 'The Centre' is a symbolic representation of hierarchy and power with monopoly over the decision-making process.

In 2001 Cornelia decided to apply for EU funding for the first time. This decision followed her participation to a *judet* meeting. On this occasion, Cornelia and other mayors asked for public funds to invest in their old roads, flowing water and gas supply. The management replied that the State had no money, but there was the alternative to access SAPARD (Special Accession Programme for Agriculture and Rural Development) funding, which "was a pain, but it could be done!"

Since Cornelia had little background to understand the rules and expectations of the EU funding, she turned to her network for support both in terms of information and practices. Other mayors had successfully accessed SAPARD funds to improve the quality of the country roads, and they offered advice on the steps involved and the criteria of eligibility.

Consequently, it became apparent that the first thing to do was the *feasibility study* [FS], detailing the technical and financial parameters of the investment. In order to minimise the risk of being taken advantage of, Cornelia used the same firm that was employed by her predecessors. The contact was mediated by another mayor with a "Let's help the lady to do a good job!" to the expert and finished with "Now that you know each other, I will let you talk," which smoothed the interaction. By borrowing from the mediator's social capital, Cornelia had transformed from mayor into client. This introduction was important because even though Cornelia did not have the financial capital to pay for the FS, the experts agreed to start working on it and receive the payment some time later. The degree of trust implied in this (initially) informal arrangement was provided by the recent history of a successful business relation and the expert's ability to distinguish between friends and foes.

However, in order to secure the payment for the FS from the local budget, Cornelia needed a bit more than trust. She had to be able to prove the council members that the investment of 78 million Romanian Lei[2] was *safe*, which meant that the money would not be lost, even if the funding was not obtained. This entailed another application to the Ministry of Agriculture to advance the funds for the FS. The approval from the Ministry of Agriculture came quite soon, because the designated road had been quickly added to the county's strategic investments list—an element which increased the importance of the investment and a fiction invented to please authorities.

> *Once they approved it, I had a council meeting, here at the county hall to approve the investment. As with all the public money, the Centre gives you the approval, you spend your own money and, once you finish and bring the paper, they refund you. The problem is that the refund comes God only knows when. It took me a year to get the money back. When I asked for the money, my FS was on the waiting list with other 49 from the same county.*

With all the approvals, Cornelia could safely outsource the FS:

> *I started to do the feasibility study in 2002, when the maximum investment for a project granted by SAPARD was €1,000,000. Of course, we went and bid for the maximum, as we thought they [*the Agency evaluators*] might cut anyway when evaluate the project.*

Despite the fact that Cornelia had her paperwork ready in 2002, the project was only approved four years later. This unexpected opportunity was created by a disaster: "In 2006 my funding was approved. Why, you ask me? Well … because 2005 was a very rainy year with lots of floods. We had floodwaters here in S. The government changed its priorities, even declared an 'emergency state' and my project fulfilled the criteria for the natural calamity." Consequently, Cornelia signed the funding contract on 10 August in Bucharest at the Ministry of Agriculture.

Political and economic environments in Romania have always been in flux after 1989, but 2006 was a particularly bad year for accessing European funding, since Romania was to join the EU in January 2007. On the one hand, this translated into new laws that completely changed or adjusted the rules and regulations of EU funding; on the other hand, it created a lot of confusion, as not even the officials from the 'centre' knew how to apply them.

Ordinance 34/2006 created only difficulties and nobody from the Centre knew what to do or tell us. We were asked to go to the Ministry of Agriculture for a meeting on the 15 of May for training. No materials were given at the training session and no valuable information was communicated. The room was full not only of mayors like me, but also consultancy companies. They did not know anything more than us, the mayors. Plus, they were asking for €5000 to 'help'. Honestly, there is no money to pay for consultancy.

Political entropy was doubled by inflation and devaluation:

Just to understand what the problem was: when I did the first project in 2002, I applied for €1,000,000 to build 6 km of road. The euro was 35,000 lei. In 2006, the euro was 42,000 lei and the roads were in a worse condition. The value of the project was the same: €1,000,000. Furthermore, the prices had doubled and the work volume was the same.

The fluctuating business conditions have led to a re-evaluation of the initial project. "A decision had to be made. The width of the road could not be changed—it was 5.5 m—as one cannot put pavement unless one covers the entire road. So, we settled for putting a thinner pavement than the original one and built two small bridges."

Formally, the re-evaluation had to be done by an expert, but these actors were hard to find. Even though they could be found in the public service (i.e., the Prefect House, the specialised directions within the Ministry of Agriculture), they could not be employed because of their quality of public servants.[3] Once again, Cornelia relied on her network to find an expert. "A mayor from a neighbouring village has a brother who is a chief in the financial control team from SAPARD. He talked to his brother and that's how I got the name of the expert."

Regardless of her social and entrepreneurial competence, Cornelia could not work alone due to time and physical constraints. Consequently, she had to set up a group of people with whom she had more frequent interactions and who "cooperated in staging the same routine" (Goffman 1969: 85). The team was meant to share the workload and ensure the task completion. Its necessity was not only determined practically, but it was also required by the EU regulations at a later stage in the process. Cornelia's team was quite small: herself, the deputy mayor, an assistant and the secretary. All the members were working in the same place, that is, at the town hall, and it was part of their job description to participate in the EU project. Within the team, the participants had maintained their social roles and status, so the power distribution was unequal as was the degree of responsibility. As opposed to the network, the team had different mechanisms to ensure cooperation and resolve conflicts.

For example, when filling in the funding application, Cornelia kept both her secretary and the assistant at the office until 1 am to finish before the deadline. The second day in the morning, she drove about 100 km to hand in the application. Despite her efforts, the Agency clerks informed her that the EU regulations do not allow them to accept handwritten applications. Cornelia got back home and asked the other participants to come to the office in order to type the documents. They ended up leaving home at 2 am, and the next day, another member of the team took over—the deputy mayor took the files to the Agency.

Cornelia asked the deputy mayor to do the re-evaluation of the indicators, but this time he did not perform well. In this case, the actions of one member reflected on the entire group and she had to step in to solve the conflict.

> *He* [the deputy mayor] *talked rubbish. He told the expert what he should not have and of course the man got upset. He flared out his feathers a bit, since HE was the expert. And that was it! You know … this is the deputy mayor: nice, clean and brainless!*

Once again Cornelia relied on her old solidarity networks to solve the conflict.

> *Now, I was left with no other choice than finding a new expert. I asked around who could do the job and there were only three people: one was a drunk, another was lazy and the third was the devil's man! My choice was the latter—he was from* C [a city close to the village]. *I called him, talked to him and told him what to do. He agreed to do the job: "Sure ma'am! I'll send it to you in two weeks", he said. When I heard it, I thought I would have a heart attack. "Two*

weeks? What am I going to do with it in two weeks? I need it in a week!" He said he could not do it, there was no chance … nothing! When my attempts to persuade him failed, I thought about talking to someone who knew him. I started to ask around for people who have worked with him, maybe in the same board/commission. Finally, poor Mr. M, God bless him, called him and the lunatic [the expert] *agreed. However, he settled to do everything by Thursday and I needed the project by Wednesday. Besides, he wanted to come to the village to see everything himself, not to put his signature randomly. I called Mr. M again to complain. Poor man, he was in the hospital but said to me: "What are you talking about ma'am? Coming to the village? Is he insane?* ***I have been there and that should be enough!"*** *In the end, he* [the expert] *gave me the documents on Wednesday and not Thursday as he wanted.*

The relationship between informal economy, formal economy and the state is not antagonistic anymore, since Cornelia is using it competently to achieve eligibility. The applicants live concomitantly within multiple spaces, each with its own frame of reference. Not only this does not create new incongruence, but it actually solves pressing situations due to the highly personal quality of the relations. In this environment, business is personal, through social control manifested as peer pressure, favour exchange and transfer of capital. The typical behaviours frequent in the first economy (i.e., visiting the place in order to make sure everything is in order before signing the document) become unacceptable in the informal sector due to the etiquette of the arrangements. Furthermore, the degree of trust is high enough to make the expert assess the risk as acceptable.[4]

With all the documentation in place and the funding approved, the only thing left to do was the construction of the road. The EU funding regulations state that any public institution using public funds should organise public bids for subcontracting parts of production or marketing. Cornelia organised three public bids for her road. The first bid was cancelled because of her; the second because of a sudden change in legislation. In the first case Cornelia made two mistakes: (a) she made all the calculations up to the last cent not taking into account the inflation (which made the business not profitable for the constructor) and (b) overpriced the technical documentation (for the public bids, the legal representative prepares a detailed technical documentation and sells it in order to recover some money for the local budget)—she tried to sell it for 40 million lei (approximately €1000). In the second case, the government had changed the regulations for organising public bids, introducing among other requirements the obligation for the public institution to advertise the bid on the Internet. This measure was intended to increase transparency and reduce the possibility of fraud. However, Cornelia managed on the third try to hire exactly the company she wanted. The procedure was quite straightforward—she reached an agreement with a constructor to build her road, and it was the constructor's job to bring in two other friends who had construction companies and who had bid higher than he. This informal arrangement is a typical example of a favour exchange and a win-win result.

A Dynamic Model of EU Funding Process: Actors and Registers of Behaviour

In the process of accessing EU funding, there are several types of actors that come into play at different moments, generically denoted as *applicants*, *consultants* and *bureaucrats*. The following section focuses on the characteristics of each category. Figure 4.2 is a visual representation of the

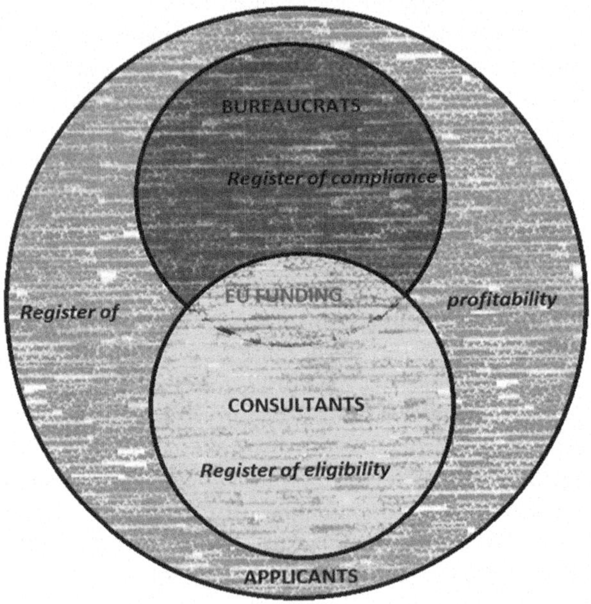

Fig. 4.2 Accessing EU funding in Romania: actors and registers of behaviour

model employed to explain the process of accessing EU funding in Romania. It builds up on the theoretical model of coordination mechanisms described in the theoretical framework.

Applicants are actors who (aim to) access EU funding in rural areas in Romania. They move between the *register of eligibility* (abiding by the formal rules and regulations imposed by the EU and Romania when applying for funding), *register of compliance* (abiding by the formal rules and regulations during the implementation stage) and the *register of profitability* (making their investment worthwhile), which transforms them from *applicants* (which is the denomination used by the EU agency) into *beneficiaries*. Despite the mirage of 'free money', a highly unstable political environment and rigid rules that shape access, EU funds seem to grant permission to a specific type of investor that has very little in common with the EU's imagined actor. This high-status actor relies on old patterns of behaviour and reciprocity rules in order to reduce uncertainty and move between state regulations, formal and informal economy. Within this category, there is a distinction between *public* and *private* applicants according to their status and role.

Consultant is a generic name denoting the category of actors that mediates and intermediates between applicants and bureaucrats. In this category, I have included actors who provide information and support to prepare the EU file and *experts*—highly specialised actors that usually provide one-off services. The category of experts includes architects, road experts, accountants and supervisors of the construction sites. Consultants commodify EU funding by treating the eligibility criteria as production factors. In this way, they construct a market that mediates the relationship between *applicants* and *bureaucrats*. Consultants have different roles, more or less formal and formalised. Firstly, they translate the EU requirements in a language accessible to the applicants by decoding the eligibility criteria into small actions and steps. Secondly, they recode the applicants' decisions into a language that is required and accepted by the EU regulations. This sort of technical knowledge is, for example, visible in filling in the funding application or making the budget. The best consultants are "the ones who can make the papers credible" (M, consultant). Thirdly, they put applicants in contact with *experts* who have specific skills and whose input is necessary for the feasibility study or any other sort of technical evaluation (as shown in Chap. 5).

Bureaucrats are public servants employed by the EU agency and its territorial offices, as well as the police and prosecution forces specialising in investigating EU funding crime (Chap. 6). They have a double role: to support the potential beneficiary by offering information and to check if the funding application and the construction fulfil the EU standards and requirements. Bureaucrats act within the framework of control and their actions are shaped by anti-corruption policies.

The model described in Fig. 4.2 should not be understood as a static description of EU funding, but as a stylised representation of a very dynamic process mediated by social embeddedness. Markets and hierarchies are decoded and enacted through a dense web network of political, religious and social interactions and affiliations. In the case described above, Cornelia accessed the market of experts through her social connections managing to submit the file before the deadline due to the power of social arrangements and transfer of capital (Bourdieu 1997). The symbolic expectations surrounding the personal nature of relationships are made possible by obtaining the expert's signature without him ever having visited the place. This gives rise to a relational economy, which entails indefinite exchanges, and transactions that encompass far more than bureaucratic norms and market prices. Gupta (1995) described the same mechanism in the case of bureaucracies in India showing that these social arenas are approached and decoded through social networks. Some researchers label this mechanism as *clientelism* (Fox 1994), but this research indicates that the inability to access markets or bureaucracies is interpreted as social incompetency and attributed to a lack of social and cultural capital. Research from Africa (De Sardan 2005), China (Yang 1994) and Russia (Ledeneva 1998) documents the same type of informal mechanisms—for example, *blat*, *guanxi*—that spring out of different cultural backgrounds at different strategic moments.

Networks are particularly adapted to counteracting contextual uncertainty by ensuring communication about prices, norms or know-how is maintained (Kanoko and Imai 1987 in Powell 1990). However, the EU funding process is not a 'regular' economic activity. Three aspects distinguish it from the pool of typical profit-enhancing activities: it is a new, excessively bureaucratised arena experiencing transnational anxiety of defrauding EU citizens' money; its regulatory framework is subject to constant revisions by Romanian bureaucracy which tries to accommodate European directives with the domestic legal framework; it effectively changes the work process through three main variables: specialisation, technology and skills (Sabel and Zeitlin 1997). These aspects create a wide gap between vernacular practices and the EU funding expectations which can barely be fulfilled by the diffuse networks. Thus, in order to accommodate the changes of this new economic arena, a new force embodied in the *consultants* assumed the role of communicator within a market framework. Essentially, excessive bureaucratisation of EU funding led to its marketisation. The next section explains in more detail each stage of the process.

Act One: Achieving Eligibility

This stage is meant to legitimise the applicant as a competent user of the European funds, and in doing so the actors are required to present documents as a proof of their competence. This is an active process of trust construction between the applicant and the bureaucrats. However, the logic is sometimes reversed, the actors changing their status in order to fulfil the criteria. This is a stage characterised by intensive networking and creative use of skills in order to deliver the best possible documents to please the 'fanatic' bureaucracy. The use of old solidarity networks (Yang 1994; Ledeneva 1998; De Sardan 1999) and gift giving (Malinowski 1922; Mauss 1925; Bourdieu 1977; Yang 1994; Ledeneva 1998) are part of the sociocultural logics of action and the economy of favours (Wedel 1986; Yang 1994; Ledeneva 1998). The networks provide support and act as buffers between the state and the individuals, offering information and providing help (Wedel 1986) in translating bureaucratic practices.

The Eligibility of the Person

The eligibility requirements for the applicant are straightforward for public actors, who are automatically involved in activities for the benefit of the community and usually get full funding. The place of residence usually represents the only caveat; as to fulfil the requirements, public actors need to be situated in rural areas.

On the contrary, the same requirements prove to be more challenging for private actors who find ways to bypass it. The necessity of rural residence applies both to the future hotel/building and the existing firm. In one case, RM, as the wife an engineer who was also involved in several private companies (construction, cable television, consulting) bought a lot in her husband's home village. She further set up a start-up company in her name and successfully applied for EU funding. She had never lived in the country and had no intention of doing so in the near future. This strategy not only solved the problem of residing in rural areas but also had the benefit of putting a new company on the market with no history of state debts. Another case was somewhat more dramatic—Mr. G had accessed EU funds to build a four-star hostel in the middle of the town and a historical area[5]; he fulfilled the criteria of eligibility by obtaining a letter from the town hall which stated that the lot of approximately 1000 square metres was outside the city. This particular case was quite ironic because it was so visible: the building had a huge banner in front which stated that the project was funded by the EU in order to support *rural* development. Mr. G's social capital was increased by such an advertisement of symbolic power (Wedel 1986; Bourdieu 1997).

"The capacity to co-fund the investment is hard to achieve and quite easy to prove" (MG, consultant). Despite the fact that the personal contribution can be between €5000 and €200,000, most investors aim for the maximum. This is due to several reasons that arise from negative anticipatory thinking: "We applied for the max because we thought they [the Agency] would cut anyway!" (Mrs C, applicant) to cost-benefit analysis—"My costs are the same irrespective of the fact that I apply for €5000 or €200,000. I still have to do the project, pay the consultants, make all the trips and get the approvals" (D, entrepreneur).

The beneficiary either has the money to do the investment or has to borrow it. The second option is quite tedious and costly; most banks have only recently started to do protocols to support EU beneficiaries, the application process is difficult and the interest rates are high. In general, the banks are stricter than the EU agency. During my fieldwork I encountered cases of daring entrepreneurs who started their projects with little amounts of personal money. In one case, S decided to take out a mortgage on his house and deposited the money into a bank account for a few days. He wanted to show the bank statement to the Agency as proof of his capacity to co-fund the investment. After showing the document to the Agency, he withdrew the money and repaid his mortgage.

In the EU logic of funding, personal and entrepreneurial histories are equally important. The potential beneficiary has to be a good citizen both financially and judicially and should present clear records to prove it. One way to overcome any problems is to set up a company under the name of a family member (close family members with a different surname are usually are preferred). In this case, the use of family for economic purposes implies a higher level of trust and a closer degree of control from both sides; the 'front' applicant aims to make a small profit by lending the legal profile and the 'real' applicant aims to minimise the degree of control on the business while pursuing profitable activities.

The Eligibility of the Project

The eligibility of the project consists in controlling both the feasibility study (FS) and the budget. These elements apply for both public and private applicants. For the public and the private applicants, the FS and the budget require the input of specialised actors—*consultants* and *experts*. Within the logic of the process, this is the first stage at which the second generic actor is involved—*the consultant*. The consultant's role is to legitimise the investment and prove its feasibility and profitability.

The FS is a technical document, quite expensive[6] and exclusively prepared by specialists recognised by the Romanian authorities. It consists of three main parts which show the necessity of the investment, its technical and financial details and the impact of the investment. The expert's role is to "open the beneficiary's mind" (M, consultant) regarding extra possibilities which would minimise future costs. For example, R wanted to build a small six-room hostel; in this case, the consultant suggested investing more in making the roof stronger, which would allow R to add another floor to the hostel later on, thus halving future costs.

The FS uses the experts' anticipatory thinking to the maximum: if the technical aspects are straightforward, the financial ones are more complex due to the unstable and risky environment (Verdery 2004; Nordstrom 2007). The FS's financial part contains details regarding the costs of goods or services and the main suppliers of each of these. This document draws heavily on consultant's creativity as in a few years' time the market can be very different (suppliers might disappear; the prices are going to change, etc.). In an attempt to incorporate future negative situations in the budget, the experts tend to slightly overestimate the prices for materials and services. However, there is a limit (Busse 2000), as the EU agency has a list with 'acceptable prices'—which aims to orientate both the expert when designing the FS and the bureaucrat when evaluating it.

The FS and the architectural project are the main documents incorporating the EU standards, which often annoyed beneficiaries:

D: *Seven sinks! I had to put seven sinks in my kitchen! One for meat, one for fish, one for fruits, one for vegetables, one for eggs, one for dishes, one for the personnel to wash their hands.* (D, applicant).

M: *Do you see this window?* [He points to a closed 50 cm window in the wall between the kitchen and the dining room]. *I never use it, but the Agency guy said I had to have it because I can't bring the food using the same door as when I carry the dirty dishes. Apparently it is not hygienic.* (M, applicant).

The EU strict regulations regarding the technical aspects of the project influence the applicant's perspective regarding the profitability of the investment. This aspect is also reflected in the budget design.

The budget is again a function of the consultant's creativity and anticipatory thinking. As a general rule, all the interviewees (irrespective of the category) pointed out that the applicant's contribution is never only 50% of the entire investment. The 50% contribution is theoretically possible, but practically improbable. First, the EU has clear regulations regarding the eligibility of expenses that can be reimbursed. For example, the beneficiary cannot deduct such items as taxes, rent, bank commissions, VAT, warranty costs and costs of buying second-hand equipment. Second, the beneficiary cannot anticipate *all* the costs, simply because the reality of the field can prove to be quite different from what was anticipated through the architectural project (type of soil or rainy season). Even if the technical indicators are adjusted later, the cost of changing the documentation is high enough to either deter the applicant from doing it, or at least increase the costs. Third, between handing in the funding application and starting the building, there is a time span of approximately one year in which the financial conditions are likely to change (the time span that I have encountered during my fieldwork is between six months and four years). Fourth, the EU reimburses only bank payments; however, Romania is still mainly a cash society for historical, technological (there are not enough banks in rural areas and no possibility to pay by card) and practical reasons (high bank fees). The unstable environment (Verdery 2004) and the different cultural practices in relation to money (Zelizer 1997) and business ultimately increase the financial contribution of the applicant (Chap. 7).

The Eligibility of the Funding Application

Assessing the eligibility of the funding application entails evaluating the correctness of the funding application and the annexes and is the ultimate expression of bureaucratic ritualism (Merton 1938).

Getting the approvals is within the job description of the actor applying for funding, and it represents a difficult exercise in networking. For a typical funding application on Measure 313,[7] a beneficiary has to get approximately 15 approvals (such as environment, construction, garbage, health and safety, water, gas and electricity). The difficulty is that each of them has an expiry date of between two weeks and three months. Furthermore, the institutional response time is generally 30 days. One viable method is to get the approvals in a certain order and hand in the funding file *before* the first approval expires. The mode of regulation is to rely on solidarity networks (Ledeneva 1998) and gift giving, the first being the more important. The barrier entailed in getting the approval was acknowledged by several respondents:

D: *A common person could not have done that! I mean ... nothing illegal, but very hard to get!*
R: *Did you give anything to get the approvals?*
D: *You mean like money or so ... No, of course not! Just a bunch of flowers here and there! [...] Some chocolate too. [...] Gave them something for a coffee....*

(D, applicant)

The 'non-common person' in this case means a person well-connected, and well-practised in the etiquette of arrangements, sometimes with high social and financial status. The use of gift giving is normalised and rationalised within the language of help and narratives of justifications (De Sardan 2005; Gupta 1995; Haller and Shore 2005).

Filling in the funding application requires a medium level of IT skills (Microsoft Office and Internet). Technically inexperienced, the future beneficiaries are assisted by consultants who double-check all the documents. This is a particularly tedious stage, as the legal representative of the project has to sign and stamp each page. The bureaucratic rules accept only blue pens and a specific type of stamp. At the moment of handing in, the beneficiary has to print four copies of the file; as one consultant put it, "It's too much paperwork! When I hand in, I have to take a jeep to carry all the papers!" (M, consultant). The close supervision relates to the payment—the consultant is usually paid a 1.5–2% commission on the amount accessed. However, in an attempt to share the risk, I have encountered cases in which the consultant only receives the entire fee if the application is approved. In the case of rejection, the consultant receives only half of the fee.

Act Two: Down to Business—The Team

The second stage in the process is less intense than the first one, but equally strategic. Once the funding is approved, the beneficiary has the first unmediated contact with the bureaucrats at the moment of signing the contract with the Agency. The contract is always signed in Bucharest (the Centre), despite the fact that the files are handed in at the regional agencies. The ceremonial aspect of the contract signing marks the end of a rite of passage, thus increasing the symbolic capital of the beneficiary. However, this moment has different meanings for the different actors involved in the process. In the bureaucratic understanding, signing the contract *is the beginning* of the process, and it is marked as such in all the guides provided for the public (see Fig. 4.1 in this chapter). For the consultants, in most cases, this moment signals *the end* of the cooperation with the beneficiary. Their role was to secure EU funding, and from this point on, their services are considered too expensive, even though necessary, as signing the contract is only the beginning of hard work. If the beneficiary wants to maintain the cooperation, another contract is put in place and different arrangements are worked out. For the beneficiary, this is an exciting moment which marks the end of a tedious application process, full of unfamiliar endeavours, and the beginning of a new one.

The period between signing the contract with the Agency and starting to build is extremely important for one reason only: it is the period in which strategies and partnerships can be worked out in order to make the most profitable business arrangements. The beneficiary has to choose a construction company to do the building in a process that has to be as transparent as possible. The EU regulations require the beneficiary to make a decision between at least three[8] offers and to advertise the requirements on the electronic system of public acquisitions, in the official monitor and sometimes even in the Official Journal of the EU. The official regulations aim to reduce the socially embedded arrangements (Polanyi 1954) and push towards a neoclassical representation of markets which brings together strangers in the act of exchange (Marshall 1936 in Thompson et al. 1991).

The public beneficiary has to organise a tender for each action (e.g., construction, supplier of materials) and, in order to do so, should prepare the appropriate documents containing the technical and financial details. In Cornelia's case, this stage proved to be challenging due to the instable economic and political environment. However, she succeeded in hiring her preferred construction company.

The main reason for working with a known partner is a higher level of trust which is favourable to doing the job and taking the necessary measures to hide unorthodox arrangements. Sometimes, there is a monetary benefit for the public actor (according to my informants the optimum price is around €1000 for small contracts with a value below €50,000 and increases with the value of the contract). There are several strategies more or less formally employed by actors to win a public tender (Chap. 5). They usually involve a two-step procedure: first, a supplier of services has to reach an agreement with a public actor. The agreement (even though quite detailed, entailing both the technical aspects of the business and the material rewards for the contractor) is not formalised in a written contract, but symbolically closed with a handshake. Second, it is the consultants' job to bring in two more friends who will bid higher in the public tender. This has been a very popular procedure for 'selecting the chosen one' until 2007 due to its inherently friendly nature. However, in 2007, the government changed the public tender rules and introduced the necessity of advertising the bids on the electronic integrated system.

Public procurement gave rise to informal practices in order to bypass the regulations. Sometimes, behaviours are on the border of legal practice but impossible to condemn legally. One of the beneficiaries I met secured a contract with a public institution (town hall) to assist with the construction of a road. In order to be able to participate in the bid, s/he had to set up a company. The latter was registered at the tribunal within a few days, just in time for the tender. Later on, during the EU routine checks, it was discovered that this firm was not registered at the Register of Commerce at the moment of the public procurement (in order to be registered at the above-mentioned institution, a firm has to wait up to 45 days). Consequently, even though legally the firm existed, from a fiscal point of view, it did not. This is an interesting aspect because later on the beneficiary was under investigation for corruption in this particular case.

Ultimately, the role of public tenders is to put together a partnership in order to proceed to the next step. This process creates a multilevelled operational team which aims to control the setting, stage the same routine and share responsibilities (Goffman 1969). After the contract signing, the EU requires that the project be managed by a team of at least three persons (the legal representative, the technical representative and the accountant). Apart from these three actors, other laws require the beneficiary to hire a supervisor for the construction site. The latter is one of the experts and *the beneficiary's watchdog* (M, broker).

Act Three: The Building—Doing the Job and Hiding the Job

The third step is the operational stage of the process involving two aspects: the construction and multiple evaluations from the EU agency in order to reimburse the expenses. It involves doing the job and hiding the informal, illegal or extralegal practices in order to receive the EU funds. At this stage the beneficiary operates more and more within the register of profitability being always aware of the necessary narratives of justification. Furthermore, the beneficiary is under the close control and supervision of the EU agency. Despite the inherent antagonistic positions, the relationship between applicants and bureaucrats was not described as tense. On the contrary, the beneficiaries were surprised and pleased by the ease and flow of the institutional communication which was unusual in comparison with other public institutions. They reported receiving reminders and support from the EU agency in order to prepare the reimbursement file (as shown in Chap. 6).

For the private applicant the building process is divided into smaller time units determined by the necessity to have one's expenses reimbursed (see Fig. 4.3). The number of instalments and the deadlines is established in agreement with the bureaucrats when signing the contract and involves a commitment from the beneficiary to reach certain stages in the construction. For example, R decided to receive the money in three instalments, the first one after finishing the building, the second after building the tennis court and the third at the end of the process. If, for whatever reason, the beneficiary cannot fulfil the contractual requirements, official extensions have to be asked for and granted. In another case, D could not

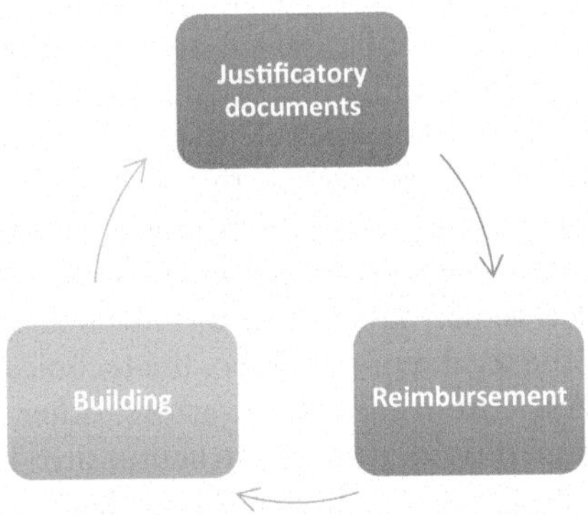

Fig. 4.3 The reimbursement process as described by the EU agency in Romania. Source: APDRP

finish the first stage in his building because the weather was too rainy which led to postponing the payments.

Reimbursement involves two types of auditing by the EU agency (more details in Chap. 6): checking the books and checking the reality in the field. For the first aspect, the beneficiary has to prepare a file including all the expenses and the corresponding invoices. Once the file is approved by the Agency, a field agent comes to check whether the building is exactly as designed. There are cases in which the controller detects differences from the designed project and makes inquiries. For example, C had to build a door 10 cm closer to the left wall than it was initially envisioned. The inspector noticed it and asked for clarification and justificatory documents. Even though the process in itself does leave room for negotiations between beneficiaries and inspectors, the latter usually ask for post factum papers. This is because the Agency has a clear mechanism in place to check the auditors both by randomly checking the documents for the approved funding projects and by doing field checks. Sometimes the field checks are conducted by high EU officials who are there to ensure that the European standards have been achieved. This mechanism limits how much can one 'negotiate' the regulations (Mars 1994; Punch 1996b) with the local officials.

It is also possible to change or amend the initial proposal. However, as in Cornelia's case shows, the request for change has to be documented by experts who prove the necessity and/or the viability of the new situation. D, for example, forgot to put a second set of stairs in her pension and the project had to be changed:

> Everyone forgot about the stairs: the architect, the Agency, even me! And the EU requirements are quite clear: you have to have a second set of stairs for the hotel! This is because after cleaning the first floor rooms the maid is not going to come down with the dirty sheets using the main stairs as the customers, right? (D, applicant)

The construction business is a 'moneymaking machine' (G, construction site supervisor) and EU funding is no exception. One of the main reasons for exercising a greater degree of control in choosing the construction company is precisely the applicant's desire to minimise costs and maximise profits. The builder has several ways of making profits from paying cash in hand in order to avoid taxation to stealing materials or purchasing them from a cheaper supplier (Mars 1994; Punch 1996b).

The beneficiary's double interest is to be part of the deals and cover it well enough in order to receive the reimbursements from the EU. The first task is within the job description of the supervisor of the construction site. The second task is shared between the accountant and the applicant.

During my fieldwork it became apparent that the supervisor of the construction site was a key actor. Within an entire county with more than 50 building sites, there were only three people who had both the accreditation and the competence to play this role. They would supervise several sites at the same time acting both as technical advisers and financial brokers on behalf of the beneficiary. This job was entirely masculinised, not only because construction industry is a highly masculine occupation in itself but also because it involved doing it in different places, some more traditional than others where there was a clear division of gender roles. Other skills required were good knowledge of the construction market—including prices, main suppliers of the materials—and access to available workforce. The latter tends to be quite important since the labour market is poorly structured, with unreliable and fluctuating workforce. Last but not least, the supervisor of the construction site had to show the capacity to do the business and conceal any informal arrangements in order to avoid difficult encounters with law enforcement.

If the beneficiary has been part of the above-mentioned transactions and wants to receive the next instalment from the EU agency, he/she then has to find ways to conceal the less orthodox arrangements. The typical way is to get invoices that prove an increased level of expenses. The easiest way to get invoices is to buy them from the bazaar (Geertz 1973). For a low price one can get as many invoices as necessary to prove the expenses. The downside of this strategy is that the invoices bought from the bazaar belong to phantom firms. If the EU experts discover invoices of this kind, they request clarifications and refunds. This impacts negatively on the reputation and credibility of the beneficiary leading to higher levels of control or even refusals to pay further instalments. Consequently, in order to avoid closer monitoring, the beneficiaries settle for getting invoices from friends (who own companies themselves) or other trustworthy members of their networks. It is part of the etiquette of arrangements to pay the VAT for the provider of the invoice.

Act Four: The Five-Year Plan

After finishing the construction and receiving the last instalment, the beneficiary is still bound by the EU contract. In the case of the public applicant, the requirements focus on the maintenance of the investment. For example, if the project has introduced flowing/piped water in a village, the requirements involve taxing the population for the service and using the difference to maintain the water pipes. The private applicant however has a few more obligations to fulfil. The most important is to keep the building running as a hotel for the next five years even if the property is sold. The final obligation relates to introducing the hotel onto the national market for tourism. This entails publicity on different official and popular websites, participating at tourism fairs and making the business profitable by any means that involve attracting customers.

Conclusion

An important role of EU funding is to Europeanise developing countries like Romania that are assumed to have little training in the 'correct' market economy as shown in the previous chapter. In other words, it aims to offer support for medium- and small-sized enterprises and development of the business sector in rural areas as a prerequisite for a market economy and democracy. It is also intended to reduce the economic and social differences between various regions, create more jobs and support alternative activities for economic growth. Ultimately, the EU funding is supposed to be a political exercise in transparency and ethical business practices that pushes entrepreneurs away from the informal economy and scandalous corrupt exchanges.

This chapter shows that EU funding has impacted positively on the bureaucratic sector making front offices user friendly. Furthermore, it has increased the number of jobs, but not necessarily within the unit of analysis (i.e., the firm). Applicants' limited background—in understanding the rules and expectations of donors—meant that a new type of actor was introduced. Consultants operate within a niche market and are specialised in decoding/translating the unfamiliar requirements of the EU demands into the more familiar language of business. This type of actor mediates and intermediates between applicants and bureaucrats and is characterised by flexible thinking and technological competence as described in the next chapter.

Despite these improvements, the process of accessing EU funding is more complicated than shown by the authorities in the official guides. The ambiguity of rules, coupled with their rigidity, makes the process difficult for the applicants. The highly unstable environment, characterised by fluctuating business conditions and political instability, further impacts on the process. Consequently, actors rely on old patterns of behaviour, which are adjusted and included in the new repertoire employed for the EU funding application. Despite the State's attempts to create formal labour markets, hiring is not necessarily done on the basis of merit. The use of old solidarity networks, transfer of capital, favour and gift exchange coexist with informal economic arrangements, thus making the distinction between legal, illegal and informal spheres superfluous.

Ultimately, EU funding ended up resembling the socialist system. The requirements for anticipatory thinking in a profoundly non-stable environment (to anticipate the budget and stick to it even though the price increases and the exchange rate changes) and the necessary fictions (paperwork required by the Agency) reinforce the 'us'—'them' gap (see Chap. 7 for more unanticipated consequences of EU funding). The papers are made to be credible and the practices are used to make the business profitable. The actors move within multiple spaces and use different practices to attract money, to be efficient and to justify their practices. They move between narratives of eligibility, profitability and justification, which will be explored in the next three substantive chapters.

Notes

1. The expression "healthy origins" was widely used during the Communist period to denote people with non-bourgeois origins. In this case, the bourgeois were all citizens that could be in any way associated with elites (be it financial, social, intellectual or big landowners).
2. Approximately €2000.
3. According to Law 188/1999, the public servants in Romania are not allowed to perform other activities that generate profit outside the public office.
4. As a further note, Cornelia had to renegotiate with another company to stamp her documents, as the expert put only the quantities and 'forgot' to put the prices.
5. The only thing that Mr M could not achieve was to demolish a 600-year-old wall. The proximity to other monuments from the same period led the authorities to suggest Mr M to build "around" the monument. Mr M

perceived it as an injustice: "C'mon, during the communism that [the wall] was a public toilet!!!" Mr. M's memory was more attached to the recent history, as a few hundred years ago the wall in question was part of a royal residence.

6. For example, in the case of Cornelia's road, the FS cost was approximately €2000.
7. On the previous financial exercise detailed in the National Programme for Rural Development for 2007–2013, Measure 313 aimed to support the development of agricultural tourism, increase the number of jobs and diversify the sources of income. The Agency for Rural Development and Fishing (APDRP, henceforth 'the Agency') was the main bureaucratic organisation dealing with this type of funding. The eligibility criteria and the ground rules for accessing funding were elaborated and presented to the public in the form of a Guide published on the main website. According to the Guide, Measure 313 was addressed to both public and private actors. The main difference was that a public actor could receive up to 100% financial support and no more than €1,000,000 and a private actor could only receive up to 50% financial support and no more than €200,000. Until January 2014, a total of 307 projects were submitted amounting to nearly €600 M, roughly 70% were selected and 44% of the applicants managed to sign a contract with the Agency (source: www.apdrp.ro).
8. I am sure the authorities must have a good reason for choosing this number, but I have not found it yet.

Bibliography

Bourdieu, P. 1977. *Outline of A Theory of Practice*. Cambridge: Cambridge University Press.

———. 1997. Le champ économique. *Actes de la recherche en sciences sociales* 119: 48–66.

Busse, E. 2000. The Embeddedness of Tax Evasion in Russia. In *Economic Crime in Russia*, ed. V. Alena Ledeneva and Marina Kurkchiyan. The Hague, London and Boston: Kluwer Law International.

De Sardan, J.P. Olivier. 1999. A Moral Economy of Corruption in Africa? *The Journal of Modern African Studies* 37 (1): 25–52.

———. 2005. *Anthropology and Development. Understanding Contemporary Social Change*. London and New York: Zed Books.

Fox, Jonathan. 1994. The Difficult Transition from Clientelism to Citizenship: Lessons from Mexico. *World Politics* 46 (2): 151–184.

Geertz, Clifford. 1973. *The Interpretation of Cultures: Selected Essays*. New York: Basic Books.

Goffman, Ervin. 1969. *The Presentation of Self in Everyday Life*. London: Allen Lane.

Gupta, A. 1995. Blurred Boundaries: The Discourse of Corruption, the Culture of Politics, and the Imagined State. *American Ethnologist* 22 (2): 375–402.
Haller, D., and C. Shore, eds. 2005. *Corruption. Anthropological Perspectives.* London: Pluto Press.
Kerr, C., J.T. Dunlop, F.H. Harbison, and C. Myers. 1973. *Industrialism and Industrial Man.* Harmondsworth, Middlesex: Penguin.
Latour, Bruno. 2005. *Reassembling the Social: An Introduction to Actor-Network-Theory.* Oxford and New York: Oxford University Press.
Ledeneva, A.V. 1998. *Russia's Economy of Favours. Blat, Networking and Informal Exchange.* Cambridge: Cambridge University Press.
Malinowski, B. 1922. *Argonauts of the Western Pacific.* London: Routledge.
Mars, G. 1994. *Cheats at Work: An Anthropology of Workplace Crime.* Aldershot: Dartmouth Publishing.
Marshall, A. 1936. *Principles of Economics.* London: Macmillan.
Mauss, M. 1925. *The Gift.* London: Routledge.
Merton, R. 1938. Social Structure and Anomie. *American Sociological Review* 3 (5): 672–682.
Nordstrom, C. 2007. *Global Outlaws.* In *Crime, Money and Power in the Contemporary World.* Berkeley, Los Angeles and London: University of California Press.
Polanyi, M. 1954. *The Great Transformation.* Boston, MA: Beacon Press.
Powell, W. 1990. Neither Market nor Hierarchy: Network Forms of Organisation. *Research in Organizational Behaviour* 12: 295–336.
Punch, Maurice. 1996b. *Dirty Business: Exploring Corporate Misconduct: Analysis and Cases.* Thousand Oaks, CA: Sage Publications.
Sabel, C.F., and J. Zeitlin, eds. 1997. *World of Possibilities. Flexibility and Mass Production in Western Industrialization.* Cambridge: Cambridge University Press.
Thompson, G., J. Frances, R. Levacic, and Jeremy Mitchell, eds. 1991. *Markets, Hierarchies and Networks. The Coordination of Social Life.* London, Thousand Oaks, and New Dehli: Sage.
Verdery, K. 2004. The Obligations of Ownership: Restoring Rights to Land in Postsocialist Transylvania. In *Property in Question. Value Transformation in the Global Economy*, ed. K. Verdery and C. Humphrey, 139–159. Oxford: Berg.
Weber, M. 1968. *Economy and society.* Vol. 1. New York: Bedminster.
Wedel, J. 1986. *The Private Poland.* New York: Facts on File Publications.
Yang, M. 1994. *Gifts, Favours and Banquets. The Art of Social Relations in China.* London: Cornell University Press.
Zelizer, V. 1997. *The Social Meaning of Money. Pin Money, Paychecks, Poor Relief, and Other Currencies.* Princeton, NJ: Princeton University Press.

CHAPTER 5

"I Make the Papers Look Credible": Consultants' Educational Role in Constructing Eligibility

After exploring the process of accessing EU funding in the previous chapter, I now turn to the first generic actor—consultants. This chapter discusses the role and impact of consultants over the economic area of EU funding. It argues that consultants are actors who mediate and intermediate between entrepreneurs and bureaucrats by translating the bureaucratic requirements into business endeavours and vice versa. In doing so, consultants commodify EU funding, through the exploitation of its symbolic, technical and economic space as a terrain on which to (re)construct market relations. Consultants act as agents of change, being both a by-product of this tectonic shift of EU integration and its exponent. As by-products of European integration, but also entangled in local historicities, consultants decode and transmit information regarding EU funding to the applicants. As exponents of European integration, consultants act as market-makers by treating criteria of eligibility as production factors.

I start by describing the legal, economic and social organisation of consultancy in Romania and show that this is a quasi-professionalised area of expertise. The second section makes the concept of consultant operational, by discussing the requirements entailed by the job. In the third section I focus on careers, trainings and motivations in becoming a consultant. The fourth section examines the social aspects of consultancy, and the fifth section establishes a connection between the function of brokerage and former patron-client relationships.

R. Bratu, *Corruption, Informality and Entrepreneurship in Romania*, Political Corruption and Governance,
https://doi.org/10.1007/978-3-319-66667-9_5

The Profession of Consultancy

The Legal and Economic Context of Consultancy

The Romanian legislative framework acknowledged consultancy as a profession in its own right by including it in the nomenclature of economic activities[1] (henceforth CAEN).[2] The Romanian Institute of Statistics classified all economic activities by assigning a unique numerical code (e.g., 7021 is the code for consultancy in the area of public relations and communication), and each economic entity had to define its object of activity according to this taxonomy. Consultancy firms providing services in the area of EU funding were covered by the 7022 CAEN code, which referred to 'Consultancy for business and management'. The nomenclature of economic activities has to be updated periodically in order to be in line with the international organisations. In Romania, the latest update was in 2008,[3] when all the economic activities were recoded and assigned new CAEN codes. The consequence was that *all* economic agents had to operate the changes in firm's status; these changes were both costly and time consuming provoking an entire chain of undesirable events.[4] In the area of EU funding, consultancy is also recognised as a valid area of expertise, since it is included on the list of eligible expenses. Consultancy for business and management can add up to 8% of the entire value of the project. However, when various types of expertise are added to consultancy, the amount can even reach 20% (e.g., architectural project or feasibility study).[5]

Despite the fact that consultants are acknowledged by the legal and political environments/frameworks, they lack a professionalised system of knowledge over which they can make legitimate claims of authority. Furthermore, there is no form of accreditation for this type of job, and the only distinction made is between consultants who have successfully written projects and the rest. On the official website[6] of the Agency, there are separate lists for successful consultants and registered consultants with the following specification: "There is no accreditation given by the Agency or any other public institution for consultancy firms offering services in the area of EU funding." This is a clear indication that at this point, the community of practice for consultancy is under construction, because the tools for thinking and the scripts for acting are not yet defined and standardised. Since there are no objective criteria to assess their level of expertise, consultants construct themselves by borrowing from the technical capital acquired in other professional areas, and the certification of expertise is established through performative devices, gut feelings and persuasion.

The Economic, Social and Professional Organisation of Consultancy

However, after 2009, consultants working in the area of EU funding have started to show the early signs of becoming a professional body. The route towards a new epistemic status has been driven on the one hand by the EU itself, by changing the eligibility criteria for consultants. Recently, a new prerequisite was introduced[7] requiring consultants who participate in the implementation of any public project to be certified by the National Council for Professional Upskilling of Adults. The tendency towards professionalisation is also based on the fact that the EU funds are heavily advertised, thus creating a highly attractive emerging market. However, the technical competences required by the job are not transmitted in a systematic way that involves structured knowledge.

Consequently, consultants have started to claim legitimacy in various forms: organise schooling, publish guides, obtain accreditation from national and international bodies, organise meetings and seminars, associate themselves with public institutions, academic establishments and prestigious NGOs, and so on. At this point, the educational offer for consultancy related to EU funding is rather diverse—the types of training on offer vary from very short term (one weekend intense training) to medium and long term (the latter involves an MSc degree in the management of structural funding offered by two universities). For example, the National School for Political and Administrative Studies (SNSPA) offers an MSc in Project Management. The curricula include courses regarding strategies and techniques for attracting EU funding, EU project management, financial analysis for EU projects, the management of the project team, evaluation and audits for the EU projects, and IT technologies used for project management. The courses combine online and face-to-face interactions, emphasise the practical component, offer a quick route to certification and emphasise the international quality of the diploma. Another example is Eurolink—House of Europe which is one of the NGOs that offers a mid-term **postgraduate online course dedicated to experts and consultants on EU-funded projects.**[8]

Some trainers are certified by international organisations (i.e., InWEnt[9]), which is more prestigious, as it enhances the reputation of the training if the educators are foreigners. For example, InWEnt—Capacity Building International Germany is a non-profit organisation (strongly connected to the German Federal Government, German business sector and the German Länder) who offered trainings and internships for new members of the EU. Since 2004, InWEnt has been shifting its focus from countries in Central Europe to Romania, Bulgaria and Western Balkan states. In 2004, InWEnt developed a three-year project aimed at helping the Romanian administration become more familiar with the EU structures. One component of the programme entailed training higher-ranking officials in the supranational intricacies of the EU projects. The project had a top-down approach, based on the idea that furthering the education of the elites (called 'training the trainers') would bring benefits to the entire country. This was based on the assumption that elites would go back and pass this knowledge on to others in subordinate positions. This indeed happened as former trainee participants in this programme are now in high-profile training positions. For example, the Romanian Institute for Training offers short-term training sessions for accessing EU funding making use of trainers previously certified by InWEnt.[10]

The technical analysis intrinsic to consultancies for EU funding is also transmitted through written materials that target both other consultants and potential clients. The public institutions dealing with EU funding have published detailed guides regarding each area of funding. However, the information is scattered on numerous websites, which are not user friendly, reflecting the overloaded bureaucratic mode of addressing the public. To counteract this problem, consultants (or consultancy firms) have created several portals dedicated to EU funding. They not only put together the information from the official sources in a comprehensible manner, but act as news agencies, discussion forums and a subtle way of advertisement.[11] By publishing newsletters (e.g., the newsletter AgroTerra is published by one of the largest consultancy companies in Romania—RGIC[12]), organising seminars and meetings and advertising their credentials from national and international bodies, consultants increase their social capital while establishing consultancy as necessary and non-illusory expert knowledge.

In order to increase their symbolic capital (Bourdieu 1984), consultants have allied themselves with powerful social authorities like academia, public institutions, the business community and NGOs. These alliances are usually constructed by strategic actors who have interacted with various areas in their professional life. In one case a consultancy firm,[13] which offers support and training for accessing EU funding, has a former minister of European Integration as a team member. According to the firm's official website, Alexandru Farcas led the negotiations for European integration between 2003 and 2004. He is now the president of this consulting company, acting as a senior consultant and coordinating the relationship with foreign companies who want to enter the local markets. Another example is a high-profile member of civil society who acts as a consultant for an institute that offers training mostly for public administration. These types of chameleonic actors are not important because they transferred their capital from one area to another (public institutions to business), but because they used their capital to *create* the market for consultancy.

> They have problematized new aspects of existence and, in the very same moment, suggested that they can help overcome the problems that they 'discovered' [*my inverted commas*]. And they have acted as powerful translation devices between [*the new*] 'authorities' and 'individuals', shaping conduct not through compulsion but through the power of truth, the potency of rationality and the alluring promises of effectivity. (Miller and Rose 1990: 5)

These powerful actors are monopolising the empty space between bureaucrats and entrepreneurs by claiming epistemic jurisdiction as 'professional' consultants and creating a *market for consultancy.* However, they do not only ground themselves in purely technical knowledge, but make use of mystique and ambiguity in order to sustain their practice (Power 1991). One way to sustain magic is through language, and the consultants' vocabulary has become flooded with foreign expressions (English is the preferred language) and technical concepts. By using EU funding slang, consultants enter a *process of estrangement*, separating themselves from other categories of participants in the project.

The Concept of Expertise

In order to cope with the uncertainties of the risk society (Beck 1992), the business environment has become professionalised by making use of external experts, who not only possessed advanced knowledge, but were also a cheaper and flexible alternative to the internal support departments. The concept of expertise refers to the "social authority ascribed to particular agents and forms of judgement on the basis of their claim to possess specialised truths and rare powers" (Miller and Rose 1990: 12). For EU-funded projects, the expert is a *sine qua non* element who constructs the 'reality' of the project through interpretative work, "discerning meaning from events by connecting them to policy ideas and text-log frames, project documents etc." (Mosse 2005: 157). Because of their representational and instrumental attributes, experts have become key resources for the modern European form of governance. The representational side is reflected by the content of expert knowledge and the ability to reference a state of the world (Preda 2005). The instrumental side, in contrast, is enacted by the fact that in the EU project expertise is mobilised to serve a particular agenda; the complex amalgam of set prices,[14] truth claims and technical procedures shapes and 'normalises' both the entrepreneurial act and the nature of the expert knowledge. Through the above features, the EU is both legitimising and regulating the forms of expertise accepted and acceptable, fashioning a highly regulated market for expertise whose main role is to ensure compliance with the dominant model (an ideology).

The expert status is explicitly recognised in the EU logic if, at a minimum, the applicant has a university degree relevant for the particular area in which s/he wishes to qualify, at least five years of experience,[15] English language skills, the ability to evaluate/review projects, and has not been found guilty of professional misconduct. Consequently, the legitimisation of experts is achieved through two main mechanisms: examination (hence the university degree in a relevant area) and on-the-job training (hence the five-year experience requirement). This reasoning is valid in the case of established professions that have achieved closure over a particular domain of knowledge and have well-established mechanisms of transmitting and regulating expertise (i.e., accountancy, architecture, engineering, etc.). In the case of consultancy (which is also expert knowledge), however, this reasoning is less sound especially in this particular context.

For the purposes of this project, I make a distinction between *experts* and *consultants*. The distinction has an empirical rationale grounded in my observations and the respondents' opinions. In this sense, I use the concept of *expert* to denote a professional who belongs to this category by means of examination and on-the-job training and who only participates in the EU project in that capacity (e.g., architect, hydrologist). The concept of *consultant* is used to denote the person who puts together the documentation and prepares the funding application without having passed an examination to attest to his/her capacity, nor do they have more than five years of on-the-job training. Even though *consultants* make use of expert knowledge in order to put together the funding application, they are, epistemologically, a different category of participants.

This section has discussed the ways in which consultancy knowledge is generated, defined and maintained as such in the area of EU funding, touching upon the concept of expertise. However, despite strong social relations, this area of work has not achieved the necessary epistemic status to become a professional organisation. In the next sections, I will explain how consultants work and make sense of their roles and status in this environment.

What Is a Consultant: Definition and Job Description

C: *Let's think about it this way: one has a Car Repairs and Servicing business, right? He might have a lot of good mechanics working for him. Every one of them knows how to fix a car—with everything that entails. The question is why isn't every one of them the owner of a Car Repairs and Servicing business?*

R: *Because they don't have the money to invest?*

C: *No, that's not true! It's because they don't know the* ***procedures*** *[respondent's emphasis]; because a car repairs business entails more than some mechanical procedures. These skilled mechanics have no knowledge of finance or legislation, they don't know what it takes to set up a business, nor where they could get the money to start a business ... there are lots of things they don't know. If they would know these things, every one of them would have a business! [...]. It's the same for me, as a consultant. In order to have a good business, I don't need to know how to fix the car, but I need to know how to lead the team, where to send the car, which pieces do I need for it, what price would I sell the car afterwards at...*

(C, consultant)

You know what Seneca[16] said ... 'The philosopher knows nothing about everything while the engineer knows everything about nothing.' It's the same with a consultant who wants to be the project manager—he has to have ideas! (M, consultant)

> *When my son was about ten years old, he came home from school and shouted at me crying: "Why can't you be a cook?!". I tried to calm him down and understand where that came from. It transpired that his teacher had asked every kid in the class to tell their colleagues what did their parents do. My son said his mom was a consultant. Nobody understood what that meant. He could not explain it either and started to cry. That was in 2004.* (L, consultant)

The above quotes show that consultants define themselves as strategic thinkers who put work routines and policy models in relationship to one another. In order to do so, they create their own blueprint providing order and coherent interpretations of events for bureaucrats, by representing the practice (of entrepreneurs) with the use of normative schema. In this sense, consultants are the promoters of a vast project of standardisation and normalisation entailed by EU funding, which sets standards for performance and creates templates for thinking and talking about events (Mosse 2005). Consultants use their anticipatory thinking and translation capacities to put in relation various systems of meaning. They guide the behaviour of the staff according to prescribed standards of performance, bearing in mind that any variation from these standards can be labelled as anything on a continuum from inefficiency to crime.

Consultants have a fragmented experience of the project, their importance decreasing over time in relationship to the entrepreneur. "For a mayor, it is very difficult to do attribution bidding for the first time. He **has** to use consultants because he could never manage otherwise. The second time, consultancy is not so necessary…" (C, consultant). However, in the beginning their role is fundamental in designing the project in such a way as to maximise its chances of approval without undermining the entrepreneur's hope for profitability. Consequently, the consultant takes responsibility over an area in which moral and legal grounds are constantly shifting.

The consultant's job description is rather complex, entailing both formal and informal requirements, manifested as imperatives of the job. I have assembled three main roles, detailed below as the imperative of translation, imperative of instruction and imperative of brokerage/mediation, that essentially describe how consultants commodify EU funding.

The Imperative of Translation

The logic of action in accessing EU funding suggests that the first important step in a chain of events is to achieve eligibility (for the project and the applicant/beneficiary) and put forward a project that is coherent, standard and accurate. Consultants construct eligibility through discursive mechanisms which involve a *process of translation*. "Language, in this sense, is more than merely 'contemplative': describing a world such that it is amenable to having certain things done to it involves inscribing reality into the calculations of government through a range of material and rather mundane techniques" (Latour 1987: 32). Callon and Latour (1981: 279) have also used the concept of translation to describe the dynamics of the actor-network relations: "By translation we understand all the negotiations, intrigues, calculations, acts of persuasion and violence thanks to which an actor or force takes or causes to be conferred on itself authority to speak or act on behalf of another actor or force." The definition is appealing because it emphasises that translation is a political process. At the same time, it opens up a vast space of discussion, by mixing human and non-human actors, and various processes and rationalities, which make it hard to use from an operational point of view.

My view of *translation* is related more to social anthropology (Olivier de Sardan 2005) and entails two main dimensions: one related to linguistics, the other one to semiotics. The first dimension is related to the fact that the concepts, principles, rules and regulations of EU funding were initially constructed and presented in a different language than Romanian (usually English or French). When translated into Romanian, they followed a foreign syntax, sometimes leaving technical concepts, which had no correspondence in Romanian, in the original language. Consultants then try to communicate the message to entrepreneurs "in a language vastly revised and corrected by urban intellectuals, whose terms are deplorably formal and schoolish" (de Sardan 2005: 171). The second dimension is related to the fact that consultants need to translate lay business language into EU language, thus bringing into relation two different semantic fields. Like M, a very experienced consultant, explained:

> I do project management, which means coordinating the technical part for the feasibility study. This means calculus, predictions etc. based on the information provided by the engineers and technologists. They give me the project done 95% and I do the rest of [the] 5%. After that, I do the business plan. But I can't do everything by myself because I need to be very careful. For example I need to make sure that the money related to one aspect is the same everywhere, because they [the bureaucrats] have specialised software to check everything. (M, consultant)

So, at one level, the semiotic dimension of translation facilitates communication between the actors involved in the process. Their work means that consultants make intelligible the EU language to entrepreneurs, formalise the business endeavour for bureaucrats and impose standards of performance upon the project and the beneficiary. At another level though, consultants need to protect the client's interests and make the business profitable, which sometimes means disguising these intentions in the project, by offering justificatory devices. In this sense, consultants merely simulate communication because the technical vocabulary is used masterfully to hide the standards of conduct instead of enforcing them.

The process of translation aims to put forward to the bureaucrats a *standardised*, *accurate* and *coherent* project. Standardisation refers to the use of discursive mechanisms that present the information in a comparable, stable, typical, combinable form. "This form enables the pertinent features of the domain to literally be re-presented in the place where decisions are to be made about them (the manager's office, the war room, the case conference and so forth)" (Miller and Rose 1990: 7). Even though the process of standardisation is necessary for the purposes of evaluation, there are cases in which it is pushed too far and takes the form of empty ritualism. For example, applicants have to hand in two printed copies of the project, with each page stamped twice (with a round and a squared stamp) and signed by the project manager in black pen. If these requirements are not fulfilled, the project is not accepted by the Agency.

Accuracy is related to the necessity of providing truthful information about the project and the beneficiary. In coping with this aspect, consultants use second-order rationalisations by making constant references to the system of control and policing (further detailed in Chap. 6). With an eye for loopholes, consultants try to tie the facts to legal heurism by adapting their techniques to the methods of control (in this sense their behaviour is similar to what Levi (1981) described in his study about fraud). Accuracy is closely connected to *credibility* and in this sense they can both be technically constructed, as the following quote explains:

> You see, a breed milk cow, if well fed, can produce up to 60 litres of milk per day. In Romania it never produces that much because of the climate, the avarice of the owner, medical issues, the type of food available or whatever other reason. The cow produces 35 litres, but the owner is very happy because his mother's cow only produced 5 litres when he was a kid. I can't make the business plan for 35 litres, because it is not efficient, so I make it

> for 50 litres. So, **the papers are done to be credible** and the fact that the Agency asks for so many papers is bloody useless. There is the business plan signed by a consultant who took the responsibility for it. The business plan is signed again by a local council. Now this should be enough. The consultant knows well how he got those figures... (M, consultant)

Coherence is also part of the consultant's ability to tell a good story. It basically entails aligning the language of the project (which is a linear progression made of inputs and outcomes) with the interests of the beneficiary, with as little discord as possible. In providing coherent interpretations of events for bureaucrats, consultants simplify the reality of the projects by ignoring resistance and conflicts and replacing them with order and unity. The papers and the 'reality' are two very different spaces, each with its own canon, requirements and narrative of justifications. In writing the project, consultants would no longer limit themselves to the calculation of actual costs, but they need to put forward a "disembedded conception of money and management relatively free of the burden of social obligations" (Mosse 2005: 146). In this sense, they need to avoid potential conflicts of interests that might arise from the papers—for example, a consultant writing a project cannot participate in the same project as a constructor. Or a bureaucrat should act as a consultant and write a project for a potential beneficiary. Furthermore, when implementing the project, the consultant works with various temporal cycles with few chances to coincide (the project cycle, the construction cycle, the profit cycle, the accountant cycle, etc.). The multiple temporalities make the consultant's job more difficult because of the close association with money cycles. So, money and time are two important disciplining metrics of the EU funding labour market.

The Imperative of Instruction

Consultants fulfil a pedagogical need of the entrepreneurial community by appropriating a communication gap between bureaucracy and the applicants. They instruct potential beneficiaries how to integrate the EU funding eligibility criteria with the practice of doing business. An essential point of the pedagogical imperative is that teaching is conducted within a market environment. By assuming the role of instructors, consultants commodify EU funding. In this sense, they make use of *two different conceptions of teaching*, one relating to giving *professional instruction* and the other one to *mentoring* and transmitting traditions (Khaldun 1967). In giving professional instruction, consultants act as agents of development, assuming some of the bureaucratic burden by transmitting the EU-accepted scripts, patterns and modes of behaviour (de Sardan 2005; Lewis and Mosse 2006). Thus consultants teach the applicants how to translate their desires and plans into EU objectives and values to the extent that the two become consonant. Indirectly, consultants also train the entrepreneurs in the 'correct' market economy by making them acquainted with the disentangled and quantified state of the world entailed by the funding procedures (Miller 2002) and by making them aware of the auditing procedures and the boundaries of acceptable behaviour. When acting as *mentors*, consultants envisage more than the register of profitability in relationship to the funding process. So, they move beyond the technicalities of EU funding into the practice of business, teaching the beneficiary a mode of self-regulation that is in accordance with the EU. In this sense, the consultant's knowledge about the area of EU funding is *predatory* (Klockars 1975) because it entails exploiting their familiarity with the domain in order to help the entrepreneur hide the unorthodox arrangements. But while predatory, the consultant is also an agent of change, by redefining opportunism and the grey areas of behaviour.

The Imperative of Mediation

The role of brokerage is closely connected to the previous imperatives because "knowledge provides resources for action, but [...] these are not only of a technical nature and do not simply entail an application of popular technical knowledge. Practice and modes of behaviour also involve social evaluations, various logics, tactics and strategies" (de Sardan 2005: 172). Consultants mediate and intermediate between bureaucrats and entrepreneurs, mobilise other experts and guide the behaviour of the project staff. As by-products of local histories, consultants are familiar with the social and symbolic stakes and make use of various logics and strategies to position themselves on the market. In this sense, there is room for the concept of *politics of consultancy/expertise*, which refers to all informal negotiations, transactions, acts of persuasion and calculations used by consultants to manage socially the participants in the project. This concept is very close to Callon and Latour's (1987) definition of *translation*, but it moves away from it by denying the pure calculative nature of mediation.

The function of brokerage (de Sardan 2005), in its political version, includes also calculation, but is based more on "the half-formed, taken for granted, indifferently systematized notions that guide the normal activities of ordinary men in everyday life" (Geertz 1973: 362).

Biographies, Training, Motivations and Career in Consultancy

Consultants' biographies and itineraries displayed a cacophonic reality, in which expert knowledge took either implicit or explicit forms. Most participants acknowledged that accessing EU funding was a developing area of business of which they had not yet had a systematic view and had little claims of epistemic authority over the field. However, competence was constructed symbolically by transferring or borrowing from the professional capital gained in other business ventures.

There are several categories of consultants, if their biographies are taken into account. The first category is represented by academics, whose entry route into consultancy is facilitated by their high level of expertise in a particular area, along with a flexible schedule and easiness in communication. D was a senior lecturer in Management at a private university in Bucharest who had successfully concluded a few EU projects. He worked mostly on his own and decided to try out this line of work because he was entrusted to teach a course about the management of EU funding at the university. Since he had no experience whatsoever, he decided to get a bit of training first and selected his first customer while on vacation. After concluding the first project successfully (he obtained funding through the PHARE programme), D decided to be bolder by approaching various clients, including mayors, and write projects on SAPARD too.

Academics usually combine both careers successfully, but sometimes opt out of academia in order to work as full-time consultants, for financial reasons. For example, C, a full-time consultant, confessed that he had stumbled across consultancy by accident. He had been an academic all his life, had a full-time position as a reader in one of the faculties from the University of Bucharest and married with three children when he met his present boss. They decided to cooperate on part-time basis for a year or so, and after that, C resigned from his position at the university in order to be a full-time consultant. His entry to the labour market as a consultant was based on meritocracy, but not in the area of consultancy. On the contrary, his employer inferred from C's past experience as a successful academic, that he would be a good consultant too.

C: *You see, I had a chance. A second chance. At 38 years old, nobody would have hired me, even if my level of education was way above average.*
R: *Why?*
C: *Because I'm just a Reader. Who would hire me? Would you hire me?*
R: *Of course.*
C: *That is only because we sat down and we talked! However, if you would see my CV, you would not hire me. You see, before an employer evaluates me, s/he evaluates my CV. My present boss hired me only on the basis of the interview. He is a very intelligent guy and decided to give me a chance. So ... just to come back ... I have a lot of courage, because I know I can do things and I believe God can help me to do a good job!*

(C, consultant)

A second category of consultants comprises people who already have other businesses and perceive consultancy as a new area worth of investment. These are usually highly qualified actors in the business area, whose skills and social capital make their lack of expertise in a new area irrelevant. They make use of the same entrepreneurial skills as in any of their other businesses. For example, L was trained as an engineer and an economist and worked in import-export. Before the Revolution, the factory where he worked ('23rd August') sent him abroad to Mozambique. Then he travelled to Argentina, Brazil, Cuba and Poland until 1993.

> When I got back in 1993, the games were done: the factory where I worked had been privatised by the director without taking me into account. What was I supposed to do? I started from scratch. I set up a firm (well, in time they multiplied) and since my last commercial relationship was with Poland, I thought I'd start from there.

He started to import coffee and products containing coffee (cappuccino) and distributed them in Romania.

L: *You see, I created the market for these products. In 1996, we had been importing for two years. I was the main sponsor of the back-then famous TV show 'The 5 o'clock tea' on the national channel. The problem was that in 1996, the Romanian government decided to put taxes on the coffee. Unfortunately, instead of taxing only the coffee, they were taxing the final product—and in my case, my product only had 20% coffee. So, it became too expensive to import the merchandise* [he was also competing with illegal importing of the same products]. *Consequently, I decided to produce it here. I found some partners and we set up a factory. The total investment was 1 million euro. Eventually I had to give up this business, even though I was sorry, but there was no other way.*

R: But how did you end up doing consultancy for EU funding?

L: Oh, that … I told you that my last job abroad was in Poland. When I got back to Romania, I helped a lot of Polish companies to enter the Romanian market. I spoke Polish, everybody knew me … I had some pedigree. So, people kept calling me and asking what to do, how to do and so on. At some point I thought … well, this calls, the other one calls … but my time is limited. So I told everyone that I would act as a consultant and **I put a price on my time**.

R: So that is how you got in touch with the area of consultancy. How about EU funding?

L: I supplied materials for a construction company working for someone who had a PHARE grant.

R: You have a construction company too?

L: Not really. I have a company that supplies materials for construction. And I know enough people who want to access the EU money.

(L, consultant)

L explained well that his entry route into EU consultancy was accidental. His entanglement with the local business environment and his network of foreign partners gradually led him to EU funding. From L's point of view, the emergence of consultancy market is captured by two sentences: "At some point I thought … well, this calls, the other one calls … but my time is limited. So I told everyone that I would act as a consultant and **I put a price on my time**." However, he did not consider this his main activity. Similarly, a female consultant (A) was educated at the LSE and returned to Romania to work first in a bank and then to set up her own consultancy company helping small businesses to prepare their documents in order to obtain financial support from the banks. She came across EU funding, through some customers, and then started to gather more information about the matter.

A third category of consultants is represented by actors who dedicate their full working day to this activity, either pursuing it on their own, or in an institutionalised environment. For example, M was one of the first five people who have worked on EU funding from the very beginning. He majored in Economics at the Academy of Economic Studies in the 1970s, worked for about 2 years in the Ministry of Finance, then for 15 years in one of the biggest factories ('23 August'). After the Revolution he moved to a research institute until 1994, when he started to work for the Ministry of Agriculture (PHARE programme).

M: *Those were wonderful years, because the nucleus was under the direct supervision of Brussels. We did a lot of trainings. And when they started the PHARE programme to set up the SAPARD Agency, I kept in touch with the people and I ended up working for SAPARD before it was set up. I was one of the five people who set up the Agency. It was extremely hard. We started from zero to do all the procedures. We never worked less than 16 hours a day including weekends. In 2002 we got the accreditation and started to work only 40hours a week.*

R: *Why did you leave the Agency?*

M: *Political reasons. The Social Democrats were in power and they sent in one of their men as a director. He did not like the old people in the Agency. I was the last one to leave out of the five people who have started the Agency. It was unfortunate because the director only lasted three more months! But I discovered consultancy!*

(M, consultant)

Thus the range of motivations to enter consultancy covers a large spectrum and is interlinked with people's biographies. Some had a desire for quick success; others were well-connected and decided to explore a new dimension in their social encounters. Some have retired and consultancy was a highly valued source of extra income (along with pensions and other benefits). Others have become professionalised and decided to invest all their time and resources in this area. Along with the financial motivation (consultancy pays better as compared to other economic areas in Romania), consultants talked about other things that motivate them: the desire to help their country, the professional pride to achieve something new. C was talking about his desire to help the community. "There are lots of people who live in the country and need water or electricity or roads. I want to help! I want to do something for this country!" M, on the other hand, talked proudly about 'a job well done' and his involvement in setting up a salami factory that was so technologically advanced that "not even a fly could go in." D (whose sister became a nun and was living in a monastery) offered to help the institution to get EU funding in order to introduce tap water. He offered to work pro bono, but was refused by the mother superior who considered charity a far easier and more reliable way of getting the necessary funds for the works (not to mention that the money would have been outside the vigilant eye of the EU control agencies. More information regarding entrepreneurs' decisions to access EU funding can be found in Chap. 7).

The EU has put forward a neoliberal model of economic exchange and enterprise, which forced upon the consultants the reorganisation of work methodologies. The career path of a consultant can be pursued as a freelancer or as an employee. The decision between individual and organisational participation lies ultimately with the consultant and depends on a multitude of reasons. In most of the cases that I came in contact with, consultants already had a full-time job or found the market for consultancy too unsettled for building up a career. One person suggested that consultancy was not for beginners: "Consultancy is the type of thing you do after you have established yourself in your professional area. Otherwise people do not trust you!" (A, consultant). In order to avoid the unpleasant situation of being self-employed in a relatively unregulated business, some consultants choose to become part of a company dealing with EU funding. They may either set up their own company or join a well-established firm. In this way, the consultant benefits from the reputation of the company, while getting trained and exposed to the trade. C explained this below:

> If I want to work with a public institution, I need to prove my expertise. But I have no experience in working either with EU funding or public institutions. However, in our company there are people who have done that. They prove it by showing their CVs and how they work in the project. Obviously if you have no experience you need to find people willing to work with you ... and if you are a nobody, people won't want to do it. We are a company who has done work for Orange and Rompetrol. This proves that the people working here are not just anybody. You see, there are some possibilities here, some potentialities ... People start working with you if you have a business card. And **this** is quite a business card. Wherever you go, you need to show your business card from the company you work for.... (C, consultant)

The skills are obtained by both formal training and on-the-job training. The formal training is rather expensive, risky and difficult to obtain. The obsession with obtaining formal training is based on the idea that the beneficiary might not be able to recover the money spend on consultancy (if the project is approved), given that the consultant was seen to be *specialised*, but not *authorised* by state authorities to perform a particular task. In this sense, consultants speak about 'hologram degrees', for courses ran by the Ministry of Labour. A course in project management is typically around €700–1000 per person for two weeks/one month. However, given that for the past four years, the regulations have been in flux and the market so unsettled, attending one course was never the end of story. Consequently, keeping up to date became a business in itself which required heavy investment. The investment was rather risky, because for a long time, the Romanian public administration did not release the EU guides for funding, which meant that the market was closed and the consultants could not get their investment back. This stagnation made several consultants re-evaluate their options and re-orient their economic endeavours. The survivors were the more experienced ones or the ones who had already been known as consultants working on the pre-accession funds.

R: *So, for how long have you been doing consultancy for EU funding?*
L: *Just for the EU? One year.*
R: *How about pre-accession funding like PHARE, ISPA, SAPARD?*
L: *No, I have not done this, but I have some employees who have worked on that before.*
R: *How many people like this do you have in the company?*
L: *Three. I sent them to school. They took the courses … there is this Italian-Romanian company that organises courses for writing a project. The company is recognised* [accredited] *by the Ministry of Labour. The course lasts for three months and it's pretty serious, with teachers from Romania and Italy … In the end, they give diplomas, you know the diplomas with hologram … it basically shows that the people who have finished the course are authorised to write projects.*
R: *And how much did you pay for the course?*
L: *€700 per person*
R: *It was not cheap*
L: *Well, in the beginning you have to invest because … now is the time to access EU funding. They are just beginning! […]I was one of the students myself, just to know what to tell them to do […] no matter how experienced you are, you still need to know what exactly is going on.* (L, consultant)

Despite the obvious need to be *authorised*, hence to take expensive courses, consultants acknowledge the value of *specialisation*. Consequently, on-the-job training constitutes a valuable preparation (both paid and tuition free) for the future.

> My first big project was a salami factory in C [a big city in Romania]. Four million euro. Ultramodern. Everything was controlled by the computers. The recipes were standardised. If the technologist logged on any computer from the factory and changed the production plan by introducing one more salami, the entire factory would adjust. In the same place I did an abattoir; it was a window-less building with artificial illumination system. There was no question to find a fly in that place ... not even theoretically. The only place where one could see a fly was in the first room where they sacrificed the animals [...] So, you see, a little bit here, a little bit there ... you learn. You need the minimum knowledge in order to manage the entire project. (M, consultant)

In general, consultancy takes place in small and medium enterprises (SMEs). The organisational setting suits this type of job as SMEs are flexible entities, easy to manoeuvre, open and closed at will, with low investments required for setup and management (Aidis and Sauka 2005). Beyond the transfer of symbolic capital and learning opportunities, the firm setting offers access to information, job security and the possibility of career development; in other words, it offers structured access to the market by rendering the actors better equipped to tackle economic uncertainty.

> For me the most important thing was to find people to work with ... and I found them through my colleagues who have introduced me to their former co-workers or friends. In this way, I found out a lot of valuable information. For example, I heard that consultancy services decreased from 10% to 8% [in terms of EU eligible payments for a project]. (A, consultant)

As a social mechanism of coordination, networks seem to function extraordinary well for small- and medium-sized enterprises, as the information provided through networks is 'thicker' and more reliable (Kaneko and Imai 1987). Furthermore, some of the environmental risks are absorbed by the organisation while providing support and resources for action.

> I have three consultants working full time for me. Up to now they have not done much [the interview was conducted before the funding lines of interest

in this case were open] … I've only sent them to school to get trained […] Yes, of course I paid for the courses. It was €700 per person […]. It does not matter that they have not anything so far, they will. They have a portfolio of clients, they know what to do and when the funding lines will open, we'll just hand in the projects. (M, consultant)

Staff shortage facilitates a fluid organisation in small- and medium-sized consultancy firms which sometimes lack clear compartmentalisation of tasks. Employees need to fulfil a wide range of tasks related to marketing, operations, customer service and human resources. The only exception to this rule tend to be the legal and accounting departments, as they require special training and authorisation. For example, M was the owner of a firm who acted as marketing director when advertising the company and finding customers, as a human resources director when employing people and deciding to send them to trainings, and as customer service director when ensuring that the quality of the service provided was consistent with the contract. He mostly needed people on the operational side, which entailed writing the projects, liaising with the public institutions for routine checks and getting the approvals for the project. M retained for himself what he considered to be the most prestigious tasks (which were incidentally related to networking) and delegated the ones that were either highly skilled (like accountancy) or involved a low level of skills (getting the approval from public institutions). The situation is similar in the case of consultants who get a foreign expert to work on the project:

C: *In Romania the language barrier is visible, even if we manage to communicate in English. They* [the foreign consultants] *have experience and having a PhD was a plus* [the Romanian consultant was an academic], *but it was not enough. Their name is very prestigious. We can consult them when we have problems … they can give us valuable information, they can help us evaluate various work offers. These are all important because we live in a society that requires you to have some international experience. On the other hand these people cannot be too involved in a project. They are very expensive and I can't pay too much. Also, it would not be good for me to let them do the fieldwork and search for information. Their role is to create the structure of the project: the main activities, the calendar of the project, the manpower, the team…. They can do all these from abroad. However, you need to have a few Romanian consultants in order to be operational. They need to have experience and know exactly what to do. In a typical project you need at least two competent consultants to take responsibility for the project. At this point we have several people who can work with us. We have their resumes and they are ready to work. It is good for them too, because consultancy pays well. In general they will do the trips, the papers, the documents ... you see we need people who can do that...*

R: *and how will you hire them?*

C: *Full time contracts ... I need them full time!*

(C, consultant)

In terms of work ethic and workload, there are no illusions. Consultants know that there is an enormous amount of work involved in putting together a project: "A consultant cannot do more than 4–5 projects at the same time. It is impossible. There is too much bureaucracy, too many trips, too many phone calls to make..." (C, consultant). Their work ethic is in line with the job demands: they need to display coherence in the project, translate the beneficiary's requirements into EU language, while keeping in mind that this is a business and they need to make sure to get the maximum results with the minimum investment from the beneficiary.

The transfer of capital between company and employee works both ways influencing the credibility of the company on the market. In general, assessing a consultancy company means looking at its size and reputation, seniority, price (system of pricing) and share of the market. Reputation is constructed by retroactively showing a list of former clients: "I have done work for BRD, Connex and Rompetrol. These are big companies, everybody knows about them" (A, consultant), by making reference to present cooperation ("I'm actually busy now because I have two contracts with some town halls" [K, consultant]) or by dropping names of well-known people who are somehow affiliated to the consultancy company (as in the case of a former minister who is part of the board of directors). When one's reputation is not clearly established, clients ask explicit questions about the affiliation of the consultancy company: "You are a consultancy firm from Bucharest? Who are you working with [making reference to the big players in the market]?" The concept of seniority denotes a solid reputation built upon both social and technical capital, in which the latter is proved by repeated and successful interactions with clients and bureaucracy. In the case of consultancy for EU funding, seniority is hard to prove, as the funding lines were only opened in 2009. Consequently, companies advertise themselves by using transfer of capital. Some firms have offered consultancy for pre-accessing funds (PHARE, ISPA and SAPARD) and use this to advertise themselves even though the process of accessing structural funds is rather different. Other companies have offered consultancy in other areas like accountancy and marketing and decided to expand their area of activity. In the case of newly established firms, a typical way to claim seniority is by inviting a senior consultant to be part of the board of directors. Reputation and seniority established by the above-mentioned mechanisms play a very important role in granting access to clients and establishing a firm's presence in the market.

Another very important element that contributes to a firm's competitiveness is pricing. In an attempt to share the risks with the applicants, some consultants are paid in three instalments: "We take some money when we sign the contract with the entrepreneur, we take the second instalment when we hand in the project to the Agency and the third one when the project is approved" (B, consultant). In this case the price is higher (approximately €3000), because it entails not only preparing the file but also coaching the beneficiary in the process of accessing funding. If funding is not granted, the applicant and the consultancy firm would rework the project and hand it in at the next call. Other consultancy firms offer ready-made files for a lower price (around €2000)—the client is charged the full amount when the file is handed in to the Agency. In this case, however, the consultancy company has no further obligation towards the applicant.

Despite their flexibility, consultancy firms, like any other SMEs in transition countries, face great challenges among which is the complex issue of taxation (either high level of taxes, the frequent changes to tax policies, the ambiguity of tax policies) (Aidis 2006), bureaucracy, corruption or unfair competition from a large informal economy. As small businesses, they are more likely to be more vulnerable in the face of environmental challenges, as they do not have the economic power to sustain activity in periods of economic crisis (Pissarides 2004). In order to counteract these challenges, some actors have started to associate themselves thus creating strong alliances which act as a safety net. For example, A had a consultancy company specialised in helping the client to prepare the file for bank loans. As she had no experience in accessing EU funding, she associated with four other consultancy firms with various competences (one was specialised in preparing the funding application, another firm was specialised in providing feasibility studies and architectural projects and the last was specialised in communication and marketing). The agreement was that each firm would rely on the others for specialised services and would recommend the partners for potential clients. At the opposite site on the spectrum, there is another example of three consultancy firms with similar competences (in writing EU funding projects), who have associated themselves in order to split the market. If one of the firms obtains a contract with a public institution that was required to organise a public tender with at least two more competitors, the other two were called in to put in courtesy bids (which were usually higher), so that the one who had negotiated the contract could legally win it. These two cases exemplify the bright and dark side of social capital, as well as the actors' ability to switch from formal to informal arrangements easily and competently.

After discussing the organisation of consultancy as a business, the work methodologies and trainings, the next section turns to analysing the social interactions between consultants, applicants and bureaucrats. It looks at the ways in which consultants construct their presentation of self, evaluate their clients, relate to bureaucracy and work together with other consultants and experts.

Social Aspects of Consultancy

In evaluating their (potential) clients, consultants assess three main aspects: *credibility, capability and commitment.* These aspects are also the basis on which consultants present themselves to the world, by employing *persuasion* in actively searching for clients. Furthermore, the same aspects form the basis of consultants' *reputation*, which is a complex mix of social, symbolic and professional capital. These aspects are by no means the only elements involved in selecting clients, nor are they used consciously and explicitly in most interactions. In fact, more experienced consultants invoke a sixth sense, an extraordinary capability that helps them detect instantly if a new economic association would be successful or not. "I smell potential clients!" said one consultant making reference to exactly this capacity (M, consultant). However, novices are less inclined to build their expertise on the basis of a gut feeling.

Credibility is the sum of verbal avowals and nonverbal signs regarding the intention to follow a particular course of action (Goffman 1970). In the first instance, the consultant makes a prima facie assessment of the client and enterprise, analysing the eligibility of the proposed project and the seriousness of the client's purpose. There is no point in starting to work on a project if the beneficiary is not convinced that the project is worth pursuing. This is usually the case with public actors who are inexperienced and find accessing EU funding too risky and time consuming, despite the fact that, in case of failure, there are few financial losses for the public actors (as the EU funding and the government cover most of the investment). The opposite is also true: sometimes the clients are so certain that they want to do the project that they avoid the services of the consultants.

> Out of the six mayors [that replied to his proposal], one is so certain/convinced that he said to me: 'Why should I spend money on consultancy? I better do it myself. I will work and finish it in six months, 'cos I know how it works.' He had done other projects on the pre-accession funds and he knew what it was about. The other mayors have never done a project and have no idea how to put together a procurement file. They are mayors and that is enough for them! (C, consultant)

After assessing the willingness and seriousness of the client, consultants consider their *capability* to do the project. Consultants need to have more grounds in order to put their faith in the client and that means evaluating whether the client has the resources to execute the project:

> I can't lie to people! You don't need 50% funding. You need about 65%! Have you got the money? No. Well, let's go to a bank and talk. This is completely free of charge [M actually said free of charge in English despite the fact that the interview was in Romanian]. I do not start working with people until I'm certain that the client responds to at least 75% of the bureaucratic issues. (M, consultant)

Most consultants are mainly concerned with the financial resources of their clients. In the case of private clients, the beneficiary needs to co-fund the investment by 50%. If they do not have the money, or they have less money, the project might not be approved, might be delayed and, *in extremis*, the funding could be withdrawn. For the public actors, consultants need to make sure that the mayor will obtain all the necessary approvals from the local council on time, or the risks are those described above.

The third aspect is *commitment*, which is the client's willingness to sign the contract of the consultancy. Despite the fact that the very soul of the economic transactions is the contract, it is not atypical for consultants to start working before signing the contract (see Chap. 4). There are cases, especially involving the public actors, in which clients are forced or lured into commitment. In one case, a president of the county council set up a consultancy firm and advertised it throughout the entire county. All the mayors 'preferred' this company because it was rumoured that whomever works with other consultancy firms might not get the necessary approvals and would have the project delayed. I was never able to verify this rumour, so there is no way to comment on the reliability of this type of data. However, the importance of this data does not lie in its truth value, but in its widespread acceptance—most of the consultants and the clients that I spoke to believed this to be true—and their belief shaped the market for consultancy in a dramatic way. It discouraged new consultants from entering the market, allowing room only for those who were in more powerful company than the president of the county council. Consequently, the 'free market' became a 'hierarchical market' that reproduced the bureaucratic ladder in a different setting (see Chap. 2 for a theoretical discussion).

Commitment relates to the likelihood that the clients would fulfil their contractual obligations and pay the consultant without any physical or psychological risks for the latter. One consultant recounted how she refused to work with some customers even though they obviously fulfilled all the technical requirements (i.e., they had more than enough money, were keen to do the project, and so on). However, the potential beneficiaries were obviously involved in illegal activities of a violent nature and did not have the conventional understanding of the law (from the first meeting they laid out their plan to get only some of the approvals necessary for the construction and forge the rest so as "not to waste so much time"). A, the consultant, declined the job as she was afraid that the clients' critical spirit was more prone to produce bruises than reflection.

In order to recruit potential customers, consultants employ a number of different strategies. I used two main criteria to make sense of the data. The first one was related to the type of contact that was first established between consultants and their clients. The second one takes into account how active or passive the consultants were in pursuing clients (it should be mentioned that all consultants are active one way or the other, but here the concept of 'active' refers more to an above average level of aggressiveness in discovering new clients).[17] The preferred strategy or the preferred mix of strategies is a function of how developed the consultancy firm is and how well established on the market.

The first type is DA (direct and active). It is well depicted by the case of C, described in the previous section. Even though he was a newcomer to consultancy, the company that employed him has done projects involving pre-accession funds. In order to recruit clients, C focused on public actors, actively pursuing them. However, his strategy would have been more at home in an urban environment, than in a highly traditional rural area, which "has room only on the margins for achieved relations of friendship" (Bearman 2005: 234).

"You know, I did a very interesting market activity. I wrote a beautiful letter, printed it in colours on excellent shiny paper. Three pages. I sent it to 300 mayors from six counties. I received six answers. So I basically got a 2% response rate in an interval between a week and a month. From these six mayors who got back to me, some already had the approval of the local council to start the project and told me to start preparing the funding file." (Initially C sent out emails because it was cheaper and he wanted to save the resources of the company. When most of the emails were returned to him with 'fail delivery reports', he realised that the country town halls are not so well established technologically. The next time, C tried to use the fax, but it was the same problem. Eventually he settled for sending the letters by post.) C chose to contact the mayors directly, despite using an atypical approach mediated by technology. The reason for preferring this strategy over face-to-face interactions, even with such a low response rate, lies in the fact that it is less time consuming, as shown below:

> I can get a meeting with a mayor from my first attempt. But I don't **want** to meet the mayors from the beginning because there are lots of mayors in this country. I talked to ten mayors and got ten meetings. It's not hard to get meetings. It's very easy. It's a lot harder to get a meeting with a businessman. With mayors it's not hard. What do you think they do all day in the town hall? I can go and hand in a flyer with my prices. But this is not useful for me; for me, my time is more precious. My time is **too precious** to waste it on the road. What I need to do is to find the people who really want to do something [...]. For example, now I work alone and when I'm away with things to solve, there is nobody to cover for me. Besides I need to find people that I can collaborate with, I need to set up a working team, I need to make a notebook detailing all the steps involved in the process...

Since C did not benefit from a well-established reputation on the market, he had to pay particular attention to establishing his credibility in the eyes of the clients. This process involved a highly performative component enacted initially in face-to-face interactions and subsequently mediated by technology. However, he realised that this activity was too time consuming and he was neglecting other important areas like establishing a network of peers and developing his capability, thus jeopardising the future commitments.

The second type of consultant, IA (indirect and active), prefers to recruit clients through mediated contact. Despite the fact that her company had a functional website, A got most of her clients through mediated contact. She advertised her new business orientation heavily both in her professional and personal circles. Her marketing activity was more traditional than in the case of C, involving heavy use of word of mouth. As a versatile businesswoman, A operated a transfer of capital from her previous professional arrangements to the consultancy firm (the transfer of capital involved not only the financial dimension but also the social and symbolic elements), joining a partnership with several prestigious firms. This was highly advantageous because it did not put any burdens on her, yet gave A access to new clients. In this joint venture, each partner had a different specialisation, so there was no internal competition and no replication of competences. The informal agreement was that whenever one of the partners would get a client, they would recommend the other partners for different parts of the project. In this case A did not have to go to extreme lengths to establish her credibility or capability in front of clients and she could afford to be more selective, thinking twice before entering into commitments.

The third type is represented by the DP (direct and passive). This is the case of L—a businessman who had several firms with very different types of activities. He had decided to set up a consultancy firm for EU funding in 2008. Despite the fact that his company was advertised on the internet, he was not interested in selecting clients, because he already had a portfolio of clients from his other businesses. Moreover, his employees brought with them clients from their previous jobs. L made it clear that he would not work with the public actors: "I only work with private entrepreneurs [...] because the public sphere involves costs that I cannot afford!" At the time of the interview, things were in standby mode because the official guides had not been published, which would explain his relaxed attitude and his lack of interest in pursuing new clients. L's reputation is very solid and so are his relationships with his clients (because they have done business before). Consequently, L's credibility and capability are well established and reflected in the terms of the commitment (although the price is sometimes higher). L does not need to enter into a partnership because his constellation of firms already includes most of the possible specialisations of potential partners (he had a company to produce construction materials, a legal firm and a consultancy firm).

The last type of entrepreneur comprised by the proposed typology is IP (indirect and passive). This is the case of highly specialised firms/consultants who recruit their customers with the help of former customers (a former client introduces a potential client). In this case, the person who makes the introduction is the guarantor of the consultant, vouching for their credibility and capability. This type of social arrangements is propitious for illegal/out-of-the-ordinary requirements. It might be the case that the client is looking for someone reliable and competent to undertake the necessary proceedings in order to make an EU project profitable, but does not have the time to develop a personal relationship and test it over a reasonable period. Consequently, the social network absorbs this demand and acts, in this particular case, as a human resources department (see also Chaps. 3 and 5).

Persuading clients to enter into commitments is a complex endeavour. Consultants socially seduce their clients by invoking substantive rewards despite the restrictive situational environment and by making use of well-established ceremonial devices (as detailed in Chap. 4). These require social care in handling the clients:

> So, until I learned how to approach the mayors, it was really hard. I had to learn what the mayors want to hear … but this is a whole story! Firstly, the mayor is a person who wants to know how things will be from the very first meeting. But without any details. To me, it seemed very important to communicate the details. The more I knew, the more I felt it was important to tell the mayor everything I knew. Wrong! They want to know that things are simple and they won't have any headaches. (C, consultant)

C's explanation shows that

> The ritual code itself requires a delicate balance, and can be easily upset by anyone who upholds it too eagerly or not eagerly enough, in terms of standards and expectations of this group. Too little perceptiveness, too little savoir-faire, too little pride and considerateness, and the person ceases to be someone who can be trusted. (Goffman 1970: 40)

During the first exploratory meetings between the consultant and the beneficiary, the interaction is loaded with uncertainties and potentialities and fuelled by an unusual diffusion of power between the actors. Consultants are generally more educated, younger, better informed, in a nutshell, better equipped to deal with this type of funding, as compared to their clients. However, clients are in a powerful position (especially the public actors who are gatekeepers for their communities). The interaction can be thwarted by the obvious social distance, but as long as the participants understand the ceremonial significance of the way they are treated and are capable of responding without abusing the symbol system, there is hope for cooperation. "Tact in regard to face-work relies for its operation on tacit agreement to do business through the language of hint—the language of innuendo, ambiguities, well-placed pauses, carefully worded jokes and so on" (Burns in Goffman 1970: 30). Expressions like 'let's understand each other,' 'let's reach an agreement like proper human beings,' 'we also know how to take care of things' signal the availability to negotiate and the willingness to do business and to achieve a win-win state of affairs. The beginning of cooperation is celebrated with a drink, usually a sample from the local production of alcohol in the case of rural areas produced by the participants in their backyard.[18]

The situational environment is highly restrictive (see Chaps. 6 and 7) on the one hand because of the elevated degree of control from the bureaucrats (control of the papers, field checks with both national and international teams). On the other hand, the situation is highly structured (because EU funding applications are over-standardised leaving little room for innovation), but highly uncertain (there is very little general agreement as to what, how and when should be done).[19] The unavoidable mistakes that accompany any economic activity, which would normally be absorbed by the social field, become too expensive. Furthermore, the familiar ways of doing business are challenged, as the EU projects impose standardised ways of conduct (e.g., starting to build without all the approvals or not having insurance for the workers lead to withdrawal of funding). In their efforts to secure commitments and without affecting the client's productive capacity, consultants use their creative spirit to bypass the situational constraints. Ultimately, the written projects are an expression of the profound mystery of creativity (Chapman et al. 2009)—they are inventions, not inventories:

> The final project has little to do with reality! You need to make the papers to be credible!! Let's say a beneficiary wants to build a greenhouse to produce vegetables. Of course, I make the project in such a way that he looks good. In order to look good and be eligible, I put ten kilos of tomatoes extra, because tomatoes are more expensive than kohlrabi and more profitable. And that's it! Or how I did with a timber factory ... when I saw that there was no way to reach the profitability indicators with hornbeam, because of the rains, I put everything on oak ... and everything worked like magic! (M, consultant)

Obviously, consultants need to pay attention to the 'magic of the project' because, as Goffman put it (1970: 166), "there is a difference between holding a job down and pulling a job off; here an act becomes a deed."

The interaction between consultants and clients is successful only if there is an agreement regarding the substantive rewards for the client. For private actors, things are more straightforward, as the client already knows the desired outcome, which is a reward in itself. However, for the public actor things are not as clear. If successful, the project might bring substantial benefit to the community; however, it is the mayor not the community that signs the contract and takes the responsibility. For assuming these risks, the mayors need to be highly motivated. The strategies of persuasion employed by consultants include moral, social and financial arguments.

The moral argument invokes higher loyalties and the demand to do one's duty.[20] The ultimate judge of fulfilled obligations is the divinity, which is accepted and relied upon even in its institutional form (according to the 2007 Barometer of Opinion, in Romania the most trusted institutions are the church and the army; on average 80% of the people said they trusted them, as opposed to 5% of people who expressed their trust in government and parliament). Once the mayor has decided to start the cooperation, the priest is called in to give the blessing and hold a short service. This tradition has several functions among which to signal the beginning of an event, to mobilise the community in case help is needed and last, but not least, to publicise the event to the entire community.

The social arguments relate to the status of the mayor and the desire to increase social prestige. By accessing EU funding, the mayor has the opportunity to make fundamental interventions in the life of the community. Introducing gas, electricity, current and water, and building roads are major, historical events that affect the everyday life of the community and change the nature of work. The alterations are dramatic, as the rhythms of life and work are inherited from the previous generations. Despite the aura granted by supporting a project with such important effects, in particular moments, mayors need extra support to enhance their social status. Such a key moment is the electoral campaign, and in this case, consultants can be instrumental.[21] They can make financial contributions to the campaign, offer their services for specific tasks or even run the campaign themselves. This type of association between consulting for EU funding and getting involved in the mayor's campaign is not seen as problematic by the consultants. As C told me: "What is the big deal about getting involved in the electoral campaign? I don't get it! It is legal to fight for what you want! It is actually moral!" Favour exchange is based on *noblesse oblige*. "Since social relationships are defined partly in terms of voluntary mutual aid, refusal of a request for assistance becomes a delicate matter, potentially destructive for the asker's face" (Goffman 1970: 29).

The efficiency of moral and social arguments is sometimes enhanced by bringing in the financial arrangements. If money is involved, the negotiations regarding the *undisclosed commission paid to the mayor* take place at the beginning of the process, before the consultancy contract has been signed. This commission (some researchers refer to it as *bribe* [Wedel 1986; Yang 1994; Gupta 1995; Ledeneva 1998; de Sardan 1999, 2005; Haller and Shore 2005; Blundo and De Sardan 2006]) can take various forms.[22]

First, there is the option of an upfront bribe offered to the mayor in return for committing to work with the consultant who offered the bribe. Despite the fact that this is the most debated option in the literature about corruption (Rose-Ackerman 1999; Van Klaveren 1999), it was almost non-existent in my fieldwork. Offering money to unknown people in the hope that they would become business partners, without anyone to vouch for the transaction, is unthinkable (not only for obvious economic reasons but also for social ones: it is considered rude to offer money in the first encounter. Besides, people are suspicious that this might be a setup from some TV channel or the police). The only case of this type that I have come across was while I was doing the media review. Journalists travelled to the eastern area of the country getting in touch with numerous mayors and pretending they were consultants for EU funds. One mayor accepted the bribe. He was filmed while making plans to talk to some of his friends who were mayors in the neighbouring villages to introduce the consultants.

A second strategy, more economically viable than the first one, would be that the consultant offers to give the mayor a commission if the project is approved. This acts as an incentive for the mayor who has something to gain at a personal level after carrying all the responsibility for the public institution. This arrangement is decoded as a bribe by the consultant and as a commission by the mayor.

A third option relates to the 1% of the money that can be spent on organising public procurements. Legally the consultant can claim the money, but it is considered rude to deprive the town hall of this small sum. However, the mayor can only use the money for the public interest, in the same project, for the same purpose. Consequently, there is little benefit to the mayor's pocket (as the money goes to the local budget), and even though this is part of the shadowy financial arrangements between the consultant and the client, neither would define this as corruption.

Fourth, it is the two-for-one campaign. The consultant might agree to do extra work for the town hall without being paid. For example, in one case a consultant was told by the mayor that he would only sign the contract if the consultant would write a second funding project for the same money. There are situations in which consultants are not forced into such commitments, but choose to pursue this course of action themselves. So, when they approach mayors, the consultants advertise themselves in this way. However, it would be highly inappropriate for the mayor to suggest such a course of action, as consultants would consider it abusive. The opposite situation became frequent after the financial crisis which heavily affected private entrepreneurs (who could not afford to co-fund the investment anymore), but it had little impact on public actors (except for the fact that the state had less money to co-fund the investment and the mayors had to rely more heavily on local budgets hoping that they would be reimbursed).

Fifth, the sign of a truly successful partnership between the consultant and the client is when they agree on the constructor because that involves 'real money'. Sometimes the consultant introduces the construction company and then new arrangements can be made. If construction is involved, then the mayor can be paid more cash; he can receive materials and even the workforce to build some parts of his/her private residence. Alternatively he can have the construction company do extra work for the same money (one mayor had funding to build a number of kilometres of road in his area. He asked the construction company to build the main roads, and as a bonus, the constructor built a road up to his house). Last but not least, if a partnership is considered profitable for the parties involved, everyone will want to repeat the experience, so they may find ways to cooperate again (in the case of private entrepreneurs there are no problems in this regard. For public actors some questions might be raised by central authorities if there is little or no variation in the companies that are chosen to conduct various works. The process of selection is supposed to be transparent through the public procurement system, but this can also be bypassed as explained in Chap. 4).

Up to this point, the section has only focused on the social aspects of brokerage involved in attracting or dealing with clients. The main reason for dedicating so much space to this aspect lies in the pivotal importance of the client for the economic arrangements. There is little use in developing a strong network of peers and experts and investing in a good relationship with the bureaucracy if the consultant has no contracts. Once the client is secured, the consultant turns his/her attention to other categories of professionals that might prove useful. Consequently the next few paragraphs focus on the social interactions with the bureaucrats, peers and experts.

Ideally, the relationship between bureaucrats[23] and consultants should be open and honest; the bureaucrats should provide the necessary information, keeping consultants up to date with the latest policy changes, and consultants should feed back to the bureaucrats some information about the dysfunctionalities encountered in the field. There are very few consultants that enjoy this type of equal relationship with the bureaucrats. Most of the time, consultants perceive the bureaucrats as being in a position of power. This provokes all sorts of negative feelings: fear, humility, revolt or anxiety. The feelings of impotence are related to the unpredictable nature of the bureaucratic response and the impossibility to change anything (neither the person nor the behaviour). "For example, there is an agronomist at the County Direction for Agriculture. If he does not like you, he kicks your ass" (M, consultant). This also contributes to a widespread perception of corruption in the system:

> You see, a bureaucrat who has the necessary negative moral structure and is in a key position can make a lot of money. An example of a key position: anywhere they give approvals. Any kind of approvals … in a ministry, like the Construction Ministry … given the fast pace of construction industry right now. Wherever there are approvals to give, there are some blotting papers who drain the money … that's what they do! Another ministry that had problems at the time was the Ministry of Agriculture. Of course it's the same thing … I'm sure nothing has changed to this day. Why do you think they are changed nowadays? [The interviewee was referring to a corruption scandal at the time that involved changing/firing/sending in early retirement a number of public servants]. Because there comes a moment when someone goes over the top … and the person who was holding him can't protect him anymore.… (L, consultant)

In order to overcome the administrative shortcomings, consultants prefer to have mediated contact with the bureaucrats. The status of the mediator is very important for the future relationship, because the social and symbolic capital of the mediator is bestowed on both the protégée and the bureaucrat doing the favour (who can expect gratitude from the asker).

"It really depends on the person who makes the introduction" (M, consultant), or "Well, I witnessed an extreme case which required the direct intervention of a minister!" (C, consultant). Bureaucracy is thus fragmented and approached with the use of social networks (Gupta 1995).

When a mediator is not found or the consultant is not intimidated by the bureaucratic power, braver strategies are employed:

> If you know how to approach the people who can solve your problems … things are ok. Because you' see, human beings are very strange animals. In order to solve your problem, you can enter the public servant's office with a big smile on your face and a confident manner … decided and slamming the door. Then, the public servant will think: 'Who is this one? Maybe he is someone important! Why is he so relaxed? In this office everyone enters bending and bowing and here he comes saying: "How are you madam? You look very good today!" How does he know me?' The other option is that the public servant takes pity on you and solves your problem. Other times you need to act a little bit crazy to solve it … depends … But when you do this every day, you are not afraid anymore. (C, consultant)

The ceremonial aspects involved in approaching the public servants display care for staging deference that is required for the success of the action. In order to maximise his chances of success C caricaturised the spirit of power by using the same external signs without having the substance. As Goffman explained:

> By easily showing a regard that he does not have, the actor can feel that he is preserving a kind of inner autonomy, holding off ceremonial order by the very act of upholding it. And of course in scrupulously observing the proper forms he may find that he is free to insinuate all kinds of disregards by carefully modifying intonation, pronunciation, pacing and so forth. (Goffman 1970: 58)

The interaction with other consultants is governed by the law of *quid pro quo*, which makes the relationships less loaded. A consultant's most important need is information, and when the bureaucracy supplies little or unreliable information, peers are a reliable (re)source. The paradox of information lies in the fact that there is too little information in an ocean of information. The media, public institutions, internet have display an abundance of information regarding EU funding; at the same time, nobody knows if the information is reliable. One consultant expressed this frustration: "It's hard to find out information. For example I have heard that consultancy will only be paid up to 8% from the project, instead of 10%, as it was before. But this is just what I've heard. I need to double check. There are too many sources of information, some of them are contradictory. I prefer to ask people who are on the market" (C, consultant). Other consultants act as a source for double-checking what the public institutions withhold.

The labour market for consultancy is not well structured, thus the hiring system is not based on impersonal criteria. Consultants prefer to work with people they know from previous jobs, conferences, childhood. "While at my post in Poland, I met a lot of people, with some I worked. The human relation is important ... and that remained. I kept in touch with those who worked in the system at that time" (L, consultant). By following each other's career paths over a number of years, consultants end up building a strong network with acquaintances in surprising social/professional positions: "I'm telling you ... go and talk to Mr. V from the Ministry of Interior. Tell him I sent you. His son in law or his son will soon get a managing position in the area of EU funding" (M, consultant). Under such circumstances, it would be difficult for the person in the public office to refuse a favour to an old friend. Besides, the bureaucrats know that positions as managers are not kept for long, because 'there are other people waiting in line.' However, there are situations in which favours are denied and the effects are drastic. The unfulfilled expectations have the value of a social delict, "throwing the persons out of gear with the social system" (Goffman 1970: 119). L had this experience:

R: *Do you have friends working for the public institutions?*
L: *I do, of course, but I'd rather not use them when I have a problem.*
R: *Why not?*
L: *Because of the inevitable debts that appear for both me and them and these put us both in uncomfortable positions.*
R: *So what do you do if you really need their help? Or what did you do in the past?*
L: *In the past I did call on them when I needed to and they refused to help so I broke up a lifetime friendship. They did not help because they were afraid they might lose their chair!* [their position].

(L, consultant)

Another option is to choose co-workers on the basis of referencing: "Always and for anything I choose people who have been recommended to me. If it works … fine; if not … fine again. I don't have time to waste" (D, consultant). However, referencing is just the beginning of a working relationship. Consultants also need to enter into commitment and sign contracts to reduce uncertainty by establishing a course of action and coerce the parts into fulfilling their obligations. The assumption that "all the parties would be bound by incorporated social norms regarding the absolute necessity of keeping one's word" (Goffman 1970: 132) is out of the question. However, the strong personal relationship acts as a buffer by securing a safe space in which consultants' innovative (even delinquent) productive capacities remain unaltered.

There are cases in which excellent working relationships between consultants come to an end, not necessarily because the business venture was not successful. Quite the opposite, consultants reported that they ended their partnerships after the business had become successful: "You see, not all friends remain friends until the end. [This is] because of the money. When you have to split the money, things are different." In this case, L was recounting a challenging episode from his past: he set up a business with foreign partners contributing with 4% in financial terms and 100% in work terms. His partners had the funds to invest and the know-how (sending specialised engineers to train the Romanian workers). However, the business was much more successful than anyone anticipated and eventually the foreign partners decided to exclude L from the business. They built a new factory which was making exactly the same products in a new area and withdrew their investment from the old factory. L could not afford to buy out their shares, so he had to sell his shares; he felt that his efforts to build up a business had been undervalued.

Working with foreign counterparts seems to raise various problems for Romanian consultants. Despite the fact that the foreign counterparts are far more experienced with EU funding and have more financial capital, the working relationships are not always successful. The social context in Romania is very different from the countries where the foreign consultants gained experience. This is an important point, because EU funding is highly dependent on the bureaucratic component and bureaucracies work at different paces in different countries. Furthermore the business culture is also remote, making it hard for

Romanian consultants to explain why a bribe might be illegal, but it is not a social crime. One of my respondents put it nicely: "How can I explain to my German partner that I need to pay some bribes??? He does not get it. So, what I need to do is either pay from my own pocket (and I'm desperate, but not an idiot!), steal from my partner (I'm not that good) or drop the partnership (because if I don't pay, setting up the contracts will take me so long that my German partner would want out!)" (K, consultant). On some occasions, brokerage firms from Romania hire foreign consultancy firms to teach them the necessary skills for managing EU funding. However, the language barriers and the spicy prices raise new problems.

In the economy of a project, the work of a consultant is credited with less than 10% of the funding. By their own admission, the job entails putting together the project in a coherent manner: "I do project management which means coordinating the technical part for the FS (feasibility study). They [the experts] give me the project 95% ready and I do the rest of 5%" (M, consultant). Ultimately, the consultant builds up his/her work on the preceding expert knowledge. There is a fundamental difference between consultant knowledge and expert knowledge, not only because the two categories have dominance over different epistemic domains but also because of the legal requirements for authorisation. In doing an EU project, consultants need experts who are *authorised* and *specialised* to do the work. These two requirements are not always met by one person, so the brokers need to be able to deal with the politics and protocols of expertise. Specialised experts are not only cheaper, but have a wider set of skills: "I had this engineer, a 'golden hand'! He could fix the equipment on the spot, so that there were no losses in the system" (L, consultant). However, the project has to be approved and signed by an authorised expert, which involves new financial arrangements. The world of experts is unusually small and it would be common for people to know each other either personally or by reputation. If the authorised expert trusts the one who did the job, then there is no need to double-check the details (see also Chap. 4); otherwise the work is done twice, as the authorised person is not willing to risk his/her job for a contract. When consultants become more established, they build a portfolio of professionals with various types of expertise and try to personalise the relationships to smooth the interaction in future contracts.

Brokerage and Former Patron-Client Relationships

In the Romanian environment consultants, entrepreneurs and bureaucrats share the same culture (like Hobbs (1988) showed for East London) and are familiar with the cultural codes of favour exchange and the

> atmosphere of generalized obligation, which can be redeemed by no accomplishments whatsoever. This atmosphere of obligation belongs among those 'microscopic', but infinitely tough threads which tie one element of society to another and thus eventually all of them together in a stable collection of life. (Klockars 1975: 395)

In this sense, a link can be established between consultancy for EU funding and patron-client relationships. The success of consultancy depends not only on the technical capacity of writing a good project but also on the social capacity of negotiations and partnership (de Sardan 2005). The set of relations established between participants on the market are greatly facilitated by a fluid institutional framework which lacks predictability and transparency. In order to counteract these shortcomings, successful consultants rely on social mediation sometimes making use of bribery and influence. It is precisely this embeddedness in the social and cultural frames that makes them particularly well equipped to deal with the market arrangements. Consultants have no need to change their ways of calculating (Callon 1998) to a neoliberal version of the market; they just need to adjust their performance to the prescribed standards.

Thus, by using familiar social mechanisms in a new economic area, consultants construct the market of EU funding (which, contrary to any expectation, is not the province of elites), while reinforcing their role in the social arena (de Sardan 2005). However, this process of market-making has nothing to do with learning the 'correct' way to do businesses. This is a historically contingent process based on hybrid forms of behaviour and alternative conceptions of legitimacy. Consultants give stellar performances working on the conventions of the business and making use of the subtleties of EU funding law, while remaining unconstrained by conventional faiths which would impede him/her seeing "what ought not to be done in what others believe one is supposed to do" (Klockars 1975).

Consultants resist the EU funding ideology by making a clear distinction between work routines and policy models. Instead of framing their actions according to the European regulations, consultants create as-if scenarios that perform eligibility for the bureaucrats (Miller 2002). In this sense, consultants are the exponents of the culture of representation in the area of EU funding, which shows that even though the ideology has changed, the practice of economic life remains the same (Miller 2002; Lewis and Mosse 2006; de Sardan 2005). However, the EU funding new metanarrative brought about variations regarding the boundaries of acceptable behaviours, criminalising formerly accepted strategies of action (see Chaps. 3 and 6 for details regarding crimes in relation to corruption and EU funding). This forced the actors to use covering strategies at the documentary level, to disguise their practices. Despite the lack of congruence between social and accountancy practices, consultants are not seen and do not regard themselves as criminals. In their work, formal and informal economic transactions or social and criminal work routines are inseparable (Ditton 1977b; Nordstrom 2007). Even though their activities might be known to their counterparts, consultants do not have a collective identity as criminals.

In this particular case, the actors do not resist 'the market'. What the consultants resist, contest and mock is the ideology of the 'free market' put forward by the EU regulatory framework and the fashionable discourse regarding corruption sustained fervently by the transnational organisations. This "neoliberal conception of individual conceals or denies the importance of social protection and relations patronage, obligation or even employment" (de Sardan 2005: 322). Consultancy practice in the area of EU funding in Romania shows that the modern concept of organisation and money brought about by the modern institution of project funding is an unfamiliar territory for all the actors involved in the process (entrepreneurs, consultants and bureaucrats).

The socially disembedded conception of money and management that excludes or minimises social obligations is the object of frustration, contestation and mockery. However, it is also the object of moral and social aspiration. The ideology of 'free market' and the EU have become the symbols of cleanness and purity as opposed to the corrupted communist practices (see Chap. 7 which shows how locals capitalise on this aspect). Thus references to consultancy are sometimes met with suspicion or resistance due to the possible use of patron-client relationships. "I hate to give bribes ... I have a small business and don't see why would I have to give 5,000,000 lei here or there [approximately £100]. I'd rather live out of charity than give the bribes!" (B, consultant). "There is so much corruption in this country that it is better to live abroad. If I would have wanted to give bribes, I would have been really far now" (C, consultant).

Conclusion

This chapter has argued that the market of consultancy related to EU funding is in fact a by-product of the EU funding process and over-regulation. It was triggered by the necessity to decode the rules associated with the process of EU funding. In this sense, consultants mediate and intermediate the relationship between entrepreneurs and bureaucrats. However, consultancy is also a niche market, in which supply and demand intersect with the purpose of constructing eligibility, while increasing profitability. Consultancy is a newly established area of expertise that shows the early signs of professional organisation. Due to the lack of adequate training and for the purposes of establishing themselves on the market, consultants make use of transfer of capital from other areas of work. Thus, the world of consultancy is very heterogeneous in terms of professional backgrounds, trainings and motivations.

An essential feature of consultants is their quality of social brokers. They not only teach entrepreneurs to actively exploit the EU funding rules to achieve profitability, but also broker among various types of experts, entrepreneurs and bureaucrats. Thus, the success of consultancy depends not only on the technical capacity of writing a good project but also on the social capacity of negotiations and partnership. Sometimes, partnerships are based on bribing officials or making use of solidarity networks. Such techniques might be illegal, but they are not socially condemned. This particular aspect shows that the morality of consultants (similar to applicants and beneficiaries) is divorced from the morality of the state; they do not decode their acts as crimes and do not have a collective identity as criminals. On the contrary, circumventing the laws to achieve eligibility is a pragmatic decision made possible by their high levels of social, financial and symbolic capital. Thus, when consultants complain about corruption, they also complain about the lack of symbolic capital to successfully complete their tasks.

Notes

1. The codification of economic activities follows international standards set up by the European Union, United Nations Organisation, International Monetary Fund and so on, thus ensuring transnational coherence on the job market.
2. CAEN is the acronym for the Classification of the Activities in the National Economy.

3. By Order 337/2007 emitted by the president of the National Institute of Statistics.
4. Changing the CAEN code was not expensive in itself—30RON (around £6), but it required an entire sequence of new changes: the constitutive act of the firm had to be altered (and that was about £70), a re-registration had to be done and so on. All the costs had to be covered by the owner, who also had to operate the changes quite fast or the activity of the firm would be blocked (a wide range of procedures running from obtaining a simple certificate for the firm to getting a bank loan could not be initiated without a change in the CAEN codes).
5. According to the official guide for measure 313: http://www.apdrp.ro/content.aspx?item=1973&lang=RO.
6. http://www.apdrp.ro.
7. http://www.apdrp.ro.
8. http://www.houseofeurope.ro/.
9. http://www.inwent.org/E+Z/content/archive-eng/02-2005/inw_art2.html.
10. The information is available at: http://www.irt.ro/ro/organizatie/echipa-irt/#trainers.
11. Just to give an example: http://www.fonduri-structurale.ro.
12. http://www.rgic.ro.
13. http://www.eurobestteam.ro/prezentare.
14. The EU and the member countries have acceptable prices for categories of experts. In Romania's case, the prices are listed on the Agency's website: http://www.apdrp.ro/.
15. http://ec.europa.eu/information_society/activities/ict_psp/cf/expert/login/index.cfm.
16. Mr. M was actually referring to George Bernard Shaw's famous comparison between a scientist and a philosopher.
17. As opposed to the popular idea that entrepreneurs prefer to have access to a wide range of suppliers, this research shows that this is not the case.
18. There are several expressions in the language that make reference to the social ritual of sealing a deal with a drink—for example, *A bea adalmasul.*
19. The EU project management is an area in which a highly structured situation is also highly uncertain (despite the apparent contradiction in terms, this seemed the best way to describe the situation).
20. In this case, the concept of *duty* is related to the role that the mayor *should* fulfil in the community. In traditional rural areas the mayor is one of the three most important people in the community (the other two being the priest and the teacher). Living in the community and being directly related to the entire village, the mayor's role has little in common with the modern understanding of the term as transcribed in the typical job description for the position.

21. Given that accessing EU funds takes a long time (in some cases more than two years), the mayor might finish the mandate before the project is approved.
22. This information was obtained while I was doing my ethnography, in unrecorded interviews or while doing participant observation. In order to protect the identity of those involved, there are no references in the text.
23. For the purposes of this section, I make no distinction between different categories of bureaucrats (working for the EU or not).

Bibliography

Aidis, R. 2006. Laws and Customs: Entrepreneurship, Institutions and Gender During Transition. In *SSEES Occasional Series*. London: University College London.

Aidis, R., and S. Sauka. 2005. *Entrepreneurship in a Changing Environment: Analyzing the Impact of Transition Stages on SME Development*. Turku: European Council for Small Businesses.

Bearman, Peter. 2005. *Doormen*. Chicago: University of Chicago Press.

Beck, U. 1992. *Risk Society: Towards a New Modernity*. New Delhi: Sage.

Blundo, G., and O. De Sardan. 2006. *Everyday Corruption and the State. Citizens and Public Officials in Africa*. London and New York: Zed Books.

Bourdieu, P. 1984. *Distinction: A Social Critique of the Judgement of Taste*. Cambridge, MA: Harvard University Press, Routledge.

Callon, M. 1998. Introduction: The Embeddedness of Economic Markets in Economics. In *Laws of the Market*, ed. Michel Callon. Oxford: OUP.

Callon, M., and B. Latour. 1981. Unscrewing the Big Leviathan: How Actors Macro-structure Reality and How Sociologists Help Them to Do So. In *Advances in Social Theory*, ed. K. Knorr-Cetina and A.V. Cicourel. London: Palgrave.

Chapman, C.S., D.J. Cooper, and P. Miller, eds. 2009. *Accounting, Organisations and Institutions: Essay in the Honour of Anthony Hopwood*. Oxford: Oxford Scholarship Online.

De Sardan, J.P. Olivier. 1999. A Moral Economy of Corruption in Africa? *The Journal of Modern African Studies* 37 (1): 25–52.

———. 2005. *Anthropology and Development. Understanding Contemporary Social Change*. London and New York: Zed Books.

Ditton, J. 1977b. *Part-time Crime: An Ethnography of Fiddling and Pilferage*. London: Macmillan Press.

Geertz, Clifford. 1973. *The Interpretation of Cultures: Selected Essays*. New York: Basic Books.

Goffman, Ervin. 1970. *Interaction Ritual*. Chicago, IL: Aldine.

Gupta, A. 1995. Blurred Boundaries: The Discourse of Corruption, the Culture of Politics, and the Imagined State. *American Ethnologist* 22 (2): 375–402.

Haller, D., and C. Shore, eds. 2005. *Corruption. Anthropological Perspectives.* London: Pluto Press.

Hobbs, D. 1988. *Doing the Business : Entrepreneurship, the Working Class and Detectives in the East End of London.* Oxford: Clarendon Press.

Khaldūn, Ibn. 1967. In *The Muqaddimah: An Introduction to History*, ed. Franz Rosenthal. Princeton, NJ: Dawood.

Klockars, C.B. 1975. *The Professional Fence.* London: Tavistock Publications.

Latour, Bruno. 1987. Vizualisation and Cognition: Thinking with Eyes and Hands. *Knowledge and Society: Studies in the Sociology of Knowledge, Past and Present* 6: 1–40.

Ledeneva, A.V. 1998. *Russia's Economy of Favours. Blat, Networking and Informal Exchange.* Cambridge: Cambridge University Press.

Levi, M. 1981. *The Phantom Capitalists: The Organisation and Control of Long-Firm Fraud.* London: Heinemann.

Lewis, D., and D. Mosse, eds. 2006. *Development Brokers and Translators: The Ethnography of Aid and Agencies.* Sterling, VA: Kumarian Press.

Miller, D. 2002. Turning Callon the Right Way Up. *Economy and Society* 31 (2): 218–233.

Miller, P., and N. Rose. 1990. Governing Economic Life. *Economy and Society* 19 (1): 1–31.

Mosse, D. 2005. *Cultivating Development : An Ethnography of Aid Policy and Practice.* London and Ann Arbor, MI: Pluto Press.

Nordstrom, C. 2007. *Global Outlaws.* In *Crime, Money and Power in the Contemporary World.* Berkeley, Los Angeles and London: University of California Press.

Pissarides, F. 2004. Financial Structures and Private Sector Development in the New Europe. In *Financial Intermediation in the New Europe: Banks, Markets and Regulation in the Accession Countries*, ed. D. Masciandoro. Northampton, MA: Edward Elgar.

Power, M. 1991. Educating Accountants: Towards A Critical Ethnography. *Accounting Organizations and Society* 16 (4): 333–353.

Preda, A. 2005. *The Sociology of Financial Markets.* Oxford: Oxford University Press.

Rose-Ackerman, S. 1999. *Corruption and Government. Causes, Consequences and Reform.* Cambridge: Cambridge University Press.

Van Klaveren, J. 1999. The Concept of Corruption. In *Political Corruption. A Handbook*, ed. A. Heidenheimer, M. Johnston, and Tanzi V. LeVine, 25–29. London: Transaction Publishers.

Wedel, J. 1986. *The Private Poland.* New York: Facts on File Publications.

Yang, M. 1994. *Gifts, Favours and Banquets. The Art of Social Relations in China.* London: Cornell University Press.

CHAPTER 6

Flat-Caps and Shackles: New Hierarchies of Bureaucratic Belonging

After discussing the *register of eligibility* and *consultants*, this chapter turns to the second generic actor—*bureaucrats*—and the *register of compliance*, by analysing the EU institutional establishment and its impact on the process of accessing EU funding. It argues that transnational anxieties regarding possible abuses of EU financial interests have put in place numerous new routines of control conducted by 'elite squads'. The institutional design of EU funding control was sustained by the specialisation of the justice circuits based on the systematic association between corruption and protection of the financial interests of the EU, as described in the first part of the chapter. However, the transnational-led control framework clashes with vernacular work routines creating its own informality. The second part of the chapter discusses the unanticipated consequences of the establishment of EU funding control through three paradoxes that relate to the discursive power of EU funding, informality and the costs of compliance.

Transnational Control in the Area of EU Funding

Designed in Brussels through direct negotiation with individual states, taking into account international interests and corporate assessments, EU funding is governed through administrative and criminal means that exercise overt control through new bureaucratic arrangements. This section looks at the new technologies of governing promoted in relationship to development, Europeanisation and international aid. It shows that the design of the EU

R. Bratu, *Corruption, Informality and Entrepreneurship in Romania*, Political Corruption and Governance,
https://doi.org/10.1007/978-3-319-66667-9_6

funding institutional establishment is based on systematic associations between development aid and corruption expressed through legal narratives, institutional expansion and law enforcement priorities. I start with an example of case prosecuted by Directia Nationala Anticoruptie (DNA) in 2009), then I juxtapose it with an example from my fieldwork and lastly I provide a picture of the EU anti-fraud establishment in Romania.

A Case

"S.I., in his capacity as the legal representative of a firm, unjustly obtained €68,288.48 and 91,824.45 RON from the EU budget through a PHARE programme. In order to secure the funding, he had faked a number of tenders in 2004, presenting false and inexact documents (in the form of three signed contracts with other firms and all the documentation relating to the tenders) and changed the destination of the funds. Instead of using the funding according to the aims of the project, he transferred the above mentioned sums in three business accounts that belonged to firms administrated by D.S.F., P.A.M., B.L. and P.E. The transfers were officially registered as payments. However, such payments were related to fictitious commercial operations and hence not due to be paid. Later on, the money was transferred to another firm where S.I. was administrator and associate. During the investigation, P.E. put moral and material pressure on two witnesses in order to make them provide false testimony. The other defendants helped S.I. to access PHARE funding by facilitating the use and circulation of fictitious documents.

The territorial branch of DNA from Craiova charged the five defendants: S.I., D.S.F., P.A.M., B.L. and P.E. under Act no. 84/P/2008 and sent them to court. S.I. was indicted for committing crimes against the financial interests of the EU (Law 78/2000 Art.18,[1] paragraphs 1 and 3, Art.18,[2] paragraphs 1 and 2) and forgery (Criminal Code, Art.290 paragraph 1). The other defendants were indicted for criminal complicity in the above mentioned crimes and the last one was also charged with attempt to determine false testimony as defined by Art.261 paragraph 1 of the Criminal Code."

Source: Translation from the DNA 2009 activity report—section regarding crime against the financial interests of the EU

This case, typical representation of DNA's activities, uncovers a few important aspects about the control of EU funding in Romania:

1. The indictments issued by the prosecutors were based on special legislation designed to protect EU financial interests *and* the Romanian Criminal Code.
2. The case entered the justice system through DNA—which is a special branch of prosecution that deals only with grand corruption and EU funding crimes (as detailed in Chap. 3). This entry route established the case as a priority, ensured a high level of prosecutorial expertise and enhanced supervision by the European institutions.
3. The investigation lasted four years (the offences were committed in 2004 and the indictment was finalised in 2008) showing the complexity of the case and the inevitable challenges in gathering evidence. It is to be expected that a number of years would pass before a final conviction would be obtained in court.
4. The value of the financial loss to the European budget is high (€68,288.48 and 91,824.45 RON).
5. Even though we do not know much about the social and economic status of the offenders, the *modus operandi* shows proficiency in conducting financial arrangements through both legal and illegal means.

These elements are excellent indicators of EU funding control apparatus in Romania and lead us to wider implications that will be discussed in the following subsections.

A New Legal Order: Implementing EU Funding

When Weber ([1922] 1968) discussed the ways in which states influence economic and social arenas, he contended that laws and regulations were linked to the concept of *order*, which was essential for the well-functioning of any economic activity: "An order will be called … *law* if it is externally guaranteed by the probability that physical or psychological coercion will be applied by a *staff* of people in order to bring about compliance or avenge violation" (Weber [1922] 1968: 34). He further argued that duration in time and political legitimacy are crucial for the concept of *order*. Weber's insights are a good place to start for an understanding of the EU funding governance structure because the criminalisation of EU funding misconduct is part and parcel of the political order that shapes the control efforts that aim to protect the financial interests of the EU. I contend that the process of criminalisation is driven by the European agenda, which prioritises European regulations over the national legislation and makes systematic associations between corruption and EU funding misconduct. In practice, this new legal order is confusing because it lacks what Weber described as essential: temporal continuity and legitimacy.

In Romania, crime in relationship to EU funding has a short history. All the legislation for the protection of the EU's financial interests was adopted between 2003 and 2011. This type of misconduct was first criminalised through Law 78/2000 (Articles $(18)^1$, $(18)^2$, $(18)^3$, $(18)^4$, $(18)^5$). Interestingly, Law 78/2000 is also the first and foremost legal instrument of criminalising corruption in Romanian legislation (Law 78/2000 on the prevention, discovery and sanctioning of corrupt acts). Consequently, by default, crime in relation to EU financial interests is also associated with corruption. However, the section regarding crime in relationship to the financial interests of the EU was introduced only in Law 161/2003, which means that the anxieties about corruption preceded concerns regarding the possibility of defrauding the EU budget.

In Article $(18)^1$, Law 78/2000 incriminates the use or presentation of false, inexact or incomplete documents or statements if such use led to the illegitimate access of EU funding. In the following paragraph, it also incriminates the act of omitting to communicate legally required information, which leads to the unjust acquisition of EU funding. The punishment for these crimes is 3–15 years of imprisonment and withdrawal of certain rights. If the consequences of these acts are very serious (this aspect is to be decided by a judge), the punishment is imprisonment from 10 to 20 years and the withdrawal of certain rights. Essentially this offence relates to forgery.

The second article $(18)^2$ criminalises any changes in the destination of EU funds that have been conducted without the careful consideration of the legal requirements. It is also punished the illegal change in the use of any due goods if this leads to an illegal diminution of the EU budget. The punishment for this crime is 6 months to 5 years of imprisonment or, if there are serious consequences, 5–15 years of imprisonment and withdrawal of certain rights.

The first two articles correspond directly to *Corpus Juris*[1] article 1, which incriminates fraud to the EU budget. Fraud here generally refers to the use or presentation of false (or incomplete/inexact) documents or declarations that cause harm the EU budget. Alternatively, this offence can take the form of omitting to present the required documents/declarations to the competent authorities in breach of a requirement to provide such documentation.

The third article $(18)^3$ prohibits the use or presentation of fake, inexact or incomplete documents or declarations which result in the illegal reduction of resources from the EU budget. It is also incriminates the omission of supplying the required information if this act has the same effects as described above. Such acts are punishable by 3–15 years of imprisonment and the withdrawal of certain rights or, if the consequences are very serious, by 10–20 years of imprisonment and withdrawal of certain rights. This article draws on the PIF Convention Art. 1, lit b. Attempting to carry out the acts is covered by Articles $(18)^2$, $(18)^3$ and $(18)^4$.

Finally, Article $(18)^5$ incriminates the misconduct of the director, administrator or any person in a position of responsibility in a company if it leads to any of the above-mentioned offences. The law specifies that the misconduct should be related to the guilty failure to carry out a duty of office or to carrying it out deficiently. Furthermore, the article also incriminates acts committed by a subordinate who acts on behalf of a specific economic agent if in connection with corruption or money laundering offences in relation to EU funding. Such acts are punishable with six months to five years of imprisonment and restraining certain rights.[2]

Romanian legislation follows *Corpus Juris* closely as regards sanctions too. *Corpus Juris* establishes as the following main types of punishment: imprisonment up to five years and/or fine; confiscation of the instruments, products or profits obtained through criminal actions; and publishing the conviction. The complementary punishments are exclusion from future subventions for five years, exclusion from future transactions for five years and prohibition for five years (at the most!) from holding public national or community office. In the Romanian legal system, the main punishment is imprisonment and the complementary punishment is exclusion from certain rights (as established by Art. 64 Criminal Code). The sentencing judge has latitude in deciding if the decision should be published in local or central newspapers. One missing aspect that might be useful would be introducing restrictions on participation in public bids for a certain period or limiting access to financial resources for a period. The punishment is individualised according to the gravity of the act, the degree of participation or guilt, as in *Corpus Juris*.

As already discussed, fraud is a general term that covers a range of behaviours. However, such behaviours are codified separately in the

Romanian Criminal Code as the Code does not include the term *per se*. The panoply of behaviours associated with fraud may include fraudulent management[3] (Art. 214), deceit[4] (Art. 215), embezzlement[5] (Art. 215), material forgery in official documents[6] (Art. 288), intellectual forgery[7] (Art. 289), forgery of documents under private signature[8] (Art. 290), use of forgery[9] (Art. 291) and forged statements[10] (Art. 292). Just to confuse things further, the new Criminal Code adopted through Law 301/2004 devoted an entire chapter to offences regarding the financial interests of the EU. However, this Criminal Code never been implemented, as successive governments have postponed its adoption.

So far, I have shown that Romania designed a special set of offences to protect the financial interest of the EU instead of assimilating them into corresponding offences already in the national criminal law, even though the crimes have the same logical content (Neagu 2010). This route of action was grounded on the one hand in the Romanian political desire to show commitment to protecting EU citizens' money. On the other hand, Romanian legal experts have long noticed an informal European trend to convergence in criminal matters (Antoniu 2009), despite the fact that European conventions specifically recommended the opposite, leaving criminal matters in the regulatory realm of the member states. However, choosing to establish new legal categories for EU funding misconduct was not followed by an "'objective' allocation of guilt" (Bauman 1997: 70). Instead, it created confusions for law enforcement that had difficulties categorising offences in which both national and European financial interests were prejudiced through the same act. As most EU grants work on the principle of co-funding, it was unclear if the offenders were to be investigated according to the special legislation regulating EU funding or to the Criminal Code.

Expansion and Specialisation of EU Funding Control Apparatus

EU funding is conditioned by institutional redesign at central and local levels, driving the implementation of new technologies of government as part of a 'modernisation' process. Following the EU recommendations (EC 2004), Romania devised a National Anti-fraud Strategy that aimed to coordinate anti-fraud efforts at the national level. Updated in 2006, this strategy had six main areas of intervention: prevention, financial public control, fiscal control, criminal investigation, financial recovery and coordination of anti-fraud efforts. Symbolically, the Anti-fraud Strategy shows

Romania's commitment to stepping up its efforts in protecting EU and the national financial interests. In this context, the anti-corruption agenda plays a major role, aiming to restrain bureaucratic discretion and strengthen external supervision through a credible, apolitical monitoring system (Rose-Ackerman 1999; Klitgaard 1988). The new agencies created (e.g., auditing agencies and integrity organisations) as part of the anti-fraud movement are embedded in a broader system of checks and balances where effectiveness depends on the separation of political powers. Thus the dynamics of anti-fraud rhetoric and practice are part of a wider political economic context that emphasises corruption as an underlying theme moulding EU funding.

Coordinating Anti-fraud Efforts

Departamentul pentru Lupta Antifrauda (Fight Against Fraud Department—henceforth DLAF) is the institution designated to implement the Anti-fraud Strategy by coordinating the adoption of laws and regulations that are in accordance with the EU conventions while ensuring their harmonisation with the domestic legal framework. This organisation was set up in 2005 as a response to the European Commission's Monitoring Report (EC 2004), which urged Romania to pay special attention to the protection of EU financial interests by setting up adequate mechanisms for investigation and the implementation of appropriate legislation. Despite a rough beginning marked by political instability, DLAF consolidated its strategic position in the anti-fraud institutional puzzle in 2011. Law 61/2011 and HG 738/2011 extended DLAF's powers to conducting administrative investigations of possible irregularities, frauds or other illicit activities that impact on the financial interests of the EU. The new legal framework also introduced new sanctions for offences in relation to EU funding (Art. 8c Law 61/2011).

An important part of the control process is in the realm of auditing agencies. Auditing is a form of symbolic action that contributes to the production of order legitimising the process of accessing EU funds. According to the Anti-fraud Strategy, financial public control is within the job description of the agencies that implement EU funding. In Romania, the main institution that ensures the technical and financial implementation of the European Fund for Rural and Agricultural Development is Agenţia de Plăţi pentru Dezvoltare Rurală şi Pescuit (APDRP). This hierarchical structure was set up in 2006 (OUG 13/27/02/2006), just before Romania joined the EU, but it was accredited by the Ministry of Agriculture one year later (on 15 December 2007). APDRP was built on the skeleton of SAPARD Agency (Special Accession Programme for Agriculture and Rural Development), which lost its reason for existing after Romania's accession in January 2007. APDRP inherited SAPARD's former employees and subsequently expanded its area of activity and its structure by establishing local branches at the regional (8) and county level (42).[11] APDRP coordinates audits through the Control and Anti-fraud Division (DCA). DCA is entitled to conduct control checks not only during the implementation phase but also for a period of five years after the project has finished (ex-post control). The control activities relate to conformity, eligibility and selection of the project, and the acquisition of goods and payments.

Directia Nationala Anticoruptie (DNA) is the only investigatory body that can prosecute offences against the financial interests of the EU. The investigations are conducted by the 'Service for fighting crimes against the financial interests of the EU', which is a subdivision of the 'Corruption Section' set up by the order of the DNA chief prosecutor in 2005. According to the DNA, in 2006, tackling EU funding misconduct was conducted by a team of four prosecutors, five police officers, three registrars and three experts (DNA 2006). Essentially, in 2006 only 3% of DNA's human resources were dedicated to EU funding-related crime—and the proportion has not changed dramatically over time. Such an allocation of human resources might indicate that, politically, this type of crime was not considered a priority as opposed to 'grand corruption' that absorbed nearly 97% of the resources.

Vertical and Horizontal Integration

The academic debates regarding foreign aid discussed in the theoretical framework of the book showed that financial support is crucially linked to the role of corruption (Sachs 2005; Easterly 2006). Easterly (2006) argues that foreign aid has been lost due to mismanagement, lack of supervisory capacity, fraud and corruption. He thus contends that the countries receiving aid should be well governed (e.g., strong institutions, powerful civil society, free media) *and* supervised by other agencies in order to ensure that the money reaches the poor. In Romania, both trends are visible, but the most important is the latter. The EU assumed the supervision role through a series of instruments that regulate law enforcement working routines and institutions.

OLAF has an important supervisory role for investigative matters at the European level. In the case of EU funding the 'supervision' of OLAF is politically displayed in the narratives of 'cooperation', even though, according to European regulations, OLAF can conduct spot checks in every EU member state. Secondary data analysis and the media review conducted for this research indicate that liaising with OLAF is a top priority for DLAF and DNA. Successive DLAF annual reports and European officials' statements indicate close cooperation between OLAF and DLAF (DLAF 2012). On the one hand, this involves transfer of knowledge from OLAF to DLAF through training and technical assistance. On the other hand, this relationship was shaped through joint investigations. For example, in 2007, Romania participated in investigating two EU-funded projects: one of them was financed through the PHARE programme and the other through a European Investment Bank loan. DLAF offered support and technical assistance to OLAF in 104 cases in 2011 (DLAF 2012) in an average time frame of 19 days per case. Furthermore, an important part of DLAF's mission is to centralise and report to OLAF the irregularities that appear in relationship to EU funding. APDRP and DNA also respond to OLAF's requests by investigating possible cases of fraud according to their legal competences and transmitting the results to the European body.

Vertical integration is doubled by a horizontal integration that ensures communication between the main control institutions dealing with EU funding in Romania. For example, in 2009 APDRP conducted 8 controls requested by DLAF, DNA and the Ministry of Public Finance; 10 file checks in response to OLAF requests; 137 document responses to DNA and DLAF; as well as 4 responses to the General Police Inspectorate. The Romanian Court of Accounts and Direction for Internal Audit had five audit mission and seven information requests. APDRP received 40 control notes from DLAF and started the procedure to recover debits.

The examples above show that the EU funding control apparatus is a hybrid form of hierarchy that reflects the contemporary changes impacting on the workplace that rejuvenate bureaucracy (Courpasson and Clegg 2006). It combines traditional hierarchical organisational principles (as described by Weber ([1922] 1968) with post-bureaucratic forms of coordination (Cascio 2000), in which people are not physically located in the same place but cooperate with supervisors and co-workers through technological means, mixing various traditions of civil service under the notion of 'supranationalism' (Tsebelis and Garrett 2001). The unique features of this bureaucratic arrangement impact on the definition of crime as a 'transnational' process, despite the fact that a crime can only be committed in a particular location at a particular time (Woodiwiss and Hobbs 2009). In fact, control has become transnational, because it is driven by international conventions and institutional supervisory arrangements, while crime has remained local. This gap between *crime* and *crime control* has been widened by European anxieties, stereotypes and perceptions of the situation that essentially define Romania as a 'systemically corrupted country' (EC 2002, 2004, 2006).

Emergent Bureaucratic Identities

The institutional arrangements described so far have created a particular work environment that inevitably impacted on the employees' professional identities. I argue that institutional prestige derived from political interpretations of Romania's state of pervasive corruption coupled with repeated positive evaluations from the European Commission (expressed through country reports) have transformed these institutions into 'elite squads'. For example, DLAF or DNA symbolic capital is constructed through repeated interactions with OLAF and other European institutions and their position as the unique administrator of the Romanian Anti-fraud Strategy and the unique investigative body for EU funding misconduct. This symbolic capital is further reflected in the composition of its staff—very young people, with postgraduate degrees preferably obtained abroad. For example, in the 2006 DLAF Report Activity, the former chief of DLAF, Mr Tudor Chiuariu, stated that the average age of the staff was 30 years. Quirke (2010) reported that all the staff was "well under the age of 40!" and that the Romanian authorities did not perceive the lack of professional experience as a problem. In his research Quirke (2010) also tried to advance the hypothesis that the lack of seniority of DLAF employees might have been "a conscious attempt to avoid employing older investigators who may have been compromised by a culture of corruption," but reported that "Romanian officials were a little evasive when asked to confirm if there was any substance to this observation" (Quirke 2010: 18). My research shows the investigators' lack of seniority is closely related to the job description as put forward by the authorities. As DLAF was designed from the beginning to be the main point of interaction with OLAF, there was a need for people who could speak at least two foreign languages, who were adaptable and willing to travel abroad (for training and investigations). It was simply more difficult to find such qualities in more experienced investigators. Finally, the last important aspect that contributes to the quality of elite squad of DLAF/DNA is the payment scheme. DLAF investigators have always been paid more than their counterparts (Quirke (2010) reports that they were paid 75% more). The justification for such high payment is related to incentivising highly specialised practitioners who might be conducting their activity under political pressure. This quality of 'elite squads' tends to impact on employees' career mobility opportunities. Such relatively stable occupational and organisational structures tend to favour on the one hand 'bounded careers' (Arthur and Rousseau 1996) that attach people to the organisation; on the other hand they favour the development of a 'career capital' in the form of professional networks without geographical boundaries and a capacity to learn and develop new skills through repeated training (Weick 1996).

Patterns of Control

Within the general EU anti-fraud framework, policies related to regulation generally aim to increase the level of control and criminalisation through *higher control rates*, *higher crime rates*, *harsher sentences* and *high-profile offenders*. Before discussing the three, it is important to highlight the challenge to explain the rising levels of crime associated with EU funding because

> statistics—whether crime or opinion polls—have an ideological function: they appear to *ground* free floating and controversial impressions in the hard, incontrovertible soil of numbers. Both the media and the public have enormous respect for the 'facts'—*hard facts*. And there is no fact so 'hard' as a number—unless it is the percentage difference between two numbers. (Hall et al. [1978] 2013: 13)

EU funding crime statistics are not solid indicators of the volume of crime (Hall et al. [1978] 2013; Hobbs 2013) because of the following: (1) the data show only a number of reported crimes and do not capture the 'dark figure'; (2) various criminal justice institutions have different recording routines; (3) EU funding crimes are investigated by the National Anti-corruption Directorate (NDA), a special branch of the criminal justice apparatus which is directly monitored by the EU through the Mechanism of Cooperation and Verification. Thus NDA is under national *and* EU pressure to 'over-perform', so is highly sensitive to EU funding and corruption, which are 'targeted crimes'; (4) political pressures and public anxiety about EU funding lead to over-reporting; (5) changes in the law make strict comparisons over time difficult; (6) the creation of new criminal labels for EU funding through special laws that double or counteract the effects of the Criminal Code thus leading to lack of consistent practice among magistrates, which in turn inflates certain crime categories; (7) in the official imagination, EU funding crimes and corruption are inextricably linked. Disentangling the two from official statistics was impossible for this researcher, and this determined the use of other methodological devices to complement the information.

Higher Control Rates

Within DLAF, two main units are important for EU funding control routines: Information Management Direction and Control Direction. The first is generally focused on preliminary verifications and cooperation with other institutions, while the second can initiate operational control activities to identify EU funding misconducts. According to the 2012 DLAF activity report, in 2011 the first unit received 645 notifications and requests from national or European authorities and solved 602 (in 225 cases controls and verifications were conducted, 151 were redirected to other institutions and in 226 cases other measures were taken). The second unit conducted 178 investigations of which 97 were finalised (53 began in the previous years and 125 began in 2011). The average time for an investigation was 110 working days (DLAF 2012). Such a time span is not unusual for economic crime—for example, Levi (1988) reports comparable time frames in his study of fraud in the UK. In the 53 cases begun before 2011, there were serious indications of fraud; in 7 cases the inspectors found irregularities, and in 37 cases there were no indications of misconduct. Thus in total, a number of 823 irregularities were investigated in 2011 by DLAF. The trend is increasing as compared to the previous years' trends, but it is not significantly different (DLAF 2007, 2008, 2009). Interpreting these trends, Ovidiu Dobleaga, the former DLAF chief, remarked:

> A high number of irregularities does not necessarily show that a state is more or less vulnerable to fraud. In fact, it shows that the control system has done its job. One can interpret irregularities in various ways. If the number increases yearly it shows that we control more and more. If the number decreases it might show that the beneficiaries become more competent and

> not necessarily that the authorities do not pay attention to fraud. One should not infer from a high number of irregularities that Romanians are 'champions of fraud' as it was interpreted last year, even though the European Commission brought clarifications on this matter. This is a bit of a sensitive aspect. (Gandul, July 2008[12])

Dobleaga was certainly right in pointing out that 'we control more and more'. Figure 6.1 shows the results of the control activities conducted by APDRP between 2004 and 2009. There is a wide gap between the number of project verified and the number of project that have been found to display irregularities with financial implications. An interesting result visible from Fig. 6.1 is that whereas control seems to increase (see the blue and red line), the number of irregularities with financial implications seems to decrease (the grey line).

As detailed in Table 6.1, during this period APDRP controlled 352 projects ex-ante, and in most cases, there were found either irregularities *without* financial implications or no irregularities at all. In more than 75% of the cases, the projects were conducted correctly, which shows that EU funding anxiety about misconduct is not justified. The number of instances of misconduct peaked in 2005, when 66% of the projects were found eligible to continue their activity. In this case, the high number of irregularities with

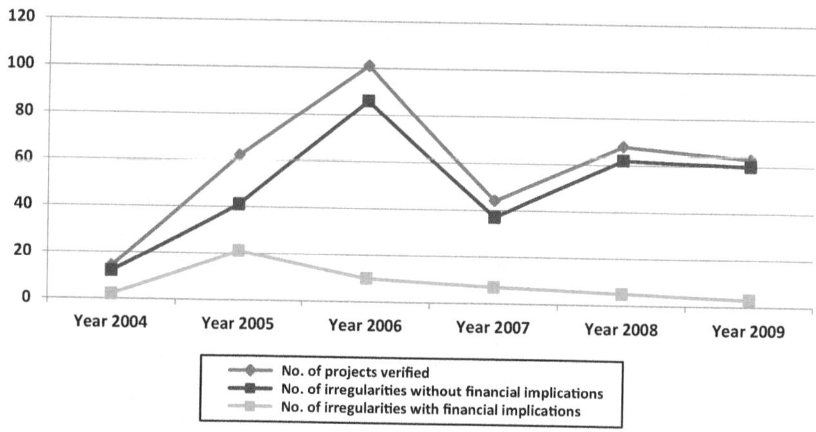

Fig. 6.1 The control activities conducted by APDRP during the implementation and execution phase before the last payment during 2004–2009. Source: Compilation from APDRP Manual/Activity Report 2010

Table 6.1 Summary of control activities conducted by APDRP during the implementation and execution phase before the last payment during 2004–2009

Year	*No. of projects verified*	*Sample size*	*Measure*	*No. of irregularities without financial implications*	*No. of irregularities with financial implications*	*No. of cancelled contracts as a result of control*	*No. of requests submitted to the police/ DNA for further investigations*
2004	14	10%	1.1	12 (86%)	2 (14%)	0	0
2005	62	10%	2.1	41 (66%)	21 (34%)	0	0
2006	54	10%	3.1	50 (93%)	4 (7%)	0	0
	47		3.4	36 (77%)	6 (13%)	2 (0.04%)	3 (0.06%)
2007	17	5%	1.1	16 (94%)	1 (6%)	0	0
	27		3.1	21 (78%)	6 (22%)	0	0
2008	29	5%	3.1	26 (90%)	2 (7%)	0	1 (3%) sent to the Financial Guard
	26	10%	2.1	23 (88.5%)	3 (11.5%)	0	0
	13	10%	3.5	13 (100%)	0	0	0
2009	63	15%	All measures	60 (95%)	3 (5%)	0	0
Total	352	N/A	N/A	N/A	N/A	N/A	N/A

Source: Compilation from APDRP Manual/Activity Report 2010

financial implications (34%) might be related to the sample size (which was unusually large including 62 projects) and to the nature of the measure investigated (Measure 2.1 envisages projects related to aquaculture). There were only two contracts cancelled as a result of the auditing activity in 2006 and only four projects were sent to the police for further investigation. This means that out of the 352 projects, only in 4 cases there were serious suspicions of fraud, which represents 1.13% over the five years under discussion. It should be taken into account that of the four cases, possibly fewer cases would enter the judiciary process and in even fewer cases would there be convictions. As compared to the number of cases where fraud is suspected, the size of the auditing efforts seems rather disproportionate. It would have been very interesting to conduct a cost-benefit analysis of the auditing system, because it seems to be based on important financial and time resources, but it was impossible to have access to such data, despite my efforts. The size of the control machine might save EU citizens' money in the long run, but "that proposition has not been examined, much less proved," as Anechiarico and Jacobs (1996: 75) remarked in the case of corruption vulnerability assessments in New York.

The ex-post control (auditing after the beneficiary has received the last payment) only became possible in 2006 through OG 13/2006. The aim of ex-post control is to monitor:

- the location of the productive activity co-funded by EU
- the distribution of property rights over the means of production
- the implementation conditions as shown in the contract
- the specific activity as specified in the contract and the funding application

The results of ex-post control between 2006 and 2008 conducted by the APDRP (Fig. 6.2) are consistent with the previous table and show that there are in fact very few irregularities (only 7 out of 164) with financial implications discovered during the ex-post control, even though arguably more than in the previous table. This might be related to the fact that the ex-post control was in fact conducted on the first projects approved in

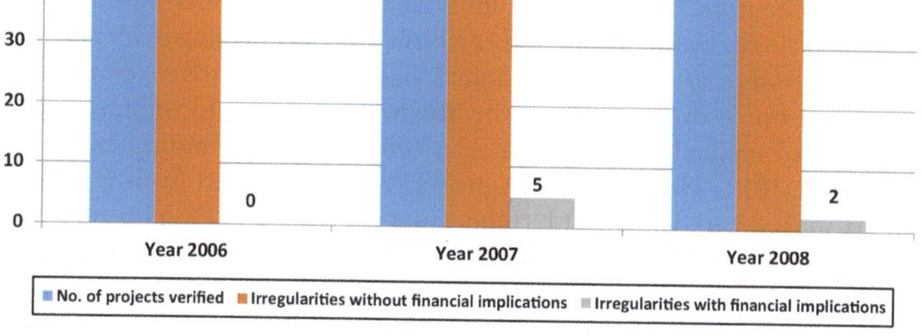

Fig. 6.2 Control activities conducted by APDRP after the last payment during 2004–2008. Source: Compilation from APDRP Manual/Activity Report 2010

Romania, probably around 2004. At the time, neither the beneficiaries nor the employees of the SAPARD Agency were familiar with EU funding procedures. It would not be surprising if future ex-post controls would reveal *fewer* irregularities with financial implications.

Higher Crime Rates

As the only prosecutorial institution able to investigate and issue indictments related to EU funding crimes, the DNA reported 97 cases solved in 2011 (DNA 2012). Compared to the number of corruption cases solved in 2011, the EU funding crimes represent 4% of the indictments that DNA issued. In its 2012 activity report, DNA indicated that the prosecutors have issued 648 indictments for corruption crimes (25%), 364 indictments for crimes associated with corruption (14%) and 590 indictments for crimes directly related to corruption (23%). Table 6.2 shows the evolution of DNA activity in relation to the protection of the financial interests of the EU between 2005 and 2011.

Table 6.2 shows a dramatic increase in the *number of cases investigated* by this organisation—from 43 cases in 2006 to 714 cases in 2011 (in 2011 the prosecutors' volume of work was 16 times higher than in 2006). Since 2008, the number of cases investigated has almost doubled every year, which means that the institutional cooperation between the organisations that are part of the anti-fraud network is functioning well. It could also indicate extreme institutional caution on the principle 'better safe than sorry'. Such supposition might be sustained by the very small number of indictments compared to the number of cases investigated. For example, in 2011 only 0.06% of the total number of cases was completed with indictments and 0.16% of the number of cases was actually solved by the DNA prosecutors. This is not an unusual situation considering the complexity of these investigations and the difficulty of obtaining evidence.

The *number of indictments* issued has also increased over the six years, but not as dramatically as the previous indicator. In total, roughly 200 cases qualified as crimes in relationship to EU funding between 2006 and 2011. However, DNA prosecutors progressed from 5 indictments in 2005 to 45 in 2011 (nine times more in 2011). This increase could be the result of accumulated experience and access to various trainings, professional meetings and informal support offered by both national and European institutions. As a validation of institutional cooperation with DLAF, the DNA included in their annual reports the

Table 6.2 The DNA's activity in relationship to the protection of the financial interests of the EU between 2005 and 2011

Year	*Total number of cases*	*Number of solved cases*	*Number of indictments*	*Number of defendants sent to court*	*Value of the financial damage*	*Measures to recover the financial damage*	*Number of cases solved as a result to DLAF notification*
2005	43	19	5	7	Not known	Yes in all cases	0
2006	Not known	Not known	11	8	598,873,339 lei	Yes in all cases	0
2007	Not known	Not known	26	51	1,573,585 euro	Yes in all cases	0
2008	95	49	32	77	2,669,285.64 euro + 1,874,599.47 lei	Yes in all cases	16
2009	266 (132 new cases)	109	23	46	7,127,000.71 euro + 1,510,933.64 lei	Yes in all cases	9
2010	545 (281 new cases)	222	29	62	446,920.97 euro + 6,859,077.7 lei	Yes in all cases	8
2011	714 (363 new cases)	276	45	95	1,539,955.91 euro + 16,133,976.46 lei	Yes in all cases	9

Source: Compilation from the DNA annul reports 2005–2012

number of cases that were finalised with indictments based on the evidence supplied by DLAF. The statistical analysis indicates stable patterns of horizontal cooperation between the two institutions probably sustained by the bureaucratic practice of 'lending prosecutors' from DNA to DLAF.[13] The number of defendants sent to court has also increased from 7 in 2005 to 95 in 2011, which shows that in six years DNA prosecutors have found 13 times more offenders for EU funding-related crimes.

Table 6.3 The courts' activity in relationship to the protection of the financial interests of the EU between 2006 and 2011

Year	*Number of definite court decisions*	*Number of convicted offenders*	*Number of indefinite court decisions*	*Acquittals and reason*	*Number of cases sent back to the prosecutor*	*Punishment*	*Custodial sentence (prison)*
2006	Not known	4	Not known	Not known	0	Not known	Not known
2007	4	Not known	Not known	Not known	0	In three cases the punishment was suspended	Two years and six months (one case)
2008	1	Not known	10	Not known	0	Three years suspended	0
2009	7	9	11	Two offenders Art. 10 Code of Criminal Procedure	1	From one year and six months to three years	One offender was sent to prison
2010	14	20	17	Two offenders Art. 10 Code of Criminal Procedure and Art. 18[1]	0	18 offenders suspended sentence	Two offenders for four years in prison
2011	31	54	20	Six offenders on Art. 18[1]	0	38 suspended sentences. The punishment ranged from less than a year (ten offenders) to six years (three offenders). Nine offenders were convicted to less than two years of imprisonment and thirty-three to less than three years	16

Source: Compilation from the DNA annul reports 2005–2012

Sentencing Patterns

The sentencing patterns displayed in Table 6.3 show a rising trend—from only 9 convictions in 2009 to 20 in 2010 and 54 in 2011, which might indicate that earlier investigatory activity has just started to produce visible results. It is expected that the number of definite sentences would increase in the next few years. A proxy indicator for the quality of the prosecution can be the number of cases sent back to the prosecutor (only one in five years 2006–2011). An important observation related to sentencing is the tendency of courts to impose suspended custodial sentences. This seems to be the case especially if the embezzled funds are partially or fully recovered (Neagu 2010). In total, over the five years 20 offenders were sent to prison for EU funding fraud and received sentences of between six months and four years. Given the offenders' high levels of financial, social and symbolic capital, some important consequences might arise from the investigations or even the adverse publicity alone, irrespective of the sentence: for this subset of fraudsters, the 'process is punishment' (Levi 2006: 18).

High-Status Offenders

Secondary analysis of the DLAF, DNA and APDRP annual reports reveals that EU funding misconduct can be assimilated to Sutherland's concept of 'white-collar crime' (1983), which refers to "a person of respectability and high social status" who commits crime "in the course of his occupation" (Sutherland 1983: 7). For example, according to the DLAF data, most offenders were public servants that would qualify as members of the local elites: seven mayors from rural areas, three local councillors, two deputy mayors from rural areas, one deputy president of the county council and one council secretary from an urban area. Other persons involved in defrauding EU funds were a director of a penitentiary facility, a university director, an educational general inspector at a county level, employees of the medical school, an inspector in the County Construction Inspectorate and a local director of APIA (Agency for Payments and Intervention in Agriculture).

Unsurprisingly, the profile of the offender displays high levels of financial, social and symbolic capital. This is due to the specifics of this economic arena, which is mostly accessible to *high-status individuals* (as already discussed in Chap. 5) that combine *professional competences* with strong social *reputations*. For example, in 2005, the DNA sent to court two defendants: BDE was the executive director of a firm and CM was the supervisor of a construction site. In order to win a construction contract BDE participated in a public bid and presented inaccurate and incomplete documents about his firms' debts to the state budget, social security and commercial litigation. BDE won the bid and obtained €5,709,791.67 from PHARE funds. With the help of CM, BDE prepared fictional records on the work in progress and submitted them to the Contracting Authority for payment. In fact, the PHARE funds were used to cover other debts of the firm. In order to recover the loss, the prosecutors seized some goods.

In another case, the value of the loss was much lower, but the case proved to be more complex. RZ was the administrator and legal representative of a firm that was implementing an EU-funded project that involved building a small hotel. DNA prosecutors indicted him for using repeatedly forged, incomplete and inaccurate documents. The forged documents were annexed to the funding application, acquisition and payment files during 2005–2006. First, in order to obtain EU funding, RZ signed a document that attested that the construction work had started on 17June 2006. In fact the work had started nearly a month earlier. Second, he persuaded three chief engineers from the construction company to draw up and sign various documents that did not correspond to the truth. In November 2006 he persuaded MH who had the position of inspector in the County Construction Inspectorate to forge an official document registered at the Inspectorate by changing the date (to put '20.06.2006', instead of '25.05.2006'). Third, he had not informed the SAPARD Agency about the changes in property rights over the terrain/land. Fourth, he did not inform the Contracting Authority about the conflict of interests created because a part of the wood used for construction had been bought from another company of which he was the administrator. The DNA prosecutors argued that the defendant had received €85,931.78 to which he was not entitled from the EU budget and in order to recover the debt seized the hotel.

As the previous examples show, the high profile of the offender is usually coupled with *significant financial losses.* DLAF (2012), for example, estimated the value of financial losses to EU funding from irregularities and crimes at €28,883,658.88. After conducting its own investigations on the basis of DLAF data, the DNA estimated the value of the financial loss at €4,615,302. The discrepancy of the estimates is normal, because the number of reported crimes is always higher than the number of investigated, prosecuted, sent to court and convicted crimes due to the level of evidence required and the technical procedures related to the justice system. Without downplaying the importance of the control activities, it should be noticed that *value of financial loss* is **not** a reliable indicator of EU funding misconduct. Until a case reaches the final stage of the judiciary procedures—a final court decision—there is little point in estimating possible financial impacts on the EU budget.

So far, I have described the newly set up institutional establishment designed for protecting the financial interests of the EU, showing that through its organisation and work arrangements, this bureaucratic apparatus was based on systematic associations between EU funding and corruption. The next section shows the effects of this control apparatus on the ground arguing that the gap between control routines and vernacular entrepreneurial practices creates relationships of complicity rather than competition between applicants, consultants and bureaucrats.

National and Local Practices of Control

My fieldwork showed that EU funding is based on two types of control and both of them are normally related to the reimbursement process. First, bureaucrats carry out careful document verifications, and second, they conduct thorough field verifications to ensure that the building is identical to the architectural plans. Field checks are usually within the job description of county bureaucrats, while the papers are verified in the regional office.

> First, the people from T [regional centre] had a list with all the documents that you needed to submit for reimbursement and they checked your file in front of you: 'Let's see, do you have this ... do you have that'. You see, they just checked first to see if you have all the documents. At the second stage, they checked thoroughly with the initial project to see if there are the same quantities, the same prices, if we added anything extra [...]. Then they also checked the documents regarding the materials—I mean the certificates of quality, provenance, conformity with the EU standards [...] We had a close relationship with the regional office, but it wasn't hard as the people working there were nice and understanding. You could talk to them. They weren't the kind to send you back home if you have done something wrong or so. They really helped us, they taught us: you need to do this, you need to bring that ... they cared about what they did. (D, beneficiary)

Field checks are also very strict:

"R: *When did the county bureaucrats conduct the verifications?*

D: *At each instalment of money. They could also have come in between payments, but most of the times they came whenever we asked for reimbursement.*

R: *How about the regional office? Did anyone come to visit the place?*

D: *No, for field checks it was only the county people. When we did the refund file, we sent copies of some documents by fax, so they came here to check the originals and stamp the copies. Then they did the field checks looking at the design [...]. 'Right ... according to the architectural plan, here you have a wall. Is there a wall in reality? OK, we can move on.' For example, we had to build a wall that was not in the initial design. We had to put it in the basement, some sort of additional support for the ceiling or so. When they checked the plan ... 'You have no wall in the plan. What have you done? You spent more money for cement and stuff. You spent EU money!' ... as if we hadn't spent enough money on that building! Or we had something else with a door—I don't remember exactly, but I think we moved it a few centimetres to the left or to the right ... We weren't allowed to do that, so we had to change the project. They approved the changes and we could move on. Otherwise you can't change anything. They really do check—I mean with the architectural plan in their hand they check the rooms, the surfaces, the positions etc—everything has to be conformed to the initial plan. If everything was OK, you received a letter saying that the construction was conforming to the plan and the next payment was approved. You know you have a successful project if you receive the reimbursement!"*

(S, beneficiary)

The above quotes point to a dramatic change in the bureaucratic culture in stark contrast with the local practices. The change is decoded and explained through enhanced communication, professionalisation, predictability and lack of traditional gift giving routines, but it also acquires an emotional note when bureaucracy is humanised through 'care' and warmth (e.g., 'they were nice and understanding'). For entrepreneurs used to exploiting their superior status in order to deal with bureaucracy, this was a surprising approach which enhanced the symbolic capital of EU funding. All these aspects make entrepreneurs sympathise with bureaucrats: "They sent some reminders every once in a while [...] I told you, they had their own monitoring, they needed to show that the money was spent [...] Otherwise they had problems with the EU because they don't spend the money. So that's why they sent those reminders—just to see if we had started, if we were on track etc." (D, entrepreneur). In another case, the reimbursements were received earlier than the deadline: "They paid me ... I got all the money that was approved ... they cut nothing. Also, I got the money quite fast in about a month and a half after submitting the request" (R, entrepreneur). Towards the end of the project, the relationship between entrepreneurs and bureaucrats almost enters a regime of affection: "Everything went well in the end—the representatives from the Ministry of Tourism came over to give me the classification and were very satisfied" (R, entrepreneur).

The relationship between entrepreneurs and EU bureaucrats becomes closer as the project progresses. In the beginning, the rapport is characterised by distance, and it is an almost faithful depiction of the Weberian model of impersonal contact. Towards the end of the project though, entrepreneurs and bureaucrats become closer due to repeated interactions. Despite the fact that field checks are very strict, surprisingly the bureaucrats are not blamed for that. On the contrary, they are pitied for the work they need to do as it is considered stressful. The blame is directed towards higher institutions expressed in an undefined *they*. It was never clear for me if *they* were the central office of the Agency or the EU itself, but it was obvious that the local bureaucrats and the entrepreneurs had formed an alliance against *them*. Such an alliance was based on geographical proximity, shared cultural codes, social ties and the need to avoid any problems in the face of hierarchical control. Sometimes, the narratives of justifications employed at the papers level were carefully constructed with the assistance of the bureaucrats. The natural tendency was to employ negotiations and avoid conflict, as the latter was bad for business. It affected not only the applicant but also the bureaucrats since any unspent money was interpreted by central bureaucracy as a personal failure. Thus, entrepreneurs and bureaucrats created coalitions to put a gloss on their performance. Everybody wanted to 'look good' (entrepreneurs for bureaucrats, local bureaucrats for central bureaucrats, central bureaucrats for European bureaucrats, European bureaucrats for the European MPs, European MPs for their governments and the voters). This process of plastic surgery that portrays a perfect way to do business at the documentary level has little in common with the realities of daily transactions or the work entanglements.

With its new regulatory framework, EU funding brings into being a space of interdependence created by money flows, cultural transmissions and socio-technological routines, characterised by plurality, constant innovation and pragmatic use of rules and prescriptions (Chaps. 4 and 5). Such trends put forward an 'EU-funded capitalism', the economic dimension of which is interpreted and enacted through cultural practices and symbolic images that fragment traditional entrepreneurial identity because of constant association with the anti-corruption institutional establishment. EU funding is a unique form of enhancing political legitimacy (for local governments) and transforming it into financial capital by fetishising anti-corruption.

The first paradox of the EU funding control apparatus is that it makes EU funding a semantic of governance by constant association with corruption. "Politics often demands the manufacturing of useful clichés" (Krastev 2004: 11). So when political elites refer to EU-funded projects accessed they are increasing their symbolic capital (Bourdieu 1997) through positive associations with the EU. Similarly, when political elites employ corruption narratives in their political campaigns to blame their opponents, they are in fact practising good politics. The discursive power of corruption is a very recent key anthropological theme (Haller and Shore 2005; Torsello 2012), which refers to practices that frame political action through corruption talk (allegations or facts). Building on high levels of perceived corruption and media reports, this typical practice becomes a common way to make sense of politics. As a result, political competition is "reduced to a confrontation between a government accused of corruption and an opposition that claims to be slightly less corrupt" (Krastev 2004: 10). The discursive power of EU funding refers to practices that frame political action through development *and* anti-corruption, with the effect of enhancing user's symbolic capital. For example, President Klaus Johannis refused to invite members of the opposition at the Presidential palace for the National Day reception (1 December 2016) arguing that they were 'criminals'. In fact, Liviu Dragnea, the leader of the Social Democratic Party (PSD), had been convicted for electoral fraud. More than six months later, the court still had not released the motivation for its decision. However, despite such dubious judiciary practices, the president managed to acquire electoral capital by such an obvious dissociation from a strong political competitor. In another case at a lower level encountered during my fieldwork (village), a candidate for the position of mayor accused his opponent of corruption by claiming that he had illegally distributed some parcels of land to his distant relatives. His opponent defended himself by arguing that if he had been corrupt, he could not have accessed EU funding twice because everybody knows that "DNA is watching you as if you were a gas tank.". The reference to the gas tank indirectly pointed to one of the EU-funded projects that aimed to introduce for the first time a gas line to the village, which made the demand for gas tanks unnecessary. For the locals, this was a massive change that impacted on daily work routines because refilling the gas tanks could only be done in the nearest city ten kilometres away. For elderly members of the community who had no cars, refilling the gas tank was a major and expensive endeavour. They tried to postpone it as much as possible by using wood from the nearby forest for cooking and heating. The gas line along with the EU funding publicity banner became two major symbols testifying that the mayor was *un bun gospodar* [a thrifty husbandman]. If the discursive power of corruption leads to 'dirty politics' through negative discourses based on accusations, in the case of EU funding, it builds on positive associations with development, anti-corruption and modernity.

For unsuccessful EU-funded projects, narratives of corruption can become partial explanations of failure. In one case, the locals were unhappy with the mayor because he "did not even manage to pave a three kilometre road, much less introduce a water supply. Why not? How come all the other villages around us have water on tap and we don't? It is because he is corrupt! The other mayors also steal, but ours steals too much!" (E, teacher).

If at local levels, direct contact with the 'reality' on the ground provides enough evidence to distinguish between practices and narratives, at regional or national levels corruption discourse becomes a way of attaching labels to entire communities. For example, allegations of corruption related to EU-funded projects can lead to municipalities/villages losing their legitimacy and trustworthiness. At the national level, the same practice can destabilise entire regions, as once labelled as corrupt less funding would be allocated in the subsequent years. In some cases, high-profile actors can use the same strategy to denounce less 'virtuous' regions at the European level.

The second paradox of the EU funding control apparatus is that it simultaneously deters breaking the law and accessing the funds. Polanyi (1954: 140) argued that "the road to free market was opened and kept open by an enormous increase in continuous, centrally organised and controlled interventionism." Conversely, my research shows that 'the centrally organised and controlled interventionism' as expressed by the EU funding regulatory framework is intimidating because it comes with imperatives that impose absolute obligations irrespective of the social and economic realities. Under such circumstances highly successful local entrepreneurs simply refuse to get involved with the complicated EU bureaucratic procedures. Essentially, EU funding regulations encourage thrift and control, while the engine of enterprise is profit and freedom (Schumpeter 1942). Such discrepancy makes this type of funding unattractive for most locals explaining to some degree the low absorption rate of Romania (33% in December 2013).

The strictness of EU funding rules is, in time, internalised by applicants who display extraordinary levels of knowledge, sometimes higher than that of consultants or bureaucrats. During my fieldwork I encountered shepherds and cowherds who mocked the public servants in the village halls who did not know how to supply them with the necessary documentation to apply for EU funding. However, unpredictable factors typically postpone the completion of projects. In the case of EU funding, delays are translated into financial penalties borne by the beneficiary. As one respondent put it, “This waiting … burns my pockets” (S, applicant). In one project that aimed to build an after-school centre unexpected new work required by the local terrain, and some irregularities discovered by the EU inspectors, not only delayed the project but also imposed financial penalties. In order to complete the work, the village hall applied for a bank loan. In another case—of a 10 million euro project to repair a road—the technical documentation had to be changed three times. Initially, the costs were estimated at 15 million euro, but then they were reduced as the EU agency considered the amount too high. After the construction had begun, it became obvious that the approved funding would not cover the costs of the project. The village hall could not co-fund the investment and had to drop the project until a bank loan or the state budget could cover the costs. For a long time, the local council voted against a bank loan arguing that the low income of the village hall would make repayment impossible. One of the locals recounted that “the project was badly designed from the beginning because they did not have enough money. So, they took out some works which were absolutely necessary. For this road, they had no money for traffic signals, sidewalks and road consolidation. It was only after they started the works that they realised that…” (F, engineer).

A typical example of EU funding rules ‘irrationality’ is the requirement to indicate at the time of application the names of the suppliers of materials and services. Local markets are not fixed and trades go out of business unexpectedly sometimes because they have to. For example, in two cases, the projects were delayed for over one year because the builder became insolvent. Excessive red tape, the length of time needed to obtain approval for refunds, the difficult procedures for organising public bids that involve long deadlines and the possibility of appeal are further reasons that many applicants are discouraged: "The circuit of the documents makes it easier to win a project than to implement it. We met with the other mayors on the halls of the county institutions for six months for our European projects ... and then ... if you are not in time, you have to pay penalties. We paid these, but it was no small money ... Nobody knows much ... In one place you are told one thing, in another place ... another thing. Eventually you find out, but it takes a while until the waters become clear. In any case, we keep going! In the end, when you look back you like the result!"(D, mayor).

The EU funding institutional framework clashes with the fluidity of the local contexts. Understaffed EU local and regional offices, the never-ending fluctuation of the regulatory framework, consultants' lack of know-how, mayors who do not know how to manage projects, consultants 'who are not serious' and deficiency of available technical expertise are typical reasons for avoiding EU funding, despite the regional pressures exerted on the local mayors to 'be proactive'. In one of the counties where I conducted my research, the local mayors had submitted to the prefect's demands/gentle threats and all accessed EU funding. In a very short time every second village in the county had a tourist centre. The villages barely had any tourist potential, but one mayor had obtained EU funding for that project and all the others felt encouraged to apply following closely his example and his project (they literally copied and pasted the project details, just changing the name and location of the centre).

The third paradox of the EU funding institutional framework is that it creates its own informality through the proliferation of rules and controls that often expand or create the very conditions for carrying out simultaneously licit and illicit activities. At one extreme hidden exchanges between bureaucrats and entrepreneurs appear in the brute form of cash on the principle 'Cash is the best type of lobbying.' At the other extreme market exchanges are so embedded in a mutual web of assistance that the distinction between public and private spheres becomes superfluous. Social networks favour a scant separation of formal business and personal roles, because as Powell noticed (1990: 317) "one's standing in one arena often determines one's place in the other." Thus the markets and hierarchies are decoded, interpreted and approached through personal relations. In between there are a lot of forms of negotiation (see Chap. 5)—for example, 'investment in electoral campaigns' hoping to be rewarded at a later stage with public contracts. When officials insist on the separation of spheres, refusing food or drink gifts is described as 'more catholic than the Pope'. This type of behaviour stands in contradiction to the local culture where conviviality and participation in social gatherings is natural. If the lack of participation in local exchanges is punished, so is over-participation, which is perceived as greed. Public servants who use their offices as rent-seeking units are strongly disliked and avoided.

As EU and national regulations forbid public servants to conduct entrepreneurial activities on the side, regional and public officials have established small businesses under the names of their family members. Most attractive are consultancy companies set up under partners' or children's names. The route of getting EU funding, as described in Chap. 4, involves writing a project and a funding application, getting approvals and then, if the funding is granted, executing the project according to the EU regulations. In one area where I conducted my research, the wife of a high-profile county official was the consultant for five different village halls. She was charging around €5000 per project. In another area, the market of consultancy was shared by the wives of two officials, who sometimes consulted in partnership and other times separately. For the village mayors, getting a well-connected consultant meant less time spent on approvals, but not necessarily a better or timely conducted project. An alternative route for the relatives of public servants is to set up NGOs that then obtain public funds for various educational, publicity or community projects. For example, a young couple who had a county official as godfather received as a 'wedding gift' a €50,000 public contract with the town hall that involved creating and distributing publicity materials to promote the city.

An EU-funded project brings in contact different actors who have various types of access to the political decision-making process and different interests. The examples given so far relate to a form of vertical integration between locals who want to access funding and high-level county officials who have the power to grant approvals and check the compliance of the project. An essential point is that vertical integration is typically achieved through interpersonal networks that give access to information, pave the way for personal interaction and reconcile different priorities. The bureaucracy is essentially approached and dissembled with the use of social networks such as those that give access to a prefect through his wife's consultancy company, to a mayor through his godson's publishing house or to a judge through his wife's NGO.

However, different layers of bureaucracy are approached through different practices. At the local level, links are established through personal ties and continued through informal networks. Husbands, wives, godfathers and sons represent strongly emotional links that smooth an EU funding applicant's way in a very direct, trustworthy and non-complicated manner. Money and goods exchange hands under the state's radar. At the county/regional level interaction is framed by an organisational form that can be a consultancy company, NGO or a firm. In this way, the interaction becomes more structured entering the realm of the market. The relationship of the 'front' or official owner with the powerful public servants is an 'open secret'. When an applicant signs a contract with such a consultancy company, there is an expectation of 'no headaches'—for example, getting the approvals very fast, being provided the right kind of information, having the file analysed in time. Establishing personal contact and close links at the national level (e.g., the EU agency, DNA and DLAF) is more difficult, because the control agencies are too professionalised. The risks of being exposed for professional misconduct at this level are very high due to the EU's close supervision. During my fieldwork, I noticed that when audited or inspected by national authorities, the beneficiaries behaved according to the bureaucratic rules: there were few or no attempts to bribe or influence the EU bureaucrats on the one hand because of fear of refusal and on the other hand because they had a good reputation and people felt there was no need for that. There were two exceptions throughout my entire fieldwork: in one case a beneficiary made the EU inspectors an offer they could not refuse. Living by the Danube, he had cooked freshly caught fish according to a local recipe and *mamaliga* (polenta). In another case a beneficiary had an unexpected biographical link with an EU inspector—they had illegally traded petrol together during the Yugoslavian war.

A typical way to formally fulfil the EU criteria is to 'manaresti' (fix) the public bid by designing the technical proposal in such a way that only one company fulfils all the criteria. This document details the special competences of the supplier of services. When one mayor wanted to hire a particular company to remove the snow in a town, he requested in the technical proposal a specific number of employees, a particular entrepreneurial background and a certain business maturity. The bid was publicly advertised through the electronic system. Several companies participated in the bidding, but did not fully fulfil the technical requirements and the 'right' company won the bid. Some mayors refuse to organise public bids altogether, preferring to divide the work into small subsections that do not reach the official financial limit. This allows them to contract the service providers through the direct award of the contract, instead of through the public bidding process.

A side effect of EU funding regulatory framework is its influence on the public bid market due to the necessity of organising public bids for almost every activity conducted through an EU project. For example, in Poland the public procurement market was estimated at 33 billion euro in December 2012, which accounted for around 8% of the GDP. Ad hoc audits of tenders involving EU funding detected irregularities in 36% of the cases. Most of irregularities related exactly to artificial divisions of work, unjustified rejections of best offers due to minor documentation errors and setting special conditions for tenders that violated the principles of fair competition. Despite the fact that Poland is considered the Eastern European 'champion' of EU funding, in stark opposition with Romania (see Chap. 3), the typical routines of doing business in the area of EU funding seem to be very similar.

Conclusion

This chapter focused on the construction and the effects of the EU funding institutional establishment in Romania, showing that the register of compliance, as well as the register of eligibility (Chap. 4), is framed by transnational anxieties that put in place extraordinary levels of supervision with ambiguous effects. The empirical analysis of the hierarchical machine indicates that in Romania, EU funding is controlled and investigated by high-profile anti-corruption and anti-fraud institutions constructed as elite squads. However, on the ground, compliance takes the form of "interpersonal bargaining within the context of a licence, a consent or permit, and often takes place in morally uncertain territory in which values, technology and business intersect" (Manning 1987: 298).

Notes

1. *Corpus Juris* is a set of European common rules regarding unification on criminal matters that are to be followed by every member state (see Appendix II: Guiding principles of *Corpus Juris* 2000. Draft agreed in Florence).
2. The restraining of certain rights refers to the rights mentioned in the Romanian Criminal Code, article 64 which reads: "The complementary punishment of restraining certain rights means the restraint of one of more of the following: (a) the right to elect and be elected to public authorities or to a public position; (b) the right to occupy a position presuming the exercise of state authority; (c) the right to occupy a position or practice a profession or activity similar to the one that the offender used to commit the offence; (d) parental rights; (e) the right to be a guardian or a curator."
3. **Art. 214.** (1) The act of causing loss to a person, in bad faith, on the occasion of administering or preserving his/her assets committed by the person charged with the administration or preservation of those assets, shall be punished by imprisonment from 6 months to 5 years. (2) Fraudulent management committed in order to acquire a material benefit shall be punished by imprisonment from 3 to 10 years, if the act is not a more serious offence. (3) If the asset is in private property, except for the case when it is wholly or partly State property, criminal action for the act in para.(1) is initiated upon prior complaint from the injured person.
4. **Art. 215.** (1) The act of deceiving a person, by presenting a false fact as being true or a true fact as being false, in order to obtain unjust material benefit for oneself or for another and, if damage was caused, shall be punished by imprisonment from 6 months to 12 years. (2) Deceit committed by using untruthful names or capacities or other fraudulent means shall be punished by imprisonment from 3 to 15 years. If the fraudulent means is in itself an offence, the rules for concurrence of offences shall apply. (3) The act of deceiving or maintaining the deceit of a person, when concluding or executing a contract, if without this deceit the person would not have concluded or executed the contract in the conditions stipulated, shall be sanctioned by the penalty provided in the previous paragraphs, according to the distinctions shown there. (4) The act of issuing a cheque with regard to a credit institution or a person, while being aware that the supply or cover necessary for its realisation does not exist, as well as the act of withdrawing the supply, wholly or in part, after the issuing, or of prohibiting the acceptor from paying before

expiry of the presentation term, for the purpose in para.(1), if damage was caused against the owner of the cheque, shall be sanctioned by the penalty provided in para.(2). (5) Deceit that resulted in particularly serious consequences shall be punished by imprisonment from 10 to 20 years and the prohibition of certain rights.

5. **Art. 215^1.** (1) The act, committed by a clerk, either for him/herself or for another, of appropriating, using or trafficking money, values or other assets in his/her management, shall be punished by imprisonment from one to 15 years. (2) In case the embezzlement had particularly serious consequences, the penalty shall be imprisonment from 10 to 20 years and the prohibition of certain rights.
6. **Art. 288.** (1) The act of forging an official document by counterfeiting the writing or the signatures or by altering it in any manner, likely to produce a legal consequences, shall be punished by imprisonment from 3 months to 3 years. (2) The forgery in the previous paragraph, if committed by a clerk during the exercise of service prerogatives, shall be punished by imprisonment from 6 months to 5 years. (3) Tickets or any other printed documents producing legal consequences are equated with official documents. (4) An attempt is punishable.
7. **Art. 289.** (1) The act of forging an official document when it is drawn up, committed by a clerk during the exercise of service prerogatives, by certifying untrue acts or circumstances or by omitting, in awareness, to insert certain data or circumstances, shall be punished by imprisonment from 6 months to 5 years. (2) An attempt is punishable.
8. **Art. 290.** (1) The forgery of a document under private signature by any of the means in Art. 288, if the perpetrator uses the forged document or gives it to another person for use, in order to produce legal consequences, shall be punished by imprisonment from 3 months to 2 years or by a fine. (2) An attempt is punishable.
9. **Art. 291.** The use of an official document or of a document under private signature, while knowing that it is forged, in order to produce legal consequences, shall be punished by imprisonment from 3 months to 3 years when the document is official and by imprisonment from 3 months to 2 years or by a fine when the document is under private signature.
10. **Art. 292.** The act of making an untruthful statement before a body or institution of the State or another unit in Art. 145, in order to produce legal consequences either for oneself or for another, when, according to the law or to the circumstances, the statement made is used to produce that consequence, shall be punished by imprisonment from 3 months to 2 years or by a fine.
11. According to the organisational scheme approved by Order 123/2009.

12. http://www.antifrauda.gov.ro/ro/presa/interviuri/interviu_ovidiu_dobleaga_22_07_2008/.
13. According to the 2010 and 2011 DNA annual reports, the Unit for Combating the Corruption Crimes committed against the Financial Interests of the European Community from DNA had to perform its activity with only two prosecutors as one was detached to DLAF.

Bibliography

Anechiarico, F., and J.B. Jacobs. 1996. *The Pursuit of Absolute Integrity. How Corruption Control Makes Government Ineffective*. Chicago and London: The University of Chicago Press.

Antoniu, G. 2009. Activitatea normativă penală a Uniunii Europene (I). *Revista de Drept Penal* 1.

Arthur, M.B., and D.M. Rousseau, eds. 1996. *The Boundaryless Career: A New Employment Principle for a New Organizational Era*. New York: Oxford University Press.

Bauman, Z. 1997. *Postmodernity and Its Discontents*. Cambridge: Polity Press.

Bourdieu, P. 1997. Le champ économique. *Actes de la recherche en sciences sociales* 119: 48–66.

Cascio, W.F. 2000. Managing a Virtual Workplace. *Academy of Management Executive* 14: 81–90.

Courpasson, D., and S. Clegg. 2006. Dissolving the Iron Cages? Tocqueville, Michels, Bureaucracy and the Perpetuation of Elite Power. *Organization* 13 (3): 319–343.

DLAF. 2006–2012. Raport Anual de Activitate. Bucuresti: DLAF.

DNA. 2009. Raport Privind Activitatea Desfasurata. http://www.pna.ro/bilant_activitate.xhtml?id=17

———. 2012. Raport Privind Activitatea Desfasurata. http://www.pna.ro/bilant_activitate.xhtml?id=25

Easterly, W. 2006. *The White Man's Burden: Why the West's Efforts to Aid the Rest Have Done So Much Ill and So Little Good*. New York: The Penguin Press.

EC 2002–2006. Regular Report on Romania's Progress Towards Accession. Brussels: European Commission.

Hall, S., C. Crittcher, T. Jefferson, J. Clarke, and B. Roberts. 2013. *Policing the Crisis. Mugging, the State and Law & Order*. 2nd ed. London: Palgrave Macmillan.

Haller, D., and C. Shore, eds. 2005. *Corruption. Anthropological Perspectives*. London: Pluto Press.

Hobbs, D. 2013. *Lush Life. Constructing Organized Crime in the UK*. Oxford: Oxford University Press.

Klitgaard, R. 1988. *Controlling Corruption*. Berkeley: University of California Press.

Krastev, I. 2004. *Shifting Obsession. Three Essays on The Politics of Anticorruption*. Budapest: CEU.

Krastev, Ivan. 2004. The Anti-American Century? *Journal of Democracy* 15 (2): 5–17.

Levi, M. 1988. *Regulating Fraud: White Collar Crime and the Criminal Process*. London: Tavistock.

Neagu, N. 2010. Accession Blues: Modest Successes and Major Difficulties in Romania. *Journal of Financial Crime* 17 (1): 47–60.

Manning, P. 1987. Ironies of Compliance. In *Private Policing*, ed. P. Shearing and C. Stenning, 293–316. Beverly Hills, CA: Sage.

Polanyi, M. 1954. *The Great Transformation*. Boston, MA: Beacon Press.

Powell, W. 1990. Neither Market nor Hierarchy: Network Forms of Organisation. *Research in Organizational Behaviour* 12: 295–336.

Quirke, B. 2010. Fighting EU Fraud: Why Do We Make Life Difficult for Ourselves? *Journal of Financial Crime* 17 (1): 61–80.

Rose-Ackerman, S. 1999. *Corruption and Government. Causes, Consequences and Reform*. Cambridge: Cambridge University Press.

Sachs, J. 2005. *The End of Poverty: Economic Possibilities for Our Time*. New York Penguin Press.

Schumpeter, J.A. 1942. *Capitalism Socialism and Democracy*. London: Allen and Unwin.

Sutherland, Edwin H. 1983. *White-Collar Crime: The Uncut Version*. Yale: Yale University Press.

Torsello, D. 2012. The New Environmentalism? Civil Society and Corruption in the Enlarged EU. *Urban Anthropology*, ed., G. Prato and I. Pardo. Surrey: Ashgate.

Tsebelis, G., and G. Garrett. 2001. The Institutional Foundations of Intergovernmentalism and Supranationalism in the European Union. *International Organization* 55 (2): 357–390.

Weber, M. 1968. *Economy and society*. Vol. 1. New York: Bedminster.

Weick, K.E. 1996. Enactment and the Boundaryless Career: Organizing as We Work. In *The Boundaryless Career*, ed. M.A. Arthur and D.M. Rousseau, 40–57. New York: Oxford University Press.

Woodiwiss, M., and Dick Hobbs. 2009. Moral Panics and the Rhetoric of Organised Crime Policing in America and Britain. *British Journal of Criminology* 49: 106–128.

CHAPTER 7

Friday Lunch with EU Funding: Profit-Making Routines

Chapter 4 described the process of accessing EU funding while touching upon the distinction between the EU-imagined actors and the Romanian actors who access this type of funding. This chapter will take that dichotomy a step further showing that while the EU regulations try to make the process of accessing funding a rational calculation based on standardised routines that produce predictable outcomes, the actors engaged in the process invent, innovate and combine their patterns of behaviour in order to adapt to unpredictable markets. The chapter starts with a short description of entrepreneurship in Romania based on quantitative assessments and moves on to describe the characteristics of the local actors and some unintended consequences of EU funding on the local contexts. In the second part of the chapter, practices of compliance are contrasted with typical profit-making routines. The conclusion shows that the perceptions of profitability of this economic process change as EU funding moves from 'free money' to 'expensive money'.

Entrepreneurship in Romania

According to the official statistics, in Romania, entrepreneurship is not well developed. The Global Entrepreneurship Monitor (Matis et al. 2010) ranks Romania among the lowest countries in the efficiency-driven economies. The early stage entrepreneurial rate is only 4.29%, which represents

R. Bratu, *Corruption, Informality and Entrepreneurship in Romania*, Political Corruption and Governance,
https://doi.org/10.1007/978-3-319-66667-9_7

the lowest value recorded in Central-Eastern European countries. The rate of owner-managers of a business in 2009 was 2.3%, and it decreased in 2010 to 1.09%. At the same time, the established business ownership rate was around 2.08%. With respect to gender, the female early stage entrepreneurship was 3.19% (the same value as in the previous year), but the male early stage entrepreneurial rate dropped to 5.13%. Between 2007 and 2010, the business discontinuation rate (measured as the percentage of the population between 18 and 64 who had sold, shut down or discontinued the owner-manager relationship with the business [Kelley et al. 2011: 64 in Matis et al. 2010]) was around 2% almost reaching 3% in 2009. In terms of motivations to start a business, more than one third of the respondents indicated increasing income as their main reason, while 10.82% were more attracted by independence.

The bleak picture of entrepreneurship in Romania offered by surveys like the one described above is based on assessment of the activity in the official and formal sphere. In other words, the informal economy is not taken into account. Thus, the results of such surveys need to be interpreted with great care and conclusions should be drawn with reluctance. It would be a mistake to infer from the above study that entrepreneurship in Romania is reduced to a mere 4% (in the above context the figure encapsulates the early stage entrepreneurship) or that the discontinuation rate was only 2% between 2007 and 2010 (the number of firms that are closed down during a year). On the contrary, this research shows that, in Romania, entrepreneurship is thriving in the informal area, taking a variety of forms that range from practical competence in dealing with the state to the use of the informal workforce for tax avoidance purposes. Such practices become more visible when contrasted with the official narratives that regulate access to EU funding.

Bani Garla: 'Free Money'

> They said on TV that after 2007 there will be **bani garla** [a river of money] from the EU for rural development. Apparently, Brussels people love rural tourism. All we need to do is prepare some projects. Now I am panicking because I did the project for a small bed and breakfast, but there is no money…. (G, applicant)

> There is a lot of work, but in the end it's worth it. After all, someone gives you money for free. Think about it: if you would take a loan, you would

> have to pay back the interest and the loan. With EU finding, you don't pay any interest and get to keep the money. Yes, it's a hassle, but who would give you money just like that? (RM, beneficiary)

At the beginning of the process of accessing EU funding, Romanian actors perceive this type of funding as a gift. The quotes above describe EU funding through an unusual concept—free money—which responds to every entrepreneur's dream of making profit. This concept brings together the financial and symbolic dimensions of money through the association with the EU and Brussels officials. Such an approach resonates with Viviana Zelizer's conceptualisation of money that describes "remarkably various ways in which people identify, classify, organise, use, segregate, manufacture, design, store and even decorate monies as they cope with their multiple social relations" (1997: 1). Thus money, and by extension EU funding, is not a universal measure of value as Simmel ([1907] 1978) argued. Starting from this point, the rest of the chapter will show that accessing EU funding is not only an economic activity, but it becomes a dazzling, elusive process when seen in its interactions with the social. It profiles entrepreneurial characteristics and defines particular profit-making routines.

Serial Entrepreneurs

The fieldwork conducted for this research shows that private actors who are successful in accessing EU funding are not only small entrepreneurs, but *serial entrepreneurs.* In some cases they run multiple businesses concomitantly while sometimes retaining their position in a state corporation. In other cases they have a history of changing various firms and/or professions. Instead of increasing the scale of their businesses vertically, by developing the magnitude of the enterprise, many actors prefer to start entirely new businesses. This is a risk-reducing strategy used for preventing bankruptcy. Jobs in public companies provide a more regular and calculable income, while the diversification of portfolios by opening up new companies offers insurance against the disruption of activity if one business fails. Serial entrepreneurs show flexibility by moving between jobs and the willingness to put up new companies on the market. For example, a pilot survey comparing Russian entrepreneurs with non-entrepreneurs (Djankov et al. 2004) suggested that entrepreneurs are more inclined to change professions, explore new avenues and have greater confidence and a broader set of skills than other people. They also appear to be driven by wishful thinking (Bernardo and Welch 2001; Arabsheibani et al. 2000), behaving as if they understand the present fairly well, but have a special outlook of the future. Thus opening up a company and closing it down is no more a failure than finding a job and then leaving it. In many cases the firms are the legal embodiment of the owner, are organised around the skills of the owner-manager and consist mostly of relations rather than assets. Since the owner-operator and the business are the same entity, it is of little importance if one firm is closed and another one is put on the market, because in this case the capital is linked to the individual, not the company. Hence, the impact on the business is only tangential as the other players on the market would be indifferent to the existence of the corporation when initiating a new business venture. Successful business relationships tend to be reproduced in different legal and commercial settings. The next two examples reflect all these trends while contextualising entrepreneurial careers in the Romanian environment.

Raluca's Story

It all started from my inability to stay at home and do nothing [...]. I trained as an engineer at the Bucharest Polytechnic and worked for almost 20 years in the local factory for electrical equipment. In the spring of 1999, the management conducted the first mass layoff. I was among the first to go, because my husband had a small company and they [the management] thought we had enough means of survival. It was a matter of social protection in the end, as they had to take care of all the people. Anyway, I was made redundant and received the unemployment allowance. I was 49 and looking for a job in this very small town. You can't find many opportunities here. Besides, I was driven mad all day in my house doing cooking, cleaning and laundry; even my two children were gone—they were already in College. Something had to be done! During that period, some of our friends wanted to do a mountain trip. I love travelling and since I had no job, I organised the trip. Everybody loved it and I realised that this was a nice activity, something that would suit me. Consequently, I enrolled in a six months course as a mountain guide. It was excellent, but this was no substitute for a real job. After six months, I was back to point zero: no job and staying at home. In the meantime, my husband's company (I mean him and his associates) installed cable television throughout this town. The board of directors decided to set up a radio channel also and I was appointed manager for the new born local radio channel. I did the job for a year and loved every second—my team was young, the work was fun, new and challenging ... it was great! The problem

> was that after a year, my husband, who had retained his position at a state company [apart from setting up a few private companies], was relocated to Bucharest. We had to move there for a year and I could not work anymore. When we came back, I was again jobless. However, this time I decided to do things differently. I wanted to have a business that I could control and do something that I liked. We [Raluca and her husband] thought a lot about what to do. I had two passions: tourism and interior design. The question was how to combine them. We considered opening a small boutique or setting up a small hotel. There were pros and cons for both, but I decided to go for the hotel because I found out about the EU funding in the end. We started to think about this in 2004 and accessed the funds in 2005. (Raluca, beneficiary)

Like most actors who I encountered during my fieldwork, Raluca's entrepreneurial career started out of need. When recounting her story, she starts from the privatisation of the factory, which she considers the beginning of her new career, as it gave her the freedom to shape her course of action. Her trajectory seems to involve moving between different business attempts until she found a match. This fluidity, which resembles some sort of 'firm shopping', is based on the fact that the transferable skills are more important than firm-specific skills. Despite the fact that she was forced into self-employment, Raluca easily acquired the taste for running her own business. Her husband's private companies along with his regular job in a state corporation must have represented a strong incentive for Raluca. She might have made more money elsewhere, without tying up a big part of the family wealth in this endeavour. However, she seemed to be driven by non-pecuniary motivations. In this sense, Raluca resembles Schumpeter's idea of an entrepreneur:

> First of all there is the dream and the will to find a private kingdom, usually, though not necessarily, also a dynasty. […] Then, there is the will to conquer: the impulse to fight, to prove one-self [sic] superior to others, to succeed for the sake, not of the fruits of success, but of success itself. From this aspect, economic action becomes akin to sport […] The financial result is a secondary consideration, or, at all events, mainly valued as an index of success and as a symptom of victory, the displaying of which very often is more important as a motive of large expenditure than the wish for the consumers' goods themselves. […] Finally, there is the joy of creating, of getting things done, or simply of exercising one's energy and ingenuity. […] Our type seeks out difficulties, changes in order to change, delights in ventures. (Schumpeter, 1934: 93–93)

However, Schumpeter's romantic description of entrepreneurs should be carefully considered and reinterpreted in the context of the following example, in which the 'joy of creating', 'exercising one's ingenuity' or the 'delight in ventures' acquire slightly different meanings. Mr G is a man in his 50s, married with two children. His wife is the director of the local branch of a well-known French bank. Mr G is involved in tourism, as the manager of a few hotels, all of which are strategically positioned in the mountains. Before the 1989 Revolution he was an engineer in a local factory. Immediately after 1989, he changed jobs and started working in the biggest city hotel, first as an accountant, then rising to the board of directors and later becoming one of the owners buying shares of the company. Like every company in the communist period (or immediately after the Revolution), the tourism company as well as all the hotels were owned by the state. The company possessed a chain of hotels and B&Bs in the mountains, which made them the only available resorts for tourists who had no alternative private accommodation.

Supported by the local bishop who is a major shareholder in the tourism company, Mr G became a board member and then executive director. He managed to remain in that position for more than ten years. During his time as executive director, Mr G led the company close to bankruptcy by letting the buildings deteriorate, destroyed the local market for tourism by closing down the hotels in the mountains for years, or kept them open but without electricity or heating, transferred or bought formerly state-owned property disregarding the true owners (hence the numerous subsequent court cases in which he was involved).

He was forced to resign from the position of executive director in 2006. In the meantime he had managed to build his own hotel in the proximity of the hotel he used to manage, thus attracting a share of the market. His exit from the state company was very profitable, as he managed to become the sole owner of a big hotel located in the nearby mountains at over 2000 m altitude. This hotel used to be the meeting point of the local and national male elite working in the area of electricity.

Mr G's humble origins were captured by one of his employee's remark that "he was the first generation wearing shoes in his family" and his astonishing upward mobility would have been difficult to conceive during communist times. His accession to a higher status was based on constant increase in his financial capital through careful exploitation of opportunities offered by transition. A very wealthy man, a millionaire in euros, as he likes to say to his employees, Mr G has turned an eye towards EU funding. He has bought a piece of land in the very centre of the town and has applied for SAPARD funding to build a small hotel. Even though this type of funding was directed to rural areas, he managed to get a document from the town hall attesting to the fact that the piece of land he had built on was outside of the town. With his wife as the director of a local bank, he easily accessed preferential credits and comfort letters documenting his financial status.

Mr G's story shows that informal economy is a consequence of the social and economic context, carrying both the characteristics of the communist regime and the traits of the newly born capitalism. In this sense, the changing geometry of informality is based on embeddedness in social and economic networks, and the reorganisation of the economy on different principles. Existing social networks provided Mr G with ideas about opportunities and sources of funding (Burton et al. 2002). In itself the context favours the existence of nuanced ethical systems due to the blurred boundaries between legal and illegal. Privatisation, for example, proved to be a lucrative business for Mr G, who brought his contribution to the dismantling of the tourism state company in his area. Using insider information he privatised a company over which he was responsible, in order to create profits for himself and a close circle of business partners. Abuses were noticed by the judiciary who opened up various investigations, but pardon was obtained at a price from sympathetic judges. Mr G's personal history can be read as the story of a *guilt-free predator* (Sutherland in Klockars 1975) who allied himself with powerful actors in order to acquire wealth. However, according to Schumpeter's definition (1939), he is a successful entrepreneur involved in 'creative destruction', having contributed to the destruction of the previous socialist economic order and the creation of the capitalist alternative. Mr G's own opinion about his activities is that "I give jobs to people! I help the local economy!" In a twisted way, Mr G is both a crook and a benefactor because while he clearly benefited personally by acting outside the law, his actions contributed to local development (Nordstrom 2007). Unsurprisingly, he had also been in the best position to access EU funding, as he was endowed with financial, social and human capital.

EU Funding's Perverse Local Effects

Cultural Capital: EU Funding as an 'Electoral Steam Engine'

For serial entrepreneurs, building up new business ventures means relying on various forms of capital (Bourdieu 1997). Social and cultural capitals discussed so far for private actors are directly linked to their capacity to secure cooperation, which is essential for framing issues and communicating goals. Cultural capital is a key variable in explaining which entrepreneurs mobilise the resources needed for accessing EU funding and how they use EU funding to enhance their cultural capital. This aspect is visible in the case of public actors who are involved in major EU-funded projects (Chap. 5). Setting up partnerships for the purposes of obtaining EU funding is a desirable, but not *sine qua non* condition for accessing such funds. As a general rule, projects that involve partnerships are more difficult to set up and implement because they alter the boundaries of local economies and involve heavy networking.

For example, in 2011 I came across a major project set up in the southern part of Romania. The project involved setting up current water and a sewer system in a few communities; it had an estimated value of €180 M. The financial distribution was roughly the following: 77% EU funding, 12% funding from the state budget, 2% contributed by the county office and the rest was the input of the regional water company. This project was not set up at the initiative of the locals, but it was designed in Bucharest and it was part of the national strategic design to improve the water system in Romania. The negotiations about which towns/communes should be added/left out of the project were related not only to the technical aspects of the project but also to the political affiliations and activism of the community leaders. The area did not suffer from deprivation by comparison with other regions, but such an investment was indeed necessary to improve the standard of living. However, participating in this project proved to be an image coup; given the high value of the project and the visibility of the investment, the endeavour was heavily publicised. The local leaders were photographed over time by the side of the responsible minister and constant associations were made with the party in power. This project was described by the local press as an 'electoral steam engine', which points to the high levels of cultural and symbolic capital associated with narratives of development, that make EU funding a semantic of governance (as shown in Chap. 6). For public actors, securing EU funding is very much a political process that makes use of resources developed over time[1] and not a simple matter of technical implementation.

Reproducing and Challenging the Existing Order

Stinchcombe (1965) had argued that entrepreneurs both reproduce and challenge the existing social order by constructing organisations that are embedded in social and cultural environments. The organisational settings reflected the distinctive societal situation under particular historical circumstances. In the case of EU funding this argument is valid for both public and private entrepreneurs. The next example shows how EU-funded entrepreneurial work routines are assimilated and integrated into the vernacular practices of doing business through the story of a village mayor.

Mr Money Chopper's Story

Mr F has been the mayor of a village in a mountain area for the last ten years. The area is well known for its tourist potential, wood quality and quantity, and mining potential. Mr F's history is full of dubious arrangements, successful networking with high-profile political leaders (or their immediate families), police investigations and court decisions that have never been enforced. His capacity to spend public money according to his personal taste without being convicted earned him the nickname of 'Mr Money Chopper'. His entrepreneurial endeavours involved hiring a few fictive employees for whom he cashed the wages, paying his phone bills out of the town hall's money and reimbursing some construction companies for works that were never done. He released property titles to his son over a terrain (about 10 hectares) that belonged to the community while validating himself as the rightful owner of 2.5 extra hectares (as the grandson of the initial owner with whom he had no blood relationship).

His management style has always been rather directive as he has little patience for democratic debates. Several deputy mayors chose to resign after escalating conflicts with F; the local police chief was threatened with losing his job and the members of the local council were subject to intimidation. In a council meeting he attacked the secretary with his desk, because there was no unanimity to vote on a decision that he supported. He explained: "So what if I turned over the desk? The secretary had not written the minutes of the meeting. Anyway, he is crazy, old fashioned, from Ceausescu's time. Let me tell you what happens … I want to do a good job at the town hall, but there are a lot of dogs who want to drive me crazy. They have no chance with me! They are all complainers, all dreamers who want to take my place. I did everything right, I had money before coming to the town hall and I will leave this place with money too—because my wife has a company that goes really well. If I were not honest, I would have never received a diploma from the National Democratic Association of Fighting Corruption!" (interview, mayor F[2]). In a rather emotional tone, Mr F contrasts two major ideologies through their local stereotypes: communism is associated with a 'crazy', 'old fashioned' time/individual, while he positions himself as a capitalist who 'wants to do a good job', 'has money' and is 'honest'.

Despite his violence and love of alcohol, F is well practised in networking with other official figures, sometimes even using them as tools in his personal vendettas. For example, after the meeting mentioned above, two of the councillors who voted against him received a team from the Financial Guard who came for a 'routine check'. The mayor himself drove the Financial Guard inspectors to the councillors' shop, which shows how far his influence extended. F's entrepreneurial skills, his pragmatic approach to the concept of legality and his social dexterity helped him find powerful allies in high public positions, who offered their protection and a hand in need. Their services were not repaid in money, but in wood (which is expensive and easily disguised in a construction site). As F was a public servant, he could not have other businesses on the side. However, his wife did not have the same legal restrictions. She is listed as the director of a company dealing with wood exploitation, but in fact, her husband is the one doing the business. A cerebral stroke in the autumn of 2008 left F incapable of working for a while. He never recovered his full capacity. This gave others access to the management of the town hall and impacted on his business arrangements by limiting his power to sell wood or the right to extract coal as he pleased. In 2011, his collection of criminal files was enriched by a new investigation of abuse in service, for allowing a company to extract coal in an area which was not in his jurisdiction. Despite his intentions he had not managed to access EU funding (so far), but he did hire someone to write projects for him. He decided to 'go European' by having his own employee at the town hall dealing with such issues. He could deal with 'implementation', as he was practised in the netiquette of local arrangements, but writing the project was beyond his understanding. However, he considered the high degree of control involved in EU funding 'distasteful' and thus refrained from any further action in this area. F did not resent the financial dimension provided through EU funding, but the regulatory routines associated with it.

Despite such concerns and in line with the county directive, F decided to hire an EU funding expert at the village hall, who could write funding bids. By 2008, it was considered that EU funding imposed the development of new organisational initiatives to secure the resources needed. Indeed, the complexity of the process pushed councils to employ professionals or create specialised teams to work with EU funding. However, the employment of such teams was not done according to meritocracy and the process of employment mocked the anti-corruption regulations, thus 'contaminating the purity' of the EU funding process. The art of locality here lies in the assimilation of this new economic space and its integration with the dominant cultural norms. Creating EU offices in public administration did not necessarily lead to a behavioural change; sometimes it was just a vivid representation of the saying 'the more things change, the more they remain the same'.

My own field experiences show that informal profit-making activities are not solitary enterprises. They are conducted in plain daylight with the willing co-participation of other civil servants, which points to the nature of risks that local entrepreneurs take in order to make a profit. In Schumpeter's view (1939) risk and uncertainty formed the basic conditions of individual entrepreneurial affairs. Ruggiero (1996) remarked that contemporary scholarship redefined risk as a potential social loss. In this case, risks are related to *compliance*—the civil servants enacted a compliance performance while getting ready to provide one at the documentary level. The use of creative skills in handling both the formal and informal norms makes the job of control difficult for various reasons as explained in the following section.

The Price of Compliance: Control in the Area of EU Funding

When applying for EU funding reimbursement, entrepreneurs need to *justify* their expenses using a multitude of documents. These documents have to present a coherent story about the project; in fact all the papers are independent signs that contribute to the general narrative that aims to create trust. As part of a ritual of purification, audit reports become social constructs useful for the production of anti-corruption/anti-fraud narrative. After all, as Braithwaite remarked (1984: 139) "government inspectors ensure the quality of your records, not the quality of your deeds":

> When you ask for reimbursement, you need to **justify all your expenses with a thousand papers** [my emphasis]. The main part of justification is to respect the initial project and most importantly the financial part. Of course you also had to respect the architectural project and so on. When we changed the door from the left to the right wall, we had to bring in justifications for that. (G, applicant)

EU funding is schizoid by default, as the authorities are mainly interested in the share of funds obtained from the EU. This dichotomy is expressed in the necessity to keep separate ledger accounts to record separately the circuit of money from the EU and the private investment (both for public and private entrepreneurs):

> You have your accountant who keeps separate files. There is this account for investments where you put everything that relates to this business and then this account is divided in two: the total investment and the EU investment. In the end you need to make sure that the value from your account is the same as the one granted initially through EU funding. Just make sure it is exactly the same! Not more, not less! (R, entrepreneur)

Good accountants are a necessity in order to provide good descriptions and justifications of decisions or to disguise any unorthodox arrangements.

> Accounts are a way to display the rationality of decisions and thus enhance their legitimacy. They help to demonstrate that alternatives were considered, trade-offs were made, and potential outcomes compared. Business accounts, as a 'rhetoric of numbers', engender legitimacy because they document the rationality of decisions in an age when that form of rationality is legitimate. (Carruthers and Espeland 1991:61)

All entrepreneurs that I encountered during my fieldwork did their own accounting while using a trusted professional on the side who could sign the balances at the end of the month and provide advice on how best to present financial transactions.

R: *How about accountancy? Did you do keep the books by yourself?*
D: *Well, together with someone else. I mean in the first instance I did the work and he just came along to sign it, as I was not authorised back then.*

(D, entrepreneur)

This need to control the financial records might indicate that budgeting is also a performative process (or simply a fiction) carefully constructed with the use of specialised idioms. The complex nature of the business and the intricate arrangements are concealed by the work of professionals who know well the weaknesses of business regulations. In this sense, accountancy and everyday practices might have little in common despite the fact that they are supposed to be congruent. "As a symbol of rationality, double-entry book-keeping legitimized business activities even when the actual accounts did not conform, or conformed only loosely to the strict method" (Carruthers and Espeland 1991: 61). Due to the high levels of control involved in EU funding, some actors choose carefully the direction of the public funds. They rely on big investments (e.g., the heating system) for which the costs are difficult to manipulate leaving the more volatile aspects to be dealt with in their private accounts. For example, the payment for the workforce is easier to manipulate and it is usually paid from the private contribution.

Profit-Making Routines

An essential part of the EU funding profit-making process relates to keeping the 'normative' and 'factual' orders (Parsons 1982) separate at the documentary level. Whereas the EU regulations will provide only one way of conducting transactions (which is usually as impersonal as possible), entrepreneurs will try to make them as personal as they can by entering informal arrangements, bribing, getting discounts, making use of their social capital to get favours and so on. Such practices lie outside the orthodoxy of the market exchange as understood by the EU Agencies. However, they do not challenge the orthodoxy of the local market in any way. As Ditton (1977b), Mars (1994) and Henry (1978) have shown in relationship to fiddling, such practices are bastards of capitalist economy who subvert the system of distributive justice implicit in the pricing of goods by confusing the spheres of exchange. However, such confusion is not out of the ordinary in this particular context marked by communism and transition to the market economy.

From the beginning of the process, entrepreneurs think about how to get *more* than what they are paying for from the EU.

P: *I want to do an asylum for elderly people. It is needed, as there are lots of old people in Romania! They are usually very lonely after their children have left home. They went to work abroad and come back twice a year—for Christmas and Easter. In my asylum their parents would be well taken care of and would never get bored or lonely, since they would have other people of the same age to keep them company.*

R: *So, you would offer free accommodation for elderly people. This sounds great!*

P: *Free accommodation? Who said anything about 'free'??? Nooo, they would have to pay! I mean their children of course. If they work abroad, they should have money! Besides, we are talking about their parents, the people who raised and took care of them! What I have in mind is a luxury resort, where people would live in their own flats, but we would cater for them, take charge of cleaning and entertainment. If they want company, they should be able to enjoy it, but if they don't, they should also be able to retreat in their own flat and not be disturbed.*

R: *Who would be in charge of such place?*

P: *Me, of course.*

R: *It sounds like a lot of work. How would you manage?*

P: *Oh, I thought about that too! I will make myself a big flat in the asylum, so I can move my family there. In this way, I am close to the church and if anybody dies, or they need anything, I'm already there, right? Besides, we would live there free of charge and spend less on food and cleaning. I can rent my flat downtown and save the money for later.*
(P, priest, entrepreneur)

The priest explained in detail how charities can become very good businesses by mixing spheres that relate to different registers. When explaining the purposes of the asylum or asking for funding, he positioned himself in a register of affection, but concomitantly assigned a value and a price to affection in an economic register. This is a typical practice, in the sense that some actors can exploit their role to enhance their financial status because of the traditional lack of financial regulation from the state apparatus and the nature of their work. The services performed by priests relate to a spiritual arena that is beyond the regulatory means of the state machine in a theological sense.[3]

I have encountered cases in which a parish was seen as a business unit and the major rites of passage (e.g., baptism, marriage or death) as profitable work opportunities. The senior priests that I encountered during my fieldwork could easily approximate the real income from any parish in the county displaying extraordinary levels of social knowledge. It is not uncommon that good parishes are sold to the highest bidder by the local bishop who has the absolute regulatory power over his jurisdiction. Bishops can also become politically involved in the state affairs and associate themselves to one party, but as a general rule, they tend to formally maintain only their association with the church. In one case, the local bishop had been a former *Securitate* colonel during communism and later became a member of parliament. He eventually withdrew because his local businesses were keeping him far busier than any other political position. He had established a candle factory issuing an order that requested all the priests from his jurisdiction to buy only candles produced in the local factory. Another large-scale business was a bread factory, but this was less successful because it would have been impossible to have the bread delivered every Sunday to *all* parishes. On the side, he had also set up an import-export company that sold aluminium window frames which have become very popular in Romania over the past ten years. All these entrepreneurial affairs were public knowledge, and the mix of economic and spiritual spheres was very much part of the local way of doing things that were acknowledged but not questioned. In fact, there were only two very young priests throughout my entire fieldwork who had considered applying for EU funding. Their more senior counterparts had politely declined the 'free money' arguing that they already had 'free-er money' from the believers and needed no state intervention. However, it would be unfair to infer that *all* priests have such skills or inclinations; like in any profession, some were good, some were less fit for the job.

For the rest of the actors, the road from the idea of the project to the final result is guided from the beginning by the EU requirements that force them into thinking through their endeavours for at least seven years (considering the usual time of implementation plus the five years monitoring afterwards). This anticipatory thinking coupled with the unstable conditions of the market forces caution and reflexivity upon entrepreneurs:

> Yeah, we had an idea about what and how to do, but in order to fulfil the requirements you had to respect certain norms. For example, we had to be careful with the requests put forward by the Ministry of Tourism because they give you the classification for the B&Bs and hotels. Because we wanted to have a four stars hotel, we had to make sure that the rooms had a particular surface [e.g. for four daisies B&Bs/hotels[4] the room has to be at least 15 square metres], which meant bigger rooms with more facilities, a restaurant ... you know ... everything [...]. Also, we thought we might extend the hotel later on, so we had to be careful about the ceiling. It had to be more solid than usual to sustain another floor. The feasibility study was done for a period of about five years because for five years you are under ... not necessarily control, but ... the Agency monitors you for this period. They want to make sure you don't change ... I mean if you have done a B&B, then, for five years, you have to keep it as a B&B [...]. After five years you can do what you want ... sell it, make it your private home, whatever. But before that, you have to keep it as you said it would be, be active and have profit. (D, entrepreneur)

Careful investments are a necessity, and as one of my respondents remarked, "[I]t is better to check our pockets before we start something, since we have the possibility to expand in time..." (V, applicant). The entrepreneurs are cautious because the context described below is characterised by high uncertainty.

Volatile Markets

However, anticipatory thinking is not enough to ensure profit. No matter how optimistic the budget approved by the Agency might be, the Romanian markets are so volatile that the applicant will most likely be forced to raise his/her contribution to the project. For example, the implementation phase starts with signing the contract of funding and making the first notebook of acquisitions (Chap. 4). Then the work can begin, using the private funds. This is the first moment when the plan handed in to the Agency is confronted with the reality of the market because the notebook of acquisitions is a document that details all the expenses incurred for completing the first part of the project. Such expenses might include materials necessary for building, costs of hiring a construction company to do the works, and personnel wages:

> That's when you find out if the prices have increased … which is usually the case … You see, it's one thing to anticipate the costs on paper and another thing to start doing the project. When you do the project you realise that the costs are very different. So, you will never be able to finish the project and keep within the approved budget. It will always be more expensive for you, as an individual. (R, entrepreneur)

The instability of the Romanian economic situation makes the budget an unpractical tool due to inflation and market dynamics (some companies might disappear by the time the project is approved, or others might appear and provide services at more competitive prices). Officially, there is the possibility to amend the initial budget[5] to reflect more realistically the economic situation and the field conditions, but it would be easier to 'put a stick in your arse'. These aspects coupled with the uncertainty of obtaining a positive answer deter the applicant from pursuing this path. At this point,

> The success of everything depends on intuition, the capacity of seeing things in a way which afterwards proves to be true, even though it cannot be established at the moment, and of grasping the essential fact, discarding

> the unessential, even though one can give no account of the principles by which this is done. Thorough preparatory work, and special knowledge, breadth of intellectual understanding, talent for logical analysis, may under certain circumstances be sources of failure. (Schumpeter 1934: 85)

> One more thing: they [the Agency] ask you to prove that you have half of the money to do this project right? But you will never be able to finish with only 50%. Apart from the fact that the prices will increase there are other things. Let's say you start the project and spend your half of the money. You do the construction and then send the reimbursement file to the Agency. There will be a time span between applying for a refund and actually getting it. This time span can be a month, two or God knows when. What are you going to do in the meantime? Stop the works? This is going to delay you entire project. So, you see, one always needs more than 50% in order to keep working to respect the final deadline. (R, entrepreneur)

Thus the costs of completing a project are higher even in very stable and predictable markets, and not only in a risky and unstable environment.

Cash Society

Other hidden costs add to the project, thus making it less profitable. A particular aspect that used to cause clashes was that the Agency only accepts bank payments/transfers. However, Romania is still very much a **cash society**. People do not commonly use bank transfers, especially if they live in remote rural areas. Not seldom, even SMEs avoid them. In one of the villages where I conducted my research, a couple of villagers received their pension through a bank transfer. However, the village had no cash machine, and in any case, they would not have known how to use it. Once a month, Veta's son, who shared the house with his parents and his wife, would collect the bank cards from his elderly relatives and head to the nearest town to withdraw the money. He carried the cards in a small brown leather bag around his waist. Each card had a post-it attached to it that carried the pin number. Most of his relatives had never used their cards—they would keep them safely in the wardrobe, under their best clothes. They chose to withdraw all the money at once for two reasons: they could not have accessed the money otherwise, and it was cheaper. For every card interrogation, the bank charged a small fee. This form of superimposed technological modernisation dissatisfied everyone because it was diminishing their income through bank fees, paying for Veta's son's trip to town or informal borrowing to cover delays, which created further social obligations. At the firm level, for small and medium enterprises, the situation is similar and even some administrative units support the cash society indirectly. For example, some taxes can only be paid on the spot, which makes it impossible to use a bank transfer. These contextual traits are in stark contradiction to the EU funding regulations, which assume *ab initio* certain conditions that characterise modernity in the EU vision.

The register of profitability is also related to aspects that do not have much in common with EU funding, but with the general commercial regulations of Romania. For example, it is far more profitable to obtain EU funding through a **firm**, than through a natural person. In both cases entrepreneurs have good chances of success, but there are other economic rationales behind this type of decision. For a natural person, it is easier to keep the accountancy for the EU project. However, a natural person cannot claim back the VAT:

> It would have been better to be a firm to claim back the VAT. You see, for their share [the financial contribution to the project through EU funding] I was exempted from paying the VAT because of the EU contribution. For my share ... I could not claim back the VAT. As a natural person you do not pay VAT in general. However, I bought everything with VAT and paid all the works with VAT, but could not claim it back. Altogether it was about 700 million lei [approximately €17.000]. If only I knew from the beginning ... I would have set up a firm in no time.... (R, entrepreneur)

The organisational setting of the firm is preferable from a financial point of view, but not from a practical point of view because it is typically accompanied by higher levels of control.

Bank Loans

In order to prove the capacity to co-fund, the applicant needs to show a letter from the bank stating the amount of funds available. If needed, one can also obtain a bank loan to reach the required percentage. However, banks are more reluctant to fund start-up firms than the Agency and require far more documentation than the EU.

> Most of the projects funded by the EU would never be endorsed by a bank. They are just not profitable enough or they might be profitable if you do not

> think about repaying the loan and covering the bank fees. You need to be a serious investor with a good entrepreneurial history or have a lot of valuable assets for a bank to give you comfort letters. (A, bank employee)

Entrepreneurs find such practices oppressive (De Meza and Southey 1996) and thus tend to rely on informal sources of capital or mortgage their properties. This is a risky strategy because the construction rarely works according to the plan and the rules of funding change very often (requiring new documentation or more time to assess compliance with the new regulations). Unsure of how the market would react, they choose to start small, avoid borrowing and rely on their own savings and personal assets (Aldrich 2005).

A loan complicates the budget, as various fees and bank commissions need to be taken into account and incorporated in the documents submitted to the Agency. This is one of the instances where expert knowledge is required:

> About your financial contribution to the project ... you either have the money or you make a loan; but when you make a loan it is more difficult to make the economic plan because you need to return the loan, take into account the bank fees for God knows how many years [...] or, if you return the loan before the deadline, you need to pay something else [...]. You need to calculate some indices [...] and these were more specialised. It was a bit too complicated for me also because it was a big project and you could not play with numbers. That's why I used a consultancy firm—they do these things on regular basis. (D, entrepreneur)

The logic behind asking for these specific documents is not entirely an epistemological nonsense. Most entrepreneurs were familiar with such procedures, which would have had to be fulfilled at some point during the process of construction, even without accessing EU funding. However, the amount of details requested through the application file was considered exaggerated due to the unstable conditions on the market. "How should I put it? It was a bit too much—I mean the prices will change anyway by the time you start building. Besides, some of the suppliers might not even be on the market at the time" (R, entrepreneur). This aspect shows a fundamental difference in patterns of thinking between entrepreneurial and bureaucratic logic. The former is more fluid, adaptive and context-dependent in accordance with the fluctuating conditions of the market (maybe even more realistic from an economic point of view). The latter is more strict, based on assumptions of stability and continuity and, thus, not necessarily suitable for this type of assessment.

Regulations

One last aspect that impacts negatively on the process of accessing EU funding is the fluidity of the regulatory framework. One year before joining the EU in 2006, and a few years afterwards (2007–2009), all the regulations had been adjusted to reflect the change from pre-accession to structural funding. New ministerial edicts and various drafts of the 'Beneficiary's Guide' were passed on regular basis. The difficulty was not only the fact that the new information was simply hard to absorb due to its quantity, but also that the new regulations were more complicated and subjected to various interpretations. Thus respecting the letter of the law was more problematic for both beneficiaries and bureaucrats. The irregularities found by the authorities in some projects had less to do with *mens rea* and more to do with an honest lack of understanding sustained by the confusion created by the multitude of official interpretations. In one case, DD, the mayor of a medium-size commune, who has held this position for over two mandates (8 years), was investigated by DNA in 2010 and convicted to 12 years of imprisonment by a local court. However, this has not deterred him, and in 2011 he obtained 4.5 million euro in EU funding for works related to the development of the commune. The case in which DD was investigated had to do with leasing a terrain to one of the town council members, who later tried to access EU funding. In reality the terrain was common property of the residents who used it for graze. The councillor was convicted for giving false declarations to the EU agency, and the mayor was convicted for releasing false documentation. However, DD defended himself by saying that he had released such documents at the express recommendation of the Agency's representatives and following the example of other mayors from neighbouring villages. Furthermore, the money received by the councillor from the Agency had immediately been transferred to the town hall account and used for the public's benefit.

Expensive Money

A close analysis of EU funding processes reveals that in the end the 'free money' is transformed into 'expensive money' due to the gaps between EU assumptions and local contexts. Most private entrepreneurs considered the process unprofitable arguing that the price of doing the project is divorced from the value of the product for small investments:

> It's not worth doing a project with EU funding if you have a small company or a small project. Let's say, instead of a €200,000 project you have a €50,000 project [...]. You have to do a lot of running around for the same papers. Expensive papers. For every approval you had to pay taxes and then, once you finished the construction you had to get the final authorisations and pay other taxes. So, for a small project, it's not worth it because you have to get papers and papers ... In the end, almost all the money you got from the EU office would be spent on taxes. (D, entrepreneur)

The length of the project, the amount of energy, attention or time as input variables are negatively correlated to the output. Consequently, to keep the business profitable, EU-funded projects have to be a collateral activity:

> This [the EU project] was never our main activity. It would have been impossible. Our business was very different. If this would have been our main activity, we would have all starved to death by now. This project only swallowed money for two and a half years. Seven hundred thousand euros [...]. If you are a natural person or have a small company with no activity—I mean you set up a company just to do the EU project—then, you either have another job or you have enough money to afford spending over the next two years. (D, entrepreneur)

The overinflated regulatory framework of EU funding is decoded by the above entrepreneurs in money, prices and profitability. In this context Schumpeter's definition of entrepreneurship (1939) needs to be amended, because EU funding represents a particular form of economic activity. In the official (i.e., bureaucratic) understanding, this is a form of assistance offered by the state, based on a specific order of meaning that gives precedence to the beneficiary over the entrepreneur. A beneficiary is subject to the EU regulations and bound to reflect the changes in the patterns of governance. In this sense, this process is an exercise in disciplinary technologies conducted with the help of trained specialists who provide the requested output and make it work in predictable ways. The entire EU funding process is based on the fundamental idea that things can be strictly calculated, and in this way, the economic process and its results are predictable. Such vision leaves little room for Schumpeter's romantic understanding of commercial adventures, in which entrepreneurs visualised their endeavours in a flash of inspiration. It also makes the process far less profitable than expected, which explains the Romanian low absorption rates.

Conclusion

This chapter has shown that EU funding is an example of an intrusive policy in the economic area in Romania, which has led to emerging syncretic cultures of entrepreneurship. In these newly created spaces, economic action that is embedded in a multiplex of social, economic, political and personal relations has to be presented as decontextualised in order to fulfil the EU regulations. The 'legitimate orders of power' (Weber 1968) that deny the opportunity-rich social environment also de-emphasise the informality of economic arrangements that turn local economies into moral economies. EU funding is essentially a process of policy learning to comply with European regulations. Actors learn to be *beneficiaries*, while always retaining their entrepreneurial ego. They perform institutional compromises when in registers of eligibility and profitability (as shown in Chaps. 5 and 6).

Through its regulations, EU funding reinforces the heavy players in the local arenas and thus fails to achieve its objectives (regarding the support offered to economic debutants). Furthermore, it is assimilated and integrated into the local panoply of business opportunities and benefits from the transfer of practices that 'contaminate' the purity (or Puritanism) of the European regulations. In practice, actors transgress the invisible boundaries between legal and illegal by making use of alternative concepts in their daily work routines. However, at the documentary level, such distinctions are preserved with great care in order to provide bureaucrats with great stories of success.

Notes

1. For example, on 6 April 2012, the Government issued a decision (GD 255/3 April 2012) regarding the allocation of the Prime Minister's reserve fund to the local budget. Most funds were directed to the communities with Liberal-Democrat leaders, despite the fact that there were other areas that were involved in EU projects. For example, in Suceava County, out of 49 communes that received funding, only 3 were from the opposition. (http://www.contributors.ro/politica-doctrine/%C8%99i-tu-fiul-meu-mru/ last visited on 8 April 2012).

2. The interview was conducted and printed by a local newspaper. In order to protect the anonymity of the research participants, the reference was removed.
3. I have encountered one case in which a man, disappointed by the work of a priest in the spiritual domain, appealed to the criminal justice system to put things right. He had called upon a priest repeatedly to perform specific services at his home, claiming that malefic spirits inhabited his house. Eventually, he appealed to the criminal justice system claiming that despite the services, the spirits had not left as he could hear strange noises in the house. Therefore, he sued the priest requesting back the service charge. This is an extreme example in which a regulatory system from one domain is called upon to rule over another domain over which it has neither jurisdiction nor competence.
4. The standardisation of hotels and B&Bs is measured differently in rural and urban areas. In rural areas the Ministry of Tourism awards *daisies* and in urban areas *stars*.
5. An essential part of the initial budget is the exchange rate at which the prices are calculated. For example, an applicant sent the file to the Agency when the exchange rate was 3.6725 RON per euro. However, this rate changed in a few months. When the applicant was awarded the grant, the funding contract was signed at the initial value of 3.6725 RON per euro.

Bibliography

Aldrich, H.E. 2005. Entrepreneurship. In *Handbook of Economic Sociology*, ed. N. Smelser and R. Swedberg, 451–477. Princeton, NJ: Princeton University Press.

Arabsheibani, G. de Meza, D.J. Maloney, and B. Pearson. 2000. And a Vision Appeared Unto them of a Great Profit: Evidence of Self-Deception Among the Self-Employed. *Economics Letters* 67: 35–41.

Bernardo, A., and I. Welch. 2001. On the Evolution of Overconfidence of Entrepreneurs. *Journal of Economics and Management Strategy* 10: 301–330.

Bourdieu, P. 1997. Le champ économique. *Actes de la recherche en sciences sociales* 119: 48–66.

Braithwaite, J. 1984. *Corporate Crime in the Pharmaceutical Industry*. London: Routledge.

Burton, M.D., J. Sorenson, and C. Beckman. 2002. Coming from Good Stock: Career Histories and New Venture Formation. In *Social Structure and Organizations Revisited*, ed. M. Lounsbury and M. Ventresca, 229–262. Amsterdam: JAI/Elsevier.

Carruthers, B.G., and W. Nelson Espeland. 1991. Accounting for Rationality: Double-Entry Bookkeeping and the Rhetoric of Economic Rationality. *American Journal of Sociology* 97 (1): 31–69.

De Meza, D., and C. Southey. 1996. The Borrower's Curse: Optimism, Finance, and Entrepreneurship. *Economic Journal* 106: 375–386.

Ditton, 1977b. *Part-time Crime: An Ethnography of Fiddling and Pilferage*. London: Macmillan Press.

Ditton, J. 1977c. *Part-Time Crime: An Ethnography of Fiddling and Pilferage*. London: Macmillan Press.

Djankov, S., Miguel, E., Qian, Y., Roland, G. and Zhuravskaya, E. V. 2004. *Entrepreneurship: First Results from Russia*. Working paper.

Henry, S. 1978. *The Hidden Economy: The Context and Control of Borderline Crime*. Oxford: Martin Robertson.

Klockars, C.B. 1975. *The Professional Fence*. London: Tavistock Publications.

Matis, D., A. Nagy, P. Tunde-Petra, and A. Benyovszki. 2010. *Entrepreneurship in Romania. 2010 Country Report*. Cluj Napoca: Universitatea Babes-Bolyai.

Mars, G. 1994. *Cheats at Work: An Anthropology of Workplace Crime*. Aldershot: Dartmouth Publishing.

Nordstrom, C. 2007. *Global Outlaws*. In *Crime, Money and Power in the Contemporary World*. Berkeley, Los Angeles and London: University of California Press.

Parsons, T. 1982. *On Institutions and Social Evolution*. Chicago, IL: University of Chicago Press.

Ruggiero, V. 1996. *Organized and Corporate Crime in Europe. Offers that Can't Be Refused*. Aldershot: Dartmouth Publishing.

Schumpeter, J.A. 1934. *The Theory of Economic Development*. Cambridge, MA: Harvard University Press.

———. 1939. *Business Cycles: A Theoretical, Historical and Statistical Analysis of the Capitalist Process*. New York: McGraw-Hill.

Simmel, G. 1907/1978. *The Philosophy of Money*. Trans. Tom Bottomore and David Frisby, Ed. David Frisby. 3rd ed. vol. 1. New York: Routledge. Original edition, 1907. Reprint, 1978.

Stinchcombe, A.L. 1965. Social Structure and Organizations. In *Handbook of Organizations*, ed. James G. March, 142–193. Chicago, IL: Rand McNally.

Weber, M. 1968. *Economy and society*. Vol. 1. New York: Bedminster.

Zelizer, V. 1997. *The Social Meaning of Money. Pin Money, Paychecks, Poor Relief, and Other Currencies*. Princeton, NJ: Princeton University Press.

Conclusion

This book showed that the process of EU funding puts in relationship three generic actors as detailed in Fig. A1: *applicants/beneficiaries* (people who want and/or access the funding), *consultants* (people who assist the applicant in accessing the funding) and *bureaucrats*.

During the project cycle, the interaction between these three generic actors spans three registers of behaviour: *register of eligibility*, *register of profitability* and *register of compliance*. The project begins with the preparation of the funding application. Due to the fact that EU funding is based on highly formalised idioms, applicants make use of consultants to construct eligibility. Consultants assist the applicants to prepare the necessary documentation by decoding the EU requirements. Once the funding application is approved, the project enters the implementation stage, and the 'applicant' becomes the 'beneficiary'. At this point, consultants usually exit the project, leaving the beneficiaries to interact directly with the bureaucrats. During implementation stage, beneficiaries and bureaucrats interact in the register of compliance, which is based on regular controls conducted by the bureaucrats in order to check work progress and authorise payments. Once the implementation is finalised, the project enters the ex-post monitoring phase in which bureaucrats can still conduct verifications, but the control is less intense than in the previous stages. Regardless of the phase of the project, people who access EU funding are always in

R. Bratu, *Corruption, Informality and Entrepreneurship in Romania*, Political Corruption and Governance,
https://doi.org/10.1007/978-3-319-66667-9

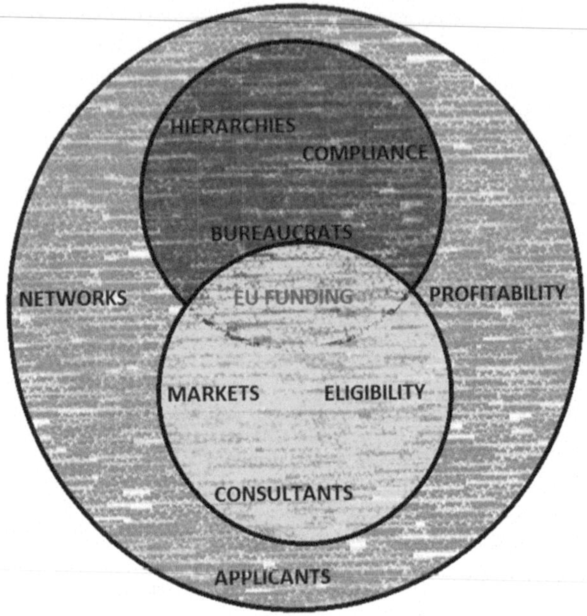

Fig. A1 The process of accessing EU funding in Romania: a stylised representation

the register of profitability, as for them EU funding is first and foremost a business.

European anxieties about the possibility of defrauding EU citizens' money have shaped the EU funding institutional establishment through systematic associations between corruption and EU funding fraud. This institutional transposition is discussed throughout the substantive chapters of this book. I have argued that the creation of anti-corruption and anti-fraud establishments was based on transfer of 'good practices' that involved a 'one size fits all' approach, which put in place impersonal institutions that failed to take into account the elements of time, space, biography and context. In order to underlie the symbolic commitment to tackle corruption and protect the financial interests of the EU, the newly designed organisations of policing and prosecution have become 'elite squads'. Their superior status is sustained by high level of financial and symbolic capital: higher wages (between 40% and 75%) than other prosecutors/

police officers, a particular profile of employees (very young, highly educated, preferably abroad, knowledge of foreign languages), access to international trainings and unmediated contact with EU officials.

In order to counteract possible misuse of EU funds, the process was over-regulated as detailed in Chaps. 4, 5 and 6. At the micro level, these massive transformations impacted visibly on the process of accessing EU funding especially in shaping the registers of compliance and eligibility. The register of compliance is based on an overwhelming number of verifications, controls, inspections and monitoring. Chapter 6 shows that this type of surveillance has unanticipated consequences for the practices and discourses related to accessing EU funding. First, the systematic associations between corruption and EU funding have transformed this economic process into a semantic of governance. The discursive power of EU funding refers to practices that frame political action through development *and* anti-corruption, with the effect of enhancing the user's symbolic capital. Second, the overinflated regulatory framework on the one hand deters people from defrauding the EU budget as reflected in the statistical trends in conviction rates. On the other hand, it also discourages people from accessing EU funds altogether, thus reducing Romania's absorption rates. Highly successful local entrepreneurs simply refuse to apply for EU funding arguing that the EU regulatory system is not adapted to the fluidity of the Romanian economic context. Third, the EU funding institutional framework creates its own informality through the proliferation of rules and controls that often expand or create the very conditions for carrying out simultaneously licit and illicit activities.

The register of eligibility is in fact a collection of rules that aim to prevent corruption and fraud to EU budget. Chapters 4 and 5 have argued that this is a performative process in which the quality of the fit with the EU criteria is constructed with the help of consultants who decode and translate EU funding regulations. Potential applicants are taken aback by highly elaborate technical idioms employed by the rules that grant access to EU funding, and so they turn to consultants to understand how to become *beneficiaries*. Consultants exploit the technical, symbolic and economic space of EU funding as a terrain on which to construct market relations. In doing so, they essentially commodify EU funding by treating eligibility criteria as production factors. Consultants become market-makers by appropriating and 'marketising' a communication gap between bureaucrats and applicants.

The regulatory framework of this economic process is based on a neoliberal conception of disembedded money, markets and management. In the process of accessing EU funding, applicants and consultants 'correct' this view by making use of social relations that emphasise the importance of social protection and obligation. The success of a project depends not only on the ability to write a good funding application but also on the ability to conduct negotiations and establish partnerships. Such skills, acquired through business interactions, become risk reduction strategies that counteract the highly uncertain, volatile markets through social embeddedness. 'Papers are made to be credible' one consultant remarked (M), and criminal law is used as business law in an attempt to obtain and preserve EU funding. Actors live in multiple spaces (legal, economic, social) and act at the intersection of several markets, guiding their actions according to the principle of profitability. In their daily work routines involved in the process of EU funding, they employ a wide range of practices that make the theoretical distinction between legal and illegal superfluous. The interactions between applicants and bureaucrats are shaped by culturally embedded profit-making routines. Gift giving, favour exchange, bribing and nepotism are part and parcel of an 'archaeology' of entrepreneurial work practices that might break criminal laws, but are based on generally accepted social values.

The findings described above actually point to the fact that political and social orders are disjointed. This aspect becomes visible in discussing the third and last major aim of this thesis, which focused on the efficacy and efficiency of EU funding in Romania. The literature regarding EU funding generally asserts the positive impact of this European tool on local economies. However, this research uncovered a few paradoxes relating to EU funding in Romania, which represent some challenges to the above-mentioned view.

Firstly, the Romanian bureaucratic apparatus is fully functional and highly praised by the EU officials. A high number of irregularities have been regularly reported to OLAF; the number of cases investigated for crimes in relationship to EU funding has increased and so has the number of convictions. However, Romania's absorption rate for the new financial exercise is very low at this point (May 2017), barely matching the national contribution to the EU budget. Under the circumstances, the low absorption rate coupled with large investments in the crime control apparatus makes EU funding efficiency questionable. One might argue that the efforts will pay off in the long run, but such an assertion would also need to be proven.

Secondly, EU funding reinforces the heavy players and excludes the medium and small entrepreneurs, thus *increasing* (instead of decreasing) the economic differences. The strict regulations, the documentation price and the requirement to co-fund restrict the access to funding (Chaps. 2 and 4). For example, in the agriculture sector less than 1% of the farms with over 100 hectares have received 50% of the EU subventions, while small farms (between 1 and 5 hectares) have received less than 25% (Luca 2009).

Thirdly, EU funding has undoubtedly created a number of jobs through the individual projects. But an unintended consequence of the regulatory framework is the creation of a market and a profession. Consultancy appeared and developed out of the necessity to translate the bureaucratic requirements for entrepreneurs (Chap. 5). The number of regulations and technical idioms used for communication deters people from accessing funds while making the epistemic status of EU funding the kingdom of consultants.

This book contributes to the academic debates on EU funding (Milio 2010; Torsello 2012), by offering grass-roots knowledge about the process of accessing EU funding in Romania based on ethnographic material analysed from a distinctively sociological perspective. It explains EU funding using a mid-level instrument of analysis that sees *markets, hierarchies* and *networks* as mapping devices that explain the coordination of contemporary social, economic and political life (Powell 1990; Thompson et al. 1991). Despite the fact that the economic sociology literature typically presents them as alternative ways to achieve coordination, I argue that in my assessment, EU funding is a hybrid space that allows for a plurality of coordinative mechanisms rather than their mutual exclusivity. The book associates the three modes of coordination with the three registers of behaviour and the three actors, as shown in Fig. A1. Each of them brings a distinctive contribution to the literature: the register of eligibility draws on sociology of markets scholarship that shows that consultants are market-makers who commodify EU funding; the register of compliance is decoded through the literature on hierarchies and the role of regulatory framework for economic life; the register of profitability draws on literature about embeddedness of economic life through social networks.

The book contributes to the economic sociology debates on markets and new industries (Stinchcombe 1965; Aldrich and Fiol 1994; Fligstein 2001) by showing that the EU funding regulatory framework promotes new entrepreneurial work routines based on flexible specialisation, technological competence and professionalisation through upskilling (Sabel and Zeitlin 1997). These variables effectively change the work process while creating a wide gap between vernacular practices and the EU funding expectations. Consultants act as merchants of EU funding, assuming a role that could not have been fulfilled by diffuse networks through a market-making process. The new market for EU funding consultancy is an example of market creation as a result of excessive bureaucratisation.

In discussing the role of hierarchies, the book argues that EU funding is not a 'normal' economic process because it is highly regulated by transnational and national edicts, laws and orders. The classical debates about the role of law in regulating economic life (Weber [1922] 1968) are taken forward through the scholarly debates regarding the new technologies of governing promoted in relationship to development (De Sardan 2005; Escobar 1995; Scott 1998), Europeanisation and international aid (Sachs 2005; Easterly 2006). Building on these arguments, the book shows that in governing EU funding flows for Romania, the theme of development through foreign funding has metamorphosed into the theme of crime through corruption narratives (Chaps. 3 and 6). Thus the dynamics of corruption rhetoric and anti-corruption practices are part of a wider political economic context; the relevance of which is critical for understanding of EU funding.

The book further contributes to the debates about transparency and anti-corruption (Anechiarico and Jacobs 1996) drawing on recent scholarship (Ledeneva 2013b) that criticises the conventional paradigm of corruption. I show that the inevitable association between corruption and EU funding led to a transfer of anxieties and practices of control from corruption to the protection of the financial interests of the EU. Investigation and prosecutions are conducted by newly set up elite squads monitored directly from Brussels. This raises an interesting point about the concept of 'transnational' that is presently applied to crime. Some argue that due to globalisation, crime has become transnational (Duyne 2011), while others (Hobbs 1998) consider that inevitably crime happens in a particular place, so it is local in its nature. In the case of EU funding in Romania, the focus turns from crime to control: the nature of the crime becomes unimportant, as the control is by default transnational. In this sense, this account should be read as a story of transnational enforcement and local subversions.

The research adds to the economic sociology debates about the embeddedness of economic process in the social (Polanyi 1954; Granovetter 1973; Hart 2000; Thrift 2001; Zelizer 2004). Markets and hierarchies are decoded and enacted through a dense web of political, religious and social interactions and affiliations. This gives rise to a relational economy which entails indefinite exchanges and transactions that encompass far more than bureaucratic norms and market prices. Networks are particularly adapted to counteracting contextual uncertainty by ensuring that communication about prices, norms or know-how is maintained through its informal mechanisms that spring from a particular cultural and social background at strategic moments.

The concept of entrepreneurship runs like a thread throughout the entire thesis and establishes the link between economic sociology and sociology deviance (Hobbs 1988, 2013; Rugierro 1996, 2012, 2013). In discussing entrepreneurship, Schumpeter (1939) argued that the key characteristic of entrepreneurs is their innovative capacity as this allows them to change the existing social order. In his strain theory, Merton (1938) showed that deviance is the result of a disjuncture between cultural goals and institutionalised means of achieving it. Innovation, in the economic initiative as well as in deviance, starts with accepting the cultural goals irrespective of the drastic or illegitimate means that it might require, as shown by research on the informal economy (Hart 1982, Sassen 1997), occupational deviance (Ditton 1977b, Henry 1978, Klockars 1975) and white-collar crime (Sutherland 1983, Cressey 1953, Levi 1981). Building on these links, the book contributes to the sociological debates by analysing the blurred boundaries between legal, informal and illegal economic activities in the area of EU funding. It argues that legality is a fluid concept and that in everyday activities people make use of alternative conceptions of legitimacy. In the process of accessing EU funding, the State is important only to some degree because entrepreneurs know that "economics is a dance of the il/legal: *a pas à deux*" (Nordstrom 2007: 206).

In the near future, the institutional establishment of EU funding is unlikely to shrink. Quite the contrary, control will probably increase and sanctions will become more severe. This prediction is based on the observation that the anti-fraud project tends to become more elaborate due to its association with corruption. For example, in September 2011 the European Commission set up a group of experts on corruption (2011/C 286/03) to advise the Commission on anti-corruption policies and to evaluate and advance the present anti-corruption instruments at the EU level. The first anti-corruption report released on the 3rd of February 2014[1] analyses corruption in the 27 EU member states and signals major threats to EU funding, by showing, for example, that "weaknesses in the prevention and repression of corruption in public procurement adversely affect the management of national and EU funds" (EC 2014: 21). This "can lead to interruption and/or suspension of payments until appropriate corrective measures have been taken by the Member State, including the strengthening of the management and control systems" (EC 2014: 26). Such an approach signals that EU supervision in the area of EU funding is likely to increase and policing/prosecuting EU funding might become even more powerful and more professionalised.

These changes will also impact on the Romanian framework of EU funding distribution and implicitly on the potential beneficiaries. The integrity standards for beneficiaries are likely to be stronger and more explicit, the rules of public procurement will probably become more detailed and auditing will proliferate. Anechiarico and Jacobs' observation about the future of anti-corruption in New York can be applied to EU funding in Romania: it is likely to have "a corruption control problem as well as a corruption problem" (1996: 193). The obvious solution to such a bleak future would be to assess the effectiveness of the present control tools before setting up new ones. This would generate some empirical analysis that might in turn lead to a more nuanced discourse about EU funding fraud and corruption. Furthermore, the control apparatus would benefit immensely from setting up a dialogue with Romanian business circles. Instead of preparing anti-fraud policies based on the input of experts that have never accessed EU funding nor conducted business in Romania, the government could cooperate more with former and present beneficiaries. Such partnership would be a win-win situation, empowering local business circles while designing more effective regulations.

This research offered a detailed account of the institutions and practices of accessing EU funding in Romania, and its findings are context-specific. In order to introduce a comparative dimension to this research, I relied on the few other ethnographic accounts (e.g., Torsello 2012) and quantitative studies from other European countries (Gounev and Ruggiero 2012; Nowak forthcoming). The latter have been used with great reluctance because EU funding works on different accession rules in various EU member states and it is highly dependent on the economic growth and social stability. Simplistic quantitative assessments which define a country as successful on the basis of size of funds accessed are examples of 'irresponsible knowledge'. Based on this point, it would also be challenging to generalise the results of this research to other contexts (e.g., post-socialist economies) because each country negotiates its own funding rules within the European framework of anxieties. For example, it is highly probable that countries that negotiate their EU accession at this point, such as Serbia, would face harsher criteria.

Bibliography

Aldrich, H.E., and M.C. Fiol. 1994. Fools Rush In? The Institutional Context of Industry Creation. *Academy of Management Review* 19: 645–670.

Anechiarico, F., and J.B. Jacobs. 1996. *The Pursuit of Absolute Integrity. How Corruption Control Makes Government Ineffective*. Chicago and London: The University of Chicago Press.

Cressey, D.R. 1953. *Other People's Money: A Study in the Social Psychology of Embezzlement*. Glencoe, IL: The Free Press.

Escobar. 1995. *Encountering Development: The Making and Unmaking of the Third World*. Princeton, NJ: Princeton University Press.

European Commission. 2008–2012. Report from the Commission to the European Parliament and the Council on Progress in Romania under the Co-operation and Verification Mechanism. European Commission, Brussels.

Fligstein. 2001. *The Architecture of Markets: An Economic Sociology of Twenty-first-Century Capitalist Societies*. Princeton, NJ: Princeton University Press.

Gounev, P., and V. Ruggiero, eds. 2012. *Corruption and Organized Crime in Europe. Illegal Partnerships*. London and New York: Routledge

Granovetter, M. 1973. The Strengths of Weak Ties. *American Journal of Sociology* 78 (6): 1360–1380.

Hart, K. 1982. *The Political Economy of West African Agriculture*. Cambridge: Cambridge University Press.

Hart, K. 2000. *Money in an Unequal World*. London: Texere Publishing Limited.
Henry, S. 1978. *The Hidden Economy: The Context and Control of Borderline Crime*. Oxford: Martin Robertson.
Hobbs, D. 1988. *Doing the Business: Entrepreneurship, the Working Class and Detectives in the East End of London*. Oxford: Clarendon Press.
Hobbs, D. 1998. Going Down the 'Glocal': The Local Context of Organised Crime. *The Howard Journal of Criminal Justice* 37 (4): 407–422.
Hobbs, D. 2013. *Lush Life. Constructing Organized Crime in the UK*. Oxford: Oxford University Press.
Merton, R. 1938. Social Structure and Anomie. *American Sociological Review* 3 (5): 672–682.
Milio, S. 2010. Twenty Years of European Funding: Italy Still Struggling with Implementation. In *Italy Today: The Sick Man of Europe*. Oxford: Routledge
Nordstrom, C. 2007. *Global Outlaws*. In *Crime, Money and Power in the Contemporary World*. Berkeley, Los Angeles and London: University of California Press.
Powell, W. 1990. Neither Market nor Hierarchy: Network Forms of Organisation. *Research in Organizational Behaviour* 12: 295–336.
Sabel, C.F., and J. Zeitlin, eds. 1997. *World of Possibilities. Flexibility and Mass Production in Western Industrialization*. Cambridge: Cambridge University Press.
Sachs, J. 2005. *The End of Poverty: Economic Possibilities for Our Time*. New York Penguin Press.
Sassen. 1997. Informalization in Advanced Market Economies. In *Issues in Development*. Discussion Paper 20. Columbia University, New York.
Schumpeter. 1939. *Business Cycles: A Theoretical, Historical and Statistical Analysis of the Capitalist Process*. New York: McGraw-Hill.
Scott. 1998. *Seeing Like a State. How Certain Schemes to Improve the Human Condition Have Failed*. New Haven and London: Yale University Press.
Stinchcombe, 1965. 1965. Social Structure and Organizations. In *Handbook of Organizations*, ed. James G. March, 142–193. Chicago, IL: Rand McNally.
Sutherland, Edwin H. 1983. *White-Collar Crime: The Uncut Version*. Yale: Yale University Press.
Thompson, G., J. Frances, R. Levacic, and Jeremy Mitchell, eds. 1991. *Markets, Hierarchies and Networks. The Coordination of Social Life*. London, Thousand Oaks, and New Delhi: Sage.
Thrift, N. 2001. 'It's the Romance, Not the Finance, That Makes the Business Worth Pursuing': Disclosing A New Market Culture. *Economy and Society* 30: 412–432.

Torsello, D. 2012. The New Environmentalism? Civil Society and Corruption in the Enlarged EU. *Urban Anthropology*, ed. G. Prato and I. Pardo. Surrey: Ashgate.

Weber. 1968. *Economy and Society*. Vol. 1. New York: Bedminster.

Zelizer, V. 1997. *The Social Meaning of Money. Pin Money, Paychecks, Poor Relief, and Other Currencies*. Princeton, NJ: Princeton University Press.

Bibliography

Adler, P. 1993. *Wheeling and Dealing: An Ethnography of an Upper Level Drug Dealing and Smuggling Community*. 2nd ed. New York: Columbia University Press.

Adler, P.A., and P. Adler. 1983. Shifts and Oscillations in Deviant Careers: The Case of Upper-Level Drug Dealers and Smugglers. *Social Problems* 31 (2): 195–207.

Agar, M. 1973. *Ripping and Running: A Formal Ethnography of Urban Heroin Addicts*. New York: Seminar Press.

Agnew, J. 1986. *Worlds Apart: The Market and the Theatre in the Anglo-American Thought 1550–1750*. New York: Cambridge University Press.

Aidis, R. 2006. Laws and Customs: Entrepreneurship, Institutions and Gender During Transition. In *SSEES Occasional Series*. London: University College London.

Aidis, R., and S. Sauka. 2005. *Entrepreneurship in a Changing Environment: Analyzing the Impact of Transition Stages on SME Development*. Turku: European Council for Small Businesses.

Aldrich, H.E. 2005. Entrepreneurship. In *Handbook of Economic Sociology*, ed. N. Smelser and R. Swedberg, 451–477. Princeton, NJ: Princeton University Press.

Alrdirch Howard, E. 1999. *Organizations Evolving*. London: Sage.

Aldrich, H.E., and M.C. Fiol. 1994. Fools Rush In? The Institutional Context of Industry Creation. *Academy of Management Review* 19: 645–670.

Alexander, C. 2004. Value, Rights, and Changing Bodies: Privatization and Property Rights in Kazakhstan. In *Property in Question. Value Transformation*

R. Bratu, *Corruption, Informality and Entrepreneurship in Romania*, Political Corruption and Governance,
https://doi.org/10.1007/978-3-319-66667-9

in the Global Economy, ed. Katherine Verdery and Caroline Humphrey, 251–273. Oxford: Berg.

Alford, F.C. 2001. *Whistle-Blowers: Broken Lives and Organizational Power*. New York: Cornell University Press.

Aligica, D.P., and V. Tarko. 2012. State Capitalism and the Rent-Seeking Conjecture. *Constitutional Political Economy* 23 (4): 357–379.

Alvazzi Del Frate, A., and Van, J. Kesteren. 2004. *Criminal Victimization in Urban Europe. Key Findings of the 2000 International Crime Survey*. Turin, Italy: UNICRI.

Alvesson, M., and P. Thompson. 2005. Post-bureaucracy? In *The Oxford Handbook of Work and Organization*, ed. R. Batt Ackroyd, P. Thompson, and P. Tolbert. Oxford: Oxford University Press.

Amundsen, I. 1999. *Political Corruption: An Introduction to the Issues*. Bergen: Chr. Michelsen Institute.

Anders, G., and M. Nuijten, eds. 2009. *Corruption and the Secret of Law: A Legal Anthropological Perspective*. London: Ashgate.

Anderson, N. 1975. *The Hobo: The Sociology of the Homeless Man*. Chicago, IL: University of Chicago Press.

Anechiarico, F., and J.B. Jacobs. 1996. *The Pursuit of Absolute Integrity. How Corruption Control Makes Government Ineffective*. Chicago and London: The University of Chicago Press.

Antoniu, G. 2009. Activitatea normativă penală a Uniunii Europene (I). *Revista de Drept Penal* 1.

APDRP. 2010/2011. *Raport Anual de Activitate*. Bucuresti: APDRP.

Arabsheibani, G. de Meza, D.J. Maloney, and B. Pearson. 2000. And a Vision Appeared Unto them of a Great Profit: Evidence of Self-Deception Among the Self-Employed. *Economics Letters* 67: 35–41.

Archard, P. 1979. *Vagrancy, Alcoholism and Social Control*. London: Macmillan.

Argetoianu, C. 1998. *Insemnari Zilnice*. Vol. 1. Bucuresti: Machiavelli.

Arthur, M.B., and D.M. Rousseau, eds. 1996. *The Boundaryless Career: A New Employment Principle for a New Organizational Era*. New York: Oxford University Press.

Aspers, P. 2006. Sociology of Markets. In *International Encyclopedia of Economic Sociology*, ed. Jens Beckert and Milan Zafirovski. London: Routledge.

Atkinson, P. 2007. *Handbook of Ethnography*. London: Sage.

Axelrod, R. 1984. *The Evolution of Cooperation*. New York: Basic Books.

Baciu, R. 2009. Premisele Combaterii Fraudei in Uniunea Europeana. In *Aspecte Teoretice Si Practice Ale Procesului De Armonizare A Dreptului Romanesc Cu Dreptul European*, ed. Cezar Tita. Craiova: Sitech.

Back, L. 2007. *The Art of Listening*. Oxford: Berg Publishers.

Badham, R. 2005. Technology and the Transformation of Work. In *Handbook of Work and Organization*, ed. S. Ackroyd, R. Batt, and P. Thompson, 115–137. Oxford: Oxford University Press.

Baird, D.G., and E.R. Morrison. 2005. *Serial Entrepreneurs and Small Business Bankruptcies.* New York: Columbia Law School. The Centre for Law and Economic Studies: Social Science Research. Network Paper Collection.

Baker, W. 1981. Markets as Networks: A Multimethod Study of Trading Networks in a Securities Market. PhD diss., Department of Sociology, Northwestern University.

Baker, W.E., R.R. Faulkner, and G.A. Fisher. 1998. Hazards of the Market: The Continuity and Dissolution of Interorganizational Market Relationships. *American Sociological Review* 63: 147–177.

Banciu, D., S. Radulescu, and D. Ioan. 2005. *Coruptia in Romania. Realitate Si Perceptie Sociala.* Bucuresti: Lumina Lex.

Banfield, E.C. 1979. Corruption as a Feature of Governmental Organization. In *Bureaucratic Corruption in Sub-Saharan Africa: Towards A Search for Causes and Consequences*, ed. M. Ekpo. Washington, DC: University Press of America.

Bardhan, P. 1997. Corruption and Development: A Review of Issues. *Journal of Economic Literature.* 35 (3): 1320–1346.

Barley, N. 1983. *The Innocent Anthropologist. Notes from a Mud Hut.* London: British Museum Publications.

Barry, A., and D. Slater. 2002. Introduction: The Technological Economy. *Economy and Society.* 31 (2): 175–193.

Barsergian, I. 2000. When Text Becomes Field. Fieldwork in 'Transitional' Societies. In *Fieldwork Dilemmas: Anthropologists in Postsocialist States*, ed. H. De Soto and N. Dudwick, 119–129. Madison, WI: University of Wisconsin Press.

Batory, A. 2012. Why Do Anti-corruption Laws Fail in Central Eastern Europe? A Target Compliance Perspective. *Regulation & Governance* 6: 66–82.

Bearman, Peter. 2005. *Doormen.* Chicago: University of Chicago Press.

Bauer, M., and G. Gaskell, eds. 2000. *Qualitative Researching with Text, Image and Sound: A Practical Handbook for Social Research.* London: Sage.

Bauman, Z. 1997. *Postmodernity and Its Discontents.* Cambridge: Polity Press.

Baumol, William J. 1993. Formal Entrepreneurship Theory in Economics: Existence and Bounds. *Journal of Business Venturing* 8 (3): 181–294.

Bayart, J.-F. 1993. *The State in Africa: The Politics of the Belly.* London: Longman.

Beauchamp, T. 1980. The Ambiguities of 'Deferred Consent'. *IRB: Ethics & Human Research* 6 (8).

———. 1982. *Philosophical Ethics.* London: McGraw-Hill.

Beck, U. 1992. *Risk Society: Towards a New Modernity.* New Delhi: Sage.

———. 2006. *Cosmopolitan Vision.* Cambridge: Polity.

Becker, H. 1951. The Professional Dance Musician and His Audience. *American Journal of Sociology* 57: 136–144.

———. 1953. Becoming a Marihuana User. *American Journal of Sociology* 59 (3): 235–242.

———. 1963. *Outsiders Studies in the Sociology of Deviance*. New York: Free Press.
———. 1964. *The Other Side*. New York: Macmillan.
———. 1967. Whose Side Are We On? *Social Problems* 14 (3): 239–247.
Becker, G.S. 1968. Crime and Punishment: An Economic Approach. *The Journal of Political Economy* 76 (2): 169–217.
Becker, G. 1993. *Human Capital*. Chicago, IL: University of Chicago Press.
Becker, M.C., T. Knudsen, and R. Swedberg, eds. 2011. *The Entrepreneur. Classic Texts by Joseph A. Schumpeter*. Stanford, CA: Stanford Business Books.
Beirne, P., and J.W. Messerschmidt. 2010. *Criminology: A Sociological Approach*. 5th ed. Oxford: Oxford University Press.
Benveniste, G. 1977. *Bureaucracy*. San Francisco: Boyd and Fraser Publishing.
Berger, P. 1963. *Invitation to Sociology*. New York: Double Day.
Berger, P., and T. Luckmann. 1966. *The Social Construction of Reality*. New York, USA: Doubleday, Allen Lane, The Penguin Press.
Bernardo, A., and I. Welch. 2001. On the Evolution of Overconfidence of Entrepreneurs. *Journal of Economics and Management Strategy* 10: 301–330.
Beynon, H. 1985. *Working for Ford*. 2nd ed. New York: Penguin.
Birch, David L. 1997. *Small Business Research Summary. In RS Number 183*. Washington, DC: United States Small Business Administration
Birch, M. and T. Miller. 2002. Encouraging Participation. Ethics and Responsibilities. In *Ethics in Qualitative Research*, ed. M. Mauthner, M. Birch, J. Jessop, T. Miller, 91–106.
Bjelopera, J.P., and K.M. Finklea. 2010. *Organized Crime: An Evolving Challenge of US Law Enforcement*. Washington, DC: Congressional Research Service.
Block, A. 1991. *The Business of Crime*. Boulder, CO: Westview Press.
———. 1998. *Masters of Paradise. Organized Crime and the Internal Revenue Service in the Bahamas*. London: Transaction Publishers.
Blundo, G., and O. De Sardan. 2006. *Everyday Corruption and the State. Citizens and Public Officials in Africa*. London and New York: Zed Books.
Boeker, W. 1988. Organizational Origins: Entrepreneurial and Environmental Imprinting at the Time of Founding. In *Ecological Models of Organization*, ed. Glenn R. Carroll, 33–51. Cambridge, MA: Ballinger.
Boissevain, J. 1974. *Friends of Friends: Networks, Manipulators and Coalitions*. New York: St. Martin's Press.
Bonger, W. 1969. *Criminality and Economic Conditions*. Bloomington: Indiana University Press.
Bourdieu, P. 1977. *Outline of A Theory of Practice*. Cambridge: Cambridge University Press.
———. 1984. *Distinction: A Social Critique of the Judgement of Taste*. Cambridge, MA: Harvard University Press, Routledge.
———. 1997. Le champ économique. *Actes de la recherche en sciences sociales* 119: 48–66.

———. 2005. *The Social Structures of the Economy*. Cambridge, UK: Polity Press.

Bourgois, P. 2003. *In Search of Respect: Selling Crack in El Barrio*. Cambridge: Cambridge University Press.

Bourgois, P., and L. Dunlap. 1992. Exorcising Sex-for-Crack Prostitution: An Ethnographic Perspective from Harlem. In *Crack Pipe as Pimp: An Eight City Ethnographic Study of the Sex for Crack Phenomenon*, ed. M. Ratnet, 97–132. Lexington, MA: Lexington Books.

Box, S. 1983. *Power, Crime, and Mystification*. London and New York: Routledge.

Braithwaite, J. 1984. *Corporate Crime in the Pharmaceutical Industry*. London: Routledge.

Bratu, R. 2013. The Former Soviet Union. In *Controlling Corruption in Europe. The Anticorruption Report*, ed. Alina Mungiu-Pippidi, 55–67. Berlin: Barbara Budrich Publisher.

Braudel, F. 1982. *The Wheels of Commerce*. New York: Harper and Row.

Braverman, H. 1974. *Labor and Monopoly Capital: The Degradation of Work in the Twentieth Century*. New York: Monthly Review Press.

Bray, J. 1999. Beyond Compliance: Corruption as a Business Risk. In *Fighting Corruption in Developing Countries and Emerging Countries: The Role of the Private Sector*. Washington, DC. http://www.fsa.ulaval.ca/personnel/vernag/eh/F/ethique/lectures/compli.htm

Bremmer, I. 2010. *The End of the Free Market: Who Wins the War Between States and Corporations*. New York: Portfolio.

Bryane, M. 2007. *Drafting Implementing Regulations for International Anti-corruption Conventions*. QEH Working Paper Series—QEHWPS150 (150).

Bryane, M., and D. Bowser. 2009. The Evolution of the Anti-corruption Industry in the Third Wave of Anti-corruption Work. http://works.bepress.com/bryane_michael/50

Bryman, A. 2004. *The Disneyization of Society*. London: Sage.

BSA. 2002. *Statement of Ethical Practice for the British Sociological Association*. Durham: BSA.

Bucur, F. G. 2010. Ocrotirea penala a intereselor financiare ale Uniunii Europene. *Revista de Drept Penal no.* 1.

Bulmer, M., ed. 1982. *Social Research Ethics*. London: Macmillan.

Burawoy, M. 1977. *Manufacturing Consent: Changes in the Labor Process under Monopoly Capitalism*. Chicago: University of Chicago Press.

———. 1985. *The Politics of Production: Factory Regimes Under Capitalism and Socialism*. London: Verso.

———. 1998. The Extended Case Method. *Sociological Theory* 16 (1): 4–33.

Burawoy, M., and K. Verdery, eds. 1999. *Uncertain Transition. Ethnographies of Change in the Postmodern World*. Oxford: Rowman and Littlefield.

Burns, T. 1963. Industry in a New Age. *New Society* 18: 17–20.

Burt, R. 1992. *Structural Holes: The Social Structure of Competition*. Cambridge: Harvard University Press.

Burton, M.D., J. Sorenson, and C. Beckman. 2002. Coming from Good Stock: Career Histories and New Venture Formation. In *Social Structure and Organizations Revisited*, ed. M. Lounsbury and M. Ventresca, 229–262. Amsterdam: JAI/Elsevier.

Busse, E. 2000. The Embeddedness of Tax Evasion in Russia. In *Economic Crime in Russia*, ed. V. Alena Ledeneva and Marina Kurkchiyan. The Hague, London and Boston: Kluwer Law International.

Caldwell, G. 2005. Corruption at the Core of Congress. *The Financial Times*, December 3.

Callon, M. 1998. Introduction: The Embeddedness of Economic Markets in Economics. In *Laws of the Market*, ed. Michel Callon. Oxford: OUP.

Callon, M., and B. Latour. 1981. Unscrewing the Big Leviathan: How Actors Macro-structure Reality and How Sociologists Help Them to Do So. In *Advances in Social Theory*, ed. K. Knorr-Cetina and A.V. Cicourel. London: Palgrave.

Calvey, D. 2008. The Art and Politics of Covert Research : Doing 'Situated Ethics' in the Field. *Sociology* 42 (5): 905–918.

Campbell, A. 1984. *The girls in the gang*. New York: Basil Blackwell.

Carlen, P. 1976. *Magistrates Justice*. Oxford: Martin Robertson.

———. 1983. *Women's Imprisonment*. London: Routledge and Kegan Paul.

———., ed. 1985. *Criminal Women*. Cambridge: Polity Press.

———. 1988. *Women, Crime and Poverty*. Milton Keynes: Open University Press.

Carroll, G.R., and M.T. Hannan. 2000. *The Demography of Corporations and Industries*. Princeton, NJ: Princeton University Press.

Carruthers, B.G., and W. Nelson Espeland. 1991. Accounting for Rationality: Double-Entry Bookkeeping and the Rhetoric of Economic Rationality. *American Journal of Sociology* 97 (1): 31–69.

Carter, N.M., W.M. Gartner, and P.D. Reynolds. 1996. Exploring Start-Up Sequences. *Journal of Business Venturing* 11: 151–166.

Cascio, W.F. 2000. Managing a Virtual Workplace. *Academy of Management Executive* 14: 81–90.

Castells, M. 1996. *The Rise of the Network Society: The Information Age: Economy, Society, and Culture*. Oxford: Blackwell.

Chambliss, W.J. 1972. *Box Man*. New York: Harper and Row.

Chapman, C.S., D.J. Cooper, and P. Miller, eds. 2009. *Accounting, Organisations and Institutions: Essay in the Honour of Anthony Hopwood*. Oxford: Oxford Scholarship Online.

Chelcea, L., and O. Mateescu, eds. 2004. *Economia Informala in Romania. Piete, Practici Sociale si Transformari ale Statului dupa 1989*. Paideia: Bucuresti.

Clinard, Marshall B., and Peter C. Yeager. 1980. *Corporate Crime*. New York: Free Press.

Coase, R. 1937. The Nature of the Firm. *Economica* 4: 386–405.

Cohen, A.K. 1955. *Delinquent Boys. The Culture of the Gang*. New York: Free Press.

Cohen, S. 1969. *Hooligans, Vandals and the Community: A Study of Social Recreation to Juvenile Delinquency*. London: University of London.

———. 1971. Introduction. In *Images of Deviance*, ed. S. Cohen. Harmondsworth: Penguin.

———. 1972. *Folk Devils and Moral Panics : The Creation of the Mods and Rockers*. London: MacGibbon and Kee.

———. 1974. Criminology and the Sociology of Deviance in Britain. In *Deviance and Social Control*, ed. P. Elliott Rock and M. McIntosh, 1–40. London: Tavistock.

Coleman, J.S. 1994. A Rational Choice Perspective on Economic Sociology. In *The Handbook of Economic Sociology*, ed. R. Swedberg and N.J. Smelser, 166–183. New York: Russell Saga Foundation.

Colosi, R. 2010. *Dirty Dancing? An Ethnography of Lap Dancing*. Cullhompton: Willan.

Comaroff, J., and J. Comaroff. 2003. Ethnography on an Awkward Scale. Postcolonial Anthropology and the Violence of Abstraction. *Ethnography* 4: 147–179.

Coolidge, J., and S. Rose-Ackerman. 2000. Kleptocracy and Reform In African Regimes: Theory and Examples. In *Corruption and Development in Africa. Lessons from Country Case Studies*, ed. Chikulo Hope. New York: St. Martin's Press.

Cooper, A.C. 1986. Entrepreneurship and High Technology. In *The Art and Science of Entrepreneurship*, ed. D. Sexton and R.W. Smilor, 153–168. Cambridge, Mass: Ballinger.

Corrigan, P. 1979. *Schooling the Smash Street Kids*. London: Macmillan.

Corrigan, O. 2003. Empty Ethics: The Problem with Informed Consent. *Sociology of Health and Illness* 25 (3): 769–792.

Coser, L., and B. Rosenberg, eds. 1989. *Sociological Theory: A Book of Readings*. 5th ed. Long Grove, IL: Waveland Press Inc.

Courpasson, D., and S. Clegg. 2006. Dissolving the Iron Cages? Tocqueville, Michels, Bureaucracy and the Perpetuation of Elite Power. *Organization* 13 (3): 319–343.

Creed, G. 1998. *Domesticating revolution. From Soviet reform to ambivalent transition in a Bulgarian village*. University Park, PA: Penn State University Press.

Cressey, P. G. 1932. *The Taxi-Dance Hall: A Sociological Study in Commercialized Recreation and City Life*. Chicago, IL: Chicago University Press.

Cressey, D.R. 1953. *Other People's Money: A Study in the Social Psychology of Embezzlement*. Glencoe, IL: The Free Press.

Cromwell, P., J. Olson, and D. Avery. 1991. *Breaking and Entering: An Ethnographic Analysis of Burglary*. Newbury Park, CA: Sage.

Crozier, Michel. 1964. *The Bureaucratic Phenomenon*. Chicago, IL: University of Chicago Press.

CSM. 2011. Raport Privind Activitatea Consiliului Superior al Magistraturii in Perioada 1995–2010. Bucuresti.

Czarniawska-Joerges, B. 1989. *Economic Decline and Organizational Control*. New York: Praeger.

Dalton, M. 1959. *Men Who Manage*. New York: John Wiley and Sons.

De Meza, D., and C. Southey. 1996. The Borrower's Curse: Optimism, Finance, and Entrepreneurship. *Economic Journal* 106: 375–386.

De Sardan, J.P. Olivier. 1999. A Moral Economy of Corruption in Africa? *The Journal of Modern African Studies* 37 (1): 25–52.

———. 2005. *Anthropology and Development. Understanding Contemporary Social Change*. London and New York: Zed Books.

De Soto, H. 1989. *The Other Path*. New York: Harper and Row.

Della Porta, D., and A. Vannucci. 1999. *Corrupt Exchanges: Actors, Resources and Mechanisms of Political Corruption*. New York: Aldine de Gruyter.

Denzin, N.K. 1989. *Interpretative Biography*. Newbury Park, CA: Sage.

DiMaggio, P. 1988. Interest and Agency in Institutional Theory. In *Institutional patterns and culture*, ed. L. Zucker, 3–22. Cambridge, MA: Ballinger Publishing Company.

DiMaggio, Paul. 1994. Culture and Economy. In *The handbook of economic sociology*, ed. J. Swedberg Richard Smelser Neil, 27–58. New York: Russell Sage Foundation.

Dimulescu, V., R. Pop, and M. Doroftei. 2013. Bottom of the Heap. The Case of Romania. In *Controlling Corruption in Europe. The Anticorruption Report*, ed. Alina Mungiu-Pippidi, 83–98. Berlin: Barbara Budrich Publishing.

Ditton, J. 1977a. Alibis and Aliases: Some Notes on the 'Motives' of Fiddling Bread Salesmen. *Sociology* 11 (2): 233–255.

———. 1977b. *Part-time Crime: An Ethnography of Fiddling and Pilferage*. London: Macmillan Press.

———. 1977c. *Part-Time Crime: An Ethnography of Fiddling and Pilferage*. London: Macmillan Press.

Djankov, S., Miguel, E., Qian, Y., Roland, G. and Zhuravskaya, E. V. 2004. *Entrepreneurship: First Results from Russia*. Working paper.

DLAF. 2006–2012. Raport Anual de Activitate. Bucuresti: DLAF.

DNA. 2009. Raport Privind Activitatea Desfasurata. http://www.pna.ro/bilant_activitate.xhtml?id=17

———. 2012. Raport Privind Activitatea Desfasurata. http://www.pna.ro/bilant_activitate.xhtml?id=25

DNA. 2003–2011. Raport de activitate. Bucuresti: DNA.

Dodge, M., and G. Geis. 2006. Fieldwork with the Elite: Interviewing White-Collar Criminals. In *The Sage Handbook of Fieldwork*, ed. D. Hobbs and R. Wright, 79–92. London: Sage.

Doig, A. 2010. Asking the Right Questions? Addressing Corruption and EU accession: The Case Study of Turkey. *Journal of Financial Crime* 17 (1): 9–21.

Doig, A., and R. Theobald. 2000. *Corruption and Democratisation*. London: Frank Cass.

Dorn, N., and M. Levi. 2006. From Delphi to Brussels, the Policy Context: Crime Prophecy, Proofing, Assessment. *Eur J Crim Policy Res* 12: 213–220.

Doucet, A. and Mauthner, M. 2002. Knowing Responsibly. Linking Ethics, Research Practice and Epistemology. In *Ethics in Qualitative Research*, ed. M. Mauthner, M. Birch, J. Jessop and, T. Miller, 123–145.

Downes, D. 1966. *The Delinquent Solution: A Study in Subcultural Theory*. London: Routledge and Kegan Paul.

Downes, D. and Rock, P. 2007. *Understanding Deviance*. 5th ed. Oxford: Clarendon Press.

Downes, David, Paul Rock, Christine Chinkin, and Conor Gearty, eds. 2007. *Crime, social control and human rights. From moral panics to states of denial. Essay in the honour of Stanley Cohen*. London: Willan Publishing.

Drucker, P.F. 1992. The New Society of Organizations. *Harvard Business Review* 70: 95–104.

Du Gay, P. 1996. *Consumption and Identity at Work*. London: Sage.

———. 2000. *In Praise of Bureaucracy: Weber, Organization, Ethics*. London: Sage.

Dumas, Lloyd J. 2010. *Confronting Corruption, Building Accountability Lessons from the World of International Development Advising*. Ed. J.W. Wedel and G. Callman. New York: Palgrave.

Duncombe, J., and J. Jessop. 2002. Rapport and the Ethics of "Faking Friendship". In *Ethics in Qualitative Research*, ed. M. Mauthner, M. Birch, J. Jessop, and T. Miller, 107–122. London: Sage.

Dunlap, E., B. Johnson, and A. Manwar. 1994. A Successful Female Crack Dealer: Case Study of a Deviant Career. *Deviant Behaviour* 15: 1–25.

Durkheim, E. 1892. The Rules of the Sociological Method. New York: Free Press.

Duyne, P. C. 2011. *Transnational Organised Crime, Laundering and the Congregation of the Gullible*. Tilburg University.

Duyne, P.C., and M. Levi. 2005. *Drugs and Money. Managing the Drug Trade and Crime. Money in Europe*. London: Routledge.

Duyne, P.C., and B. Vander. 2009. The Incantations of the EU Organised Crime Policy Making. *Crime Law and Social Change* 51: 261–281.

Easterly, W. 2006. *The White Man's Burden: Why the West's Efforts to Aid the Rest Have Done So Much Ill and So Little Good*. New York: The Penguin Press.

EBRD. 1994–2004. Transition Report. London.

Eccles, Robert G. 1985. *The Transfer Pricing Problem: A Theory for Practice*. New York: Lexington Books.

European Commission. 2014. Report from the Commission to the Council and the European Parliament. EU Anti-corruption Report. https://ec.europa.eu/

home-affairs/sites/homeaffairs/files/elibrary/documents/policies/organized-crime-and-human-trafficking/corruption/docs/acr_2014_en.pdf

EC 2002–2006. *Regular Reports on Romania's Progress Towards Accession*. Brussels: European Commission.

Edelman, L.B. 1992. Legal Ambiguity and Symbolic Structures: Organizational Mediation of Civil Rights Law. *American Journal of Sociology* 97: 1531–1576.

Edwards, R and Mauthner, M. 2002. Ethics and Feminist Research: Theory and Practice. In *Ethics in Qualitative Research*, ed. M. Mauthner, M. Birch, J. Jessop, T. Miller, 14-31.

Egan, M.P., N. Nugent, and W.E. Paterson, eds. 2010. *Research Agendas in EU Studies: Stalking the Elephant*. Basingstoke, UK: Palgrave Macmillan.

Enemu, F.C. 2000. Problems and Prospects of Local Governance. In *African Perspectives On Corruption*, ed. G. Hyden, D. Olowu, and H. Ogendo, 29–62. Trenton/Asmara: Africa World Press.

Escobar, A. 1991. Anthropology and the Development Encounter: The Making and Marketing of Development Anthropology. *American Ethnologist* 18 (4): 658–682.

———. 1995. *Encountering Development: The Making and Unmaking of the Third World*. Princeton, NJ: Princeton University Press.

ESRC. 2005. *Research Ethics Framework*. Swindon: ESRC.

European Commission. 2008–2012. Report from the Commission to the European Parliament and the Council on Progress in Romania under the Co-operation and Verification Mechanism. European Commission, Brussels.

Eyal, G., I. Szelenyi, and E. Townlsey. 1998. *Making Capitalism Without Capitalists: Class Formation and Elite Struggles in Post-Communist Central Europe*. London and New York: Verso.

Farrell, C.M., and J. Morris. 2003. The Neo-Bureaucratic State: Professionals and Managers and Professional Managers in Schools, General Practices and Social Work. *Organisation* 10 (1): 129–157.

Fielding, N. 1982. *The National Front*. London: Routledge & Kegan Paul.

———. 2005. The Resurgence, Legitimation and Institutionalization of Qualitative Methods *Forum Qualitative Sozialforschung/Forum: Qualitative Social Research* 6 (2). doi: 10.17169/fqs-6.2.455.

Finley, M. 1973. *The Ancient Economy*. Berkeley: University of California Press.

Fisman, R., and E. Miguel. 2010. *Economic Gangsters: Corruption, Violence, and the Poverty of Nations*. Princeton, NJ: Princeton University Press.

Fligstein, N. 1996. Markets as Politics: A Political-Cultural Approach to Market Institutions. *American Sociological Review* 61: 656–673.

———. 2001. *The Architecture of Markets: An Economic Sociology of Twenty-First-Century Capitalist Societies*. Princeton, NJ: Princeton University Press.

Foucault, M. 1979. *Discipline and Punish : The Birth of the Prison*. Harmondsworth: Penguin.

Fox, Jonathan. 1994. The Difficult Transition from Clientelism to Citizenship: Lessons from Mexico. *World Politics* 46 (2): 151–184.

Frankfurt, H. 1968. On Bullshit. *Raritan Quarterly Review* 6 (2): 81–100.

Freedom House. 2005. *Politicile Anticoruptie ale Guvernului Romaniei*. Bucuresti: Raport de Evaluare.

Freeman, J.H. 1983. Entrepreneurs as Organizational Products: Semiconductor Firms and Venture Capital Firms. In *Advances in the Study of Entrepreneurship, Innovation, and Economic Growth*, ed. G. Libecap, 33–52. Greenwich, CT: JAI Press.

Freilich, M., ed. 1970. *Marginal Natives: Anthropologists at Work*. New York and London: Harper & Row.

Frieden, J. 2006. *Global Capitalism: Its Fall and Rise in the Twentieth Century*. New York: W.W. Norton.

Friedman, E., J. Simon, K. Daniel, and P. Zoido-Lobaton. 2000. Dodging the Grabbing Hand: The Determinants of Unofficial Activity in 69 Countries. *Journal of Public Economics* 76 (3): 459–493.

Friedrich, Carl J. 1972. Corruption Concepts in Historical Perspective. In *Political Corruption. A Handbook*, ed. A. Heidenheimer, J. Johnston, M. LeVine, and V. Tanzi, 15–24. London: Transaction Publishers.

Galtung, F. 1998. Criteria for Sustainable Corruption Control. *The European Journal of Development Research* 10 (1): 105–128.

Gambetta, D. 2002. Corruption: An Analytical Map. In *Political Corruption in Transition: A Skeptic's Handbook*, ed. S.A. Sajo Kotkin. Budapest: CEU.

Garfinkel, H. 1967. *Studies in Ethnomethodology*. Englewood Cliffs, NJ: Prentice Hall.

Garland, D. 2002. *The Culture of Control: Crime and Social Order in Contemporary Society*. Oxford: OUP.

Gartner, W.B., B. Bird, and J. Starr. 1992. Act as If: Differentiating Entrepreneurial from Organizational Behavior. *Entrepreneurship: Theory and Practice* 16: 13–32.

Garud, R., S. Jain, and A. Kumaraswamy. 2002. Institutional Entrepreneurship in the Sponsorship of Common Technological Standards: The Case of Sun Microsystems and Java. *Academy of Management Journal* 45: 196–214.

Geertz, Clifford. 1973. *The Interpretation of Cultures: Selected Essays*. New York: Basic Books.

Gelsthorpe, L. 1990. Feminist Methodologies in Criminology: A New Approach or Old Wine in New Bottles? In *Feminist Perspectives in Criminology*, ed. L. Gelsthorpe and A. Morris. Milton Keynes: Open University Press.

———. 1997. Feminism and Criminology. In *The Oxford Handbook of Criminology*, ed. R. Morgan, R. Reiner, and M. Maguire, 511–534. Oxford: Oxford University Press.

Gelsthorpe, L., and A. Morris. 1988, Spring. Feminism and Criminology in Britain. *British Journal of Criminology* 28 (2): 93–110.

———. 1990. *Feminist Perspectives in Criminology*. Milton Keynes: Open University Press.

Gennep, Van. 1960. *The Rites of Passage*. Milton Park: Psychology Press.

Glaeser, E.L., and R.E. Saks. 2006. Corruption in America. *Journal of Public Economics* 90 (6-7): 1053–1072.

Glaser, B.G., and A.L. Strauss. 1967. *The Discovery of Grounded Theory: Strategies for Qualitative Research*. Chicago, |IL: Aldine Publishing Company.

Godard, J. 2004. A Critical Assessment of the High-Performance Paradigm. *British Journal of Industrial Relations* 42 (2): 349–378.

Goffman, E. 1968. *Asylums*. Harmondsworth: Penguin.

Goffman, Ervin. 1969. *The Presentation of Self in Everyday Life*. London: Allen Lane.

———. 1970. *Interaction Ritual*. Chicago, IL: Aldine.

Gold, R. 1958. Roles in Sociological Field Observation. *Social Forces* 36: 217–233.

Goldsmith, A. 1999. Slapping the Grasping Hand: Correlates of Political Corruption in Emerging Markets. *American Journal of Economics and Sociology* 58 (4): 865–883.

Gomez y Paloma, Sergio, and Segrè Andrea. 1993. Agriculture in the Transition from a Command to a Market Economy: The Case of Latvia. *Agriculture and Human Values* 10 (1): 60–69.

Goode, E. 2010. *Deviant Behaviour*. 9th ed. London: Pearson.

Gottschalk, P. 2010. Categories of Financial Crime. *Journal of Financial Crime* 17 (4): 441–458.

Gouldner, A. 1964. *Patterns of Industrial Bureaucracy*. New York: Free Press.

———. 1975. *For Sociology: Renewal and Critique in Sociology Today*. Harmondsworth: Pelican.

Gounev, P., and V. Ruggiero, eds. 2012. *Corruption and Organized Crime in Europe. Illegal Partnerships*. London and New York: Routledge.

Granovetter, M. 1973. The Strengths of Weak Ties. *American Journal of Sociology* 78 (6): 1360–1380.

———. 1974. *Getting a Job: A Study of Contacts and Careers*. Cambridge: Harvard University Press.

Greer, C., and Y. Jewkes. 2008. Emerging Imaginaries of Regulation, Control & Repression. *Social Justice* 32 (1): 20–31.

Grzymala-Busse, A., and I. Abby. 2003. Great Expectations: The EU and Domestic Political Competition in East Central Europe. *East European Politics and Societies* 17 (1): 64–73.

Gupta, A. 1995. Blurred Boundaries: The Discourse of Corruption, the Culture of Politics, and the Imagined State. *American Ethnologist* 22 (2): 375–402.

Hagedorn, J. 1988. *People and Folks: Gangs, Crime and the Underclass in a Rustbelt City*. Chicago, IL: Lake View.

Hall, S., C. Critcher, T. Jefferson, J. Clarke, and B. Roberts. 2013. *Policing the Crisis. Mugging, the State and Law & Order*. 2nd ed. London: Palgrave Macmillan.

Hall, S., and T. Jefferson, eds. 1976. *Resistance Through Rituals*. London: Hutchinson.

Hall, P.A., and D. Soskice. 2001. *Varieties of Capitalism. The Institutional Foundations of Comparative Advantage*. Oxford: OUP.

Haller, D., and C. Shore, eds. 2005. *Corruption. Anthropological Perspectives*. London: Pluto Press.

Hammersley, M., and P. Atkinson. 1995. *Ethnography: Principles in Practice*. London, New York: Routledge.

Hann, C. 1994. After Communism: Reflections on East European Anthropology and the 'Transition'. *Social Anthropology* 2 (3): 229–249.

Haraway, D.J. 1991. A Cyborg Manifesto. Science, Technology, and Socialist Feminism in the Late Twentieth Century. In *Simians, Cyborgs and Women: The Reinvention of Nature*, 149–181. New York: Routledge.

Haraway, D. J. 1997. The Virtual Speculum in the New World Order. *Feminist Review* 55 (Consuming Cultures): 22–72.

Harrison, E. 2010. Unpacking the Anticorruption Agenda: Dilemmas for Anthropologists. *Oxford Development Studies* 34 (1): 15–29.

Hart, K. 1982. *The Political Economy of West African Agriculture*. Cambridge: Cambridge University Press.

Hart, A. 1998. *Buying and Selling Power*. Colorado: Westview Press.

Hart, K. 2000. *Money in an Unequal World*. London: Texere Publishing Limited.

Heidenheimer, A.J. 1970. Perspectives on the Perception of Corruption. In *Political Corruption. A Handbook*, ed. A. Heidenheimer, J.M. Johnston, M. LeVine, and V. Tanzi, 149–163. London: Transaction Publishers.

Heidenheimer, A., J.M. Johnston, M. LeVine, and V. Tanzi. 1989. The Evolution of Public Office Roles. In *Political Corruption. A Handbook*, ed. A. Heidenheimer, J.M. Johnston, M. LeVine, and V. Tanzi, 67–72. London: Transaction Publishers.

Heidensohn, F. 1996. *Women and Crime*. Basingstoke: Macmillan Press. Reprint, 2nd revised.

Hellman, J., Geraint, J., Kaufman, D. 2000. Size the State, Seize the Day. State Capture, Corruption and Influence In Transition. Policy Research Paper, No. 2444 no. World Bank Institute.

Hill, Stephen. 1988. *The Tragedy of Technology: Human Liberation Versus Domination in the Late Twentieth Century. Responsibility: Stephen Hill*. London: Pluto Press. Imprint.

Henig, D., and N. Makovicky. 2015. *Economies of Favour After Socialism*. Oxford: OUP.

Henry, S. 1978. *The Hidden Economy: The Context and Control of Borderline Crime*. Oxford: Martin Robertson.

———. 2009. *Social Deviance*. Cambridge: Polity.

Herrera, C. 1999. Two Arguments for 'Covert Methods' in Social Research. *British Journal of Sociology* 5 (2): 331–343.

Heyat, F. 2002. Women and the Culture of Entrepreneurship in Soviet and Post-Soviet Azerbaijan. In *Markets and Moralities*, ed. R. Mandel and C. Humphrey, 19–32. New York: Berg.

Heyl, B.S. 1979. *The Madam as Entrepreneur*. New Brunswick, NJ: Transaction.

———. 2007. Ethnographic Interviewing. In *Handbook of Ethnography*, ed. S. Delamont, A. Coffey, J. Lofland, P. Atkinson, and L. Lofland. London: Sage.

Hobbs, D. 1988. *Doing the Business : Entrepreneurship, the Working Class and Detectives in the East End of London*. Oxford: Clarendon Press.

———. 1995. *Bad Business: Professional Crime in Modern Britain*. Oxford: Oxford University.

———. 1998. Going Down the 'Glocal': The Local Context of Organised Crime. *The Howard Journal of Criminal Justice* 37 (4): 407–422.

———. 2013. *Lush Life. Constructing Organized Crime in the UK*. Oxford: Oxford University Press.

Hobbs, D., P. Hadfield, S. Lister, and S. Winlow. 2003. *Bouncers : Violence and Governance in the Night-Time Economy*. Oxford: Oxford University Press.

Hobbs, D., and T. May, eds. 1993. *Interpreting the Field. Accounts of Ethnography*. Oxford: Clarendon Press.

Hobbs, D., and R. Wright, eds. 2006. *The Sage Handbook of Fieldwork*. London: Sage.

Hobsbawm, E.J. 1985. *Bandits*. Harmondsworth: Penguin.

Homan, R. 1991. *The Ethics of Social Research*. London: Macmillan.

Hörschelmann, K. 2002. History After the End: Postsocialist Difference in a (Post) modern World. *Transactions of the Institute of British Geographers NS* 27: 52–66.

Howse, T. 2010. Concluding Reflections: Towards a New Strategy for Anti-Fraud Cooperation: Notes on the EU Panel of the British Society of Criminology Conference, 2009. *Journal of Financial Crime* 17 (1): 163–167.

Hudson, A. 1990. Elusive Subjects: Researching Young Women in Trouble. In *Feminist Perspectives in Criminology*, ed. L. Gelsthorpe and A. Morris. Milton Keynes: Open University Press.

Hughes, E.C. 1971. *The Sociological Eye. Selected Papers on Institutions and Race*. Vol. 1. Chicago: Aldine.

Humphrey, C., and R. Mandel. 2002. The Market in Everyday Life: Ethnographies of Postsocialism. In *Markets and Moralities*, ed. R. Mandel and C. Humphrey, 1–18. Oxford: Berg.

Humphreys, L. 1970. *Tearoom Trade: A Study of Homosexual Encounters In Public Places*. London: Duckworth.

Huntington, S.P. 1968. *Political Order in Changing Societies*. New Haven, CT: Yale University Press.

Hutter, B. 2011. Understanding the New Regulatory Governance: Business Perspectives. *Law & policy* 33 (4): 459–476.

Ianni, F. 1972. *A Family Business: Kinship and Social Control in Organized Crime*. New York: Russell Sage Foundation.

Ierunca, Virgil. 1990. *Fenomenul Pitesti.* Bucuresti: Humanitas.

Institutul Naţional De Statistică. 2013. Ocuparea Si Somajul in Anul 2012. Cercetarea statistică asupra forţei de muncă în gospodării (AMIGO). Comunicat de Presa no 92, April 17. http://www.insse.ro/cms/files/statistici/comunicate/com_anuale/ocup-somaj/somaj_2012r.pdf

Ionita, S., O. Nutu, L. Stefan, and A. Mungiu-Pippidi. 2011. Beyond Perception. Has Romania's Governance Improved after 2004? *Governance and Corruption: Romanian Journal of Political Science* 11 (1): 23–56.

Iorga, E., V. Alexandru, and L. Ercuş. 2011. *Fondurile Structurale—De La Oportunitate De Dezvoltare La Buget De Pradă. Şansele Redresării României Prin Fonduri Structurale.* Bucuresti: Institutul pentru Politici Publice.Partea I si Partea a II a.

Irwin, J. 1970. *The Felon.* Englewood Cliffs, NJ: Prentice Hall.

Irwin, J., and D.R. Cressey. 1962. Thieves, Convicts and the Inmate Culture. *Social Problems* 10 (2): 142–155.

Jacobs, B. 1999. Crack to Heroin: Drug Markets and Transition. *British Journal of Criminology* 39 (4): 555–574.

Jaques, E. 1990. In Praise of Hierarchy. *Harvard Business Review* (January–February): 127–133.

Jensen, M.C., and W.H. Meckling. 1976. Theory of the Firm: Managerial Behavior, Agency Costs, and Ownership Structure. *Journal of Financial Economics* 3: 305–340.

Jiglău, G., and S. Gherghina. 2011. The Ideological Institutionalization of the Romanian Party System. *Governance and Corruption: Romanian Journal of Political Science* 11 (1): 56–76.

Jipson, A.J., and C.E. Litton. 2000. Whiteness: Endangered Knowledge, Endangered Species? In *Danger in the Field: Risk and Ethics in Social Research*, ed. G. Lee-Treweek and S. Linkogle. London, New York: Routledge.

Johannisson, B. 1988. Business Formation: A Network Approach. *Scandinavian Journal of Management* 3: 83–99.

Johnston, M. 1996. The Search for Definitions: The Vitality of Politics and the Issue of Corruption. *International Social Science Journal* 48 (149): 639–658.

Josephson, M. 1962. *The Robber Barons.* New York: Harcourt, Brace and World.

Junker, B. 1960. *Field Work.* Chicago, IL: University of Chicago Press.

Kaminski, M. 2004. *Games Prisoners Play.* Princeton, NJ: Princeton University Press.

Kaneff, D. 2002. The Shame and Pride of Market Activity: Morality, Identity and Trading in Postsocialist Rural Bulgaria. In *Markets and Moralities*, ed. R. Mandel and C. Humphrey, 33–51. New York: Berg.

Karklins, R. 2005. *The System Made Me Do It. Corruption in Post-Communist Societies.* London and New York: M.E. Sharpe.

Kegley, C.W., and E. Wittkopf. 2006. *World Politics Trends and Transformation.* 10th ed. Belmont, CA: Thomson Wadsworth.

Keohane, R. 1986. Reciprocity in International relations. *International Organizations* 40 (1): 1–27.

Kerr, C., J.T. Dunlop, F.H. Harbison, and C. Myers. 1973. *Industrialism and Industrial Man*. Harmondsworth, Middlesex: Penguin.

Key, V. 1999. Techniques of Political Graft. In *Political Corruption. A Handbook*, ed. A. Arnold Heidenheimer, J. Johnston, M. LeVine, and V. Tanzi, 39–49. London: Transaction Publishers.

Khaldūn, Ibn. 1967. In *The Muqaddimah: An Introduction to History*, ed. Franz Rosenthal. Princeton, NJ: Dawood.

Kim, Phillip H., and E. Alrdirch Howard. 2005. Entrepreneurship and Social Capital. *Foundations and Trends in Entrepreneurship* 1 (2): 1–52.

Kinsey, R., J. Lea, and J. Young. 1986. *Losing the Fight Against Crime*. Oxford: Blackwell.

Klein, N. 2007. *The Shock Doctrine. The Rise of Disaster Capitalism*. London: Allen Lane.

Klitgaard, R. 1988. *Controlling Corruption*. Berkeley: University of California Press.

Klockars, C.B. 1975. *The Professional Fence*. London: Tavistock Publications.

Kornai, J. 1992. *The Socialist System: The Political Economy of Communism*. Oxford: Clarendon Press.

Kpundeh, S.J. 2004. *Building State Capacity in Africa*. Washington: World Bank Publications.

Krastev, I. 2004. *Shifting Obsession. Three Essays on The Politics of Anticorruption*. Budapest: CEU.

Krastev, Ivan. 2004. The Anti-American Century? *Journal of Democracy* 15 (2): 5–17.

Krizner, I.M. 1973. *Competition and Entrepreneurship*. Chicago and London: University of Chicago Press.

———. 1997. Entrepreneurial Discovery and the Competitive Market Process: An Austrian Approach. *Journal of Economic Literature* 35 (1): 60–85.

Kuehnast, K. 2000. Ethnographic Encounters in Post-Soviet Kyrgyzstan. Dilemmas of Gender, Poverty, and the Cold War. In *Fieldwork Dilemmas. Anthropologists in Postsocialist States*, ed. H.G. DeSoto and N. Dudwick, 100–118. Madison, WI: University of Wisconsin Press.

Kurer, O. 2005. Corruption: An Alternative Approach to Its Definition and Measurement. 53(1): 222–239.

Lambsdorff, J.G. 1999. *Corruption in International Research—A Review*. Berlin: TI.

Lampland, M. 2002. The Advantages of Being Collectivized. Cooperative Farm Managers in the Postsocialist Economy. In *Postsocialism. Ideals, Ideologies and Practices in Eurasia*, ed. C.M. Hann, 31–56. London: Routledge.

Langlois, R.N. 2003. Schumpeter and the Obsolescence of the Entrepreneur. *Advances in Austrian Economics* 6: 283–298.

Langseth, P., R. Stapenhurst, and J. Pope. 1999. National Integrity Systems. In *Curbing Corruption: Toward a Model for Building National Integrity*, ed. R. Stapenhurst and J. Kpundeh Sahr, 127–150. Washington: World Bank.

Lapavitsas, C. 2005. The Social Relations of Money as Universal Equivalent: A Response to Ingham. *Economy and Society* 34 (3): 389–403.

Lash, S., and J. Urry. 1987. *The End of Organised Capitalism*. Cambridge: Polity Press.

Latour, Bruno. 1987. Vizualisation and Cognition: Thinking with Eyes and Hands. *Knowledge and Society: Studies in the Sociology of Knowledge, Past and Present* 6: 1–40.

———. 2005. *Reassembling the Social: An Introduction to Actor-Network-Theory*. Oxford and New York: Oxford University Press.

Lea, J., and J. Young. 1984. *What Is to Be Done About Law and Order?* London: Pluto.

Ledeneva, A.V. 1998. *Russia's Economy of Favours. Blat, Networking and Informal Exchange*. Cambridge: Cambridge University Press.

———. 2006. *How Russia Really Works. The Informal Practices That Shaped Post-Soviet Politics and Business*. Ithaca and London: Cornell University Press.

Ledeneva, A. 2013a. A Critique of the Global Corruption "Paradigm". In *Postcommunism from Within. Social Justice, Mobilization and Hegemony*, ed. Jan Kubik and Amy Linch, 297–332. New York and London: New York University Press.

———. 2013b. *Can Russia Modernise? Sistema, Power Networks and Informal Governance*. Cambridge: Cambridge University Press.

———. 2013c. A Critique of the Global Corruption "Paradigm". In *Postcommunism from Within. Social Justice, Mobilization and Hegemony*, ed. Jan Kubik and Amy Linch, 297–332. New York and London: New York University Press.

Ledeneva, A.V., and M. Kurkchiyan, eds. 2000. *Economic Crime in Russia*. The Hague, London and Boston, MA: Kluwer Law International.

Lee-Treweek, G., and S. Linkogle, eds. 2000. *Danger in the Field: Risk and Ethics in Social Research*. London: Routledge.

Leff, N. 1964. Economic Development Through Bureaucratic Corruption. In *Political Corruption. A Handbook*, ed. A. Heidenheimer, J. Johnston, M. LeVine, and V. Tanzi, 389–403. Piscataway, NJ: Transaction Publishers. Original edition.

Lerner, Miri, Candida Brush, and Robert Hisrich. 1997. Israeli Women Entrepreneurs: An Examination of Factors Affecting Performance. *Journal of Business Venturing* 12 (4): 315–339.

Letherby, G. 2000. Dangerous Liaisons: Auto/Biography in Research and Research Writing. In *Danger in the Field: Risk and Ethics in Social Research*, ed. G. Lee-Treweek and S. Linkogle. London: Routledge.

Levi, M. 1981. *The Phantom Capitalists: The Organisation and Control of Long-Firm Fraud*. London: Heinemann.

———. 1988. *Regulating Fraud: White Collar Crime and the Criminal Process*. London: Tavistock.

———. 2010. Hitting the Suite Spot: Sentencing Frauds. *Journal of Financial Crime* 17 (1): 116–132.

Levi, M., N. Dorn, and S. White. 2008. Do European Procurement Rules Generate or Prevent Crime? *Journal of Financial Crime* 15 (3): 243–260.

Levi, M., and D. Nicholas. 2006. Regulation and Corporate Crime: Managers and Auditors. *Eur J Crim Policy Res* 12: 229–255.

Levitt, S.D., and S.J. Dubner. 2009. *Super Freakonomics*. London: Allen Lane.

Lewis, B. 2008. *Hammer and Tickle. A History of Communism Told Through Communist Jokes*. London: Weidenfeld & Nicolson.

Lewis, D., and D. Mosse, eds. 2006. *Development Brokers and Translators: The Ethnography of Aid and Agencies*. Sterling, VA: Kumarian Press.

Liazos, A. 1972. The Poverty of the Sociology of Deviance: Nuts, Sluts and Perverts. *Social Problems* 20: 103–120.

Licht, A. N. and Siegel, J. I. 2006. The Social Dimensions of Entrepreneurship. In *Oxford Handbook of Entrepreneurship*, ed. M. Yeung and Bernard Casson. Oxford: Oxford University Press.

Liebow, E. 1967. *Tally's Corner*. Boston, MA: Little Brown.

Lily, R., F. Cullen, and F. Ball. 2007. *Criminological Theory: Context and Consequences*. 4th ed. London: Sage.

Lomnitz, L. 1995. Ritual, Rumour and Corruption in the Constitution of Polity in Modern Mexico. *Journal of Latin American Anthropology* 1 (1): 20–47.

Lorenz, E.H. 1989. Neither Friends, nor Strangers: Informal Networks of Subcontracting in French Industry. In *Trust: Making and Breaking of Cooperative Relations*, ed. D. Gambetta, 194–210. Oxford: Basil Blackwell.

Lounsbury, M. 2001. Institutional Sources of Practice Variation: Staffing College and University Recycling Programs. *Administrative Science Quarterly* 46: 29–56.

Luca, Lucian. 2009. *O Țară Și Două Agriculturi:România Și Reforma Politicii Agricole Comune A UE*, ed. Cristian Ghinea. Bucharest: Centrul Roman de Politici Europene.

Luckmann, T. 1967. *The Invisible Religion: The Problem of Religion in Modern Society*. London: Macmillan.

Lugosi, P. 2006. Between Overt and Covert Research. *Qualitative Inquiry* 12 (3): 541–561.

Macdonald, S. 2007. British Social Anthropology. In *Handbook of Ethnography*, ed. S. Delamont, A. Coffey, J. Lofland, , P. Atkinson, L. Lofland. London: Sage.

Mackenzie, D., and J. Wajcman, eds. 1999. *The Social Shaping of Technology*. 2nd ed. Buckingham: Open University Press.

Maguire, M. ed. 1996. Street Crime. In *The International Library of Criminology, Criminal Justice and Penology*, ed. G. Mars and D. Nelken. Brookfield: Dartmouth Publishing Company.

Maguire, S., C. Hardy, and T.B. Lawrence. 2004. Institutional Entrepreneurship In Emerging Fields: HIV/AIDS Treatment Advocacy in Canada. *Academy of Management Journal* 47: 657–679.
Malinowski, B. 1922. *Argonauts of the Western Pacific*. London: Routledge.
Mandel, R., and C. Humphrey, eds. 2002. *Markets and Moralities. Ethnographies of Postsocialism*. Oxford: Berg.
Manning, P. 1987. Ironies of Compliance. In *Private Policing*, ed. P. Shearing and C. Stenning, 293–316. Beverly Hills, CA: Sage.
Mankiw, G. N. 1990. A Quick Refresher Course in Macroeconomics. *Journal of Economic Literature* 28 (December): 1645-1660.
Manor, J. 1999. *The Political Economy of Democratic Decentralization*. Washington DC: World Bank.
Marcus, George. 1998. *Ethnography Through Thick and Thin*. Princeton, NJ: Princeton University Press.
Mars, G. 1994. *Cheats at Work: An Anthropology of Workplace Crime*. Aldershot: Dartmouth Publishing.
Marshall, A. 1936. *Principles of Economics*. London: Macmillan.
Martinelli, A. 2006. Entrepreneurship. In *International Encyclopaedia of Economic Sociology*, ed. Jens Beckert, Milan Zafirovski. London: Routledge.
Matis, D., A. Nagy, P. Tunde-Petra, and A. Benyovszki. 2010. *Entrepreneurship in Romania. 2010 Country Report*. Cluj Napoca: Universitatea Babes-Bolyai.
Matza, D. 1969. *Becoming Deviant*. Englewood Cliffs, NJ: Prentice Hall.
Mauro, P. 1995. Corruption and Growth. *Quarterly Journal of Economics* 110 (3): 681–712.
———. 1997a. The Effects of Corruption on Growth, Investment and Public Expenditure: A Cross Country Analysis. In *Corruption and the Global Economy*, ed. K.A. Elliot, 83–107. Washington, DC: Institute for International Economics.
———. 1997b. *Why Worry About Corruption*. Washington, DC: IMF. Economic Issues 97/6.
Mauss, M. 1925. *The Gift*. London: Routledge.
Mauthner, M., M. Birch, J. Jessop, and T. Miller, eds. 2002. *Ethics in Qualitative Research*. London: Sage.
Mayhew, H. 2010. *London Labour and the London Poor*, Ed. R. Douglas-Fairhurst. Oxford: Oxford University Press.
McCorkel, J.A., and K. Myers. 2003. What Difference Does Difference Make? Position and Privilege in the Field. *Qualitative Sociology* 26: 199–231.
McLaughlin, E., J. Muncie, and G. Hughes, eds. 2003. *Criminological Perspectives. Essential Readings*. 2nd ed. London: Sage.
Mcleod, E. 1982. *Women Working*. London: Croom Helm.
McLoughlin, C. 1999. Culturally Responsive Technology Use: Developing an Online Community of Learners. *British Journal of Educational Technology* 30 (3): 231–245.

McRobbie, A. 1980. Settling Accounts with Subcultures: A Feminist Critique. *Screen Education* 39: 37–49.

Medard, J.-F. 1986. Public Corruption in Africa: A Comparative Perspective. *Corruption and Reform* 1 (2): 115–131.

———. 1997. La Corruption Internationale Et l'Afrique. *Revue Internationale De Politique Comparee* 4: 413–440.

Merton, R. 1938. Social Structure and Anomie. *American Sociological Review* 3 (5): 672–682.

———. 1957. *Social Theory and Social Structure*. New York: The Free Press.

Mieczkowski, T. 1990. Crack Distribution in Detroit. *Contemporary Drug Problems* 17 (1): 19–30.

Mihailescu, V. 2013. *Povestea Maidanezului Leutu. Cartier Antropologic*. Bucuresti: Cartier.

Milio, S. 2010. Twenty Years of European Funding: Italy Still Struggling with Implementation. In *Italy Today: The Sick Man of Europe*. Oxford: Routledge.

Miller, E. 1986. *Street Women*. Philadelphia, PA: Temple.

Miller, J. 1998. Up It Up: Gender and the Accomplishment of Street Robbery. *Criminology* 36 (1): 37–66.

Miller, D. 2002. Turning Callon the Right Way Up. *Economy and Society* 31 (2): 218–233.

Miller, T., and L. Bell. 2002. Consenting to What? Issues of Access, Gate-Keeping and 'Informed Consent'. In *Ethics in Qualitative Research*, ed. M. Mauthner, M. Birch, J. Jessop, and T. Miller, 53–69. London: Sage.

Miller, P., and N. Rose. 1990. Governing Economic Life. *Economy and Society* 19 (1): 1–31.

Millman, M. 1975. She Did It All for Love: A Feminist View of the Sociology of Deviance. In *Another Voice*, ed. M. Millman and, R. Moss Kanter. New York: Anchor Books.

Mills, Wright, C. 1959. *The Sociological Imagination*. Oxford: Oxford University Press.

Miroiu, Adrian, and Şerban Cerkez. 2013. *Competitia Politica in Romania*. Iaşi: Polirom.

Morgan, R., and R.V. Clarke. 2006. Legislation and Unintended Consequences for Crime. *European Journal on Criminal Policy and Research* 12: 189–211.

Morovan, I. 2010. *Suntem în grafic? 2010: primul bilanţ—Utilizarea fondurilor structurale*. Bucuresti: Centrul Roman de Politici Europene.

Mosse, D. 2005. *Cultivating Development : An Ethnography of Aid Policy and Practice*. London and Ann Arbor, MI: Pluto Press.

———., ed. 2011. *Adventures in Aidland. The Anthropology of Professionals in International Development*. New York and Oxford: Berghahn Books.

Motzafi-Haller, P. 1997. Native Anthropologists and the Politics of Representation. In *Auto/ethnography: Rewriting the Self and the Social*, ed. D. Reed-Danahay, 169–195. Oxford: Berg Publishers.

Mouzelis, N.P. 1967. *Organisation and Bureaucracy: An Analysis of Modern Theories*. Chicago, IL: Aldine Publishing.
Mullen, P. 1990. Which Internal Market? The NHS White Paper and International Markets. *Financial Accountability and Management* 6 (1): 33–50.
Muncie, J., and E. McLaughlin, eds. 2001. *The Problem of Crime*. 2nd ed. London: Sage.
———. eds. 2005. *The Sage Dictionary of Criminology*. 2nd ed. London: Sage.
Mungiu-Pippidi, A. 2004. *Nations in Transit*. Washington, DC: Freedom House.
———. 2006. Corruption: Diagnosis and Treatment. *Journal of Democracy* 17 (3): 86–99.
———. 2009. Romania: Outsmarting The EU's Smart Power. In *Democracy's Plight in the European Neighbourhood*. Brussels: Centre for European Policy Studies (CEPS).
Mungiu-Pippidi, A., and G. Althabe. 2002. *Secera și Buldozerul: Scornicești și Nucșoara. Mecanisme de Aservire a Țăranului Român*. Iasi: Polirom.
Mungiu-Pippidi, Alina, ed. 2013. *Controlling Corruption in Europe. The Anticorruption Report*. Berlin: Barbara Budrich Publisher.
Murphy, E., and Dingwall, R. 2007. The Ethics of Ethnography. In *Handbook of Ethnography*, ed. S. Delamont, A. Coffey, J. Lofland, P. Atkinson, and L. Lofland. London: Sage.
Myrdal, G. 1968. *Asian Drama: An Enquiry into the Poverty of Nations*. Vol. 2. New York: The Twentieth Century Fund.
Neagu, N. 2010. Accession Blues: Modest Successes and Major Difficulties in Romania. *Journal of Financial Crime* 17 (1): 47–60.
Nee, Vi. 1989. A Theory of Market Transition: From Redistribution to Markets in State Socialism. *American Sociological Review* 54 (5): 663–681.
Newburn, T. 1999. *Understanding and Preventing Police Corruption: Lessons from the Literature*, Ed. B. Webb. London: Home Office, Policing and Reducing Crime Unit, Research, Development and Statistics Directorate.
NHMRC, Australian National Health and Medical Research Council. 1999. *National Statement on Ethical Conduct in Research Involving Humans*. Canberra: Commonwealth of Australia.
Nordstrom, C. 2007. *Global Outlaws*. In *Crime, Money and Power in the Contemporary World*. Berkeley, Los Angeles and London: University of California Press.
North, D. 1981. *Structure and Change in Economic History*. New York: W. W. Norton.
Nye, J.S. 1967. Corruption and Political Development: A Cost-Benefit Analysis. *The American Political Science Review* 61 (2): 417–427.
Oberschall, Anthony. 1996. Opportunities and Framing in the Eastern European Revolts of 1989. In *Comparative Perspectives on Social Movements: Political Opportunities, Mobilizing Structure and Cultural Framings*, ed. D. McAdam, J. McCarthy, and M. Zald, 93–121. Cambridge: Cambridge University Press.

O'Malley, P. 2010. Simulated Justice. Risk, Money and Telemetric Policing. *British Journal of Criminology* 50: 795–807.
Paldam, M. 1999. *The Big Pattern of Corruption: Economics, Culture and the Seesaw Dynamics*. Aarhus: Department of Economics, University of Aarhus.
Pardo, I., and G. Prato, eds. 2004. *Between Morality and the Law. Corruption, Anthropology and Comparative Society*. London: Ashgate.
Parker, H. 1974. *View from the Boys: A Sociology of Down Town Adolescents*. Newton Abbott: David and Charles.
Parry, J. 2000. The Crisis of Corruption and the Idea of India—A Worm's Eye View. In *Morals of Legitimacy: Between Agency and System*, ed. I. Pardo, 27–56. Oxford: Berghahn Books.
Parsons, T. 1982. *On Institutions and Social Evolution*. Chicago, IL: University of Chicago Press.
Patrick, J. 1973. *A Glasgow Gang Observed*. London: Eyre Methuen.
Pearce, F., and S. Tombs. 1998. *Toxic Capitalism: Corporate Crime and the Chemical Industry*. Aldershot: Dartmouth.
Pearson, G. 1993. Foreword. Talking a Good Fight: Authenticity and Distance in the Ethnographer's Craft. In *Interpreting the Field. Accounts of Ethnography*, ed. D. Hobbs and T. May, vii–vxx. Oxford: Clarendon Press.
———. 2009. The Researcher as Hooligan. *International Journal of Social Research Methodology* 12 (3): 244–255.
Pearson, G., and D. Hobbs. 2003. King Pin? A Case Study of a Middle Market Drug Broker. *The Howard Journal* 42 (4): 335–347.
Perrotta, L. 2002. Coping with the Market in Rural Ukraine. In *Markets and Moralities*, ed. R. Mandel and C. Humphrey. New York: Berg.
Persson, A., B. Rothstein, and J. Teorell. 2010. The Failure of Anti-corruption Policies: A Theoretical Mischaracterization of the Problem. *QoG Working Paper Series* 9: 1–19.
Pine, F. 2002a. Dealing with Money: Zlotys, Dollars and Other Currencies in the Polish Highlands. In *Markets and Moralities*, ed. R. Mandel and C. Humphrey, 75–97. Oxford: Berg.
———. 2002b. Retreat to the Household? Gendered Domains in Postsocialist Poland. In *Postsocialism. Ideals, Ideologies and Practices in Eurasia*, ed. C. Hann, 95–113. London: Routledge.
Pine, F., and S. Bridger. 1998. Introduction: Transitions to Postsocialism and Cultures of Survival. In *Surviving Post-Socialism. Local Strategies and Regional Responses in Eastern Europe and the Former Soviet Union*, ed. S. Pine and F. Bridger, 1–15. London: Routledge.
Piore, M.J. 2011. Beyond Markets: Sociology, Street-Level Bureaucracy, and the Management of the Public Sector. *Regulation & Governance* 5: 145–164.
Piore, M.J., and C.F. Sabel. 1984. *The Second Industrial Divide*. New York: Basic Books.

Pissarides, F. 2004. Financial Structures and Private Sector Development in the New Europe. In *Financial Intermediation in the New Europe: Banks, Markets and Regulation in the Accession Countries*, ed. D. Masciandoro. Northampton, MA: Edward Elgar.

Polanyi, M. 1954. *The Great Transformation*. Boston, MA: Beacon Press.

Polsky, N. 1971. *Hustlers, Beats and Others*. Harmondsworth: Pelican.

Popescu-Birlan, L. 1994. Privatisation and Corruption in Romania. *Crime, Law and Social Change* 21 (4): 375–379.

Portes, A. 1994. The Informal Economy and Its Paradoxes. In *The Handbook of Economic Sociology*, ed. R. Swedberg and N.J. Smelser, 426–453. New York: Russell Sage Foundation.

Portes, A., M. Castells, and L.A. Benton. 1989. *The Informal Economy: Studies in Advanced and Less Developed Countries*. Baltimore and London: John Hopkins University Press.

Portes, A., W.J. Haller, and L.E. Guarnizo. 2002. Transnational Entrepreneurs: An Alternative Form of Immigrant Economic Adaptation. *American Sociological Review* 67: 278–298.

Powell, W. 1990. Neither Market nor Hierarchy: Network Forms of Organisation. *Research in Organizational Behaviour* 12: 295–336.

Powell, Walter W., and L. Smith-Doerr. 1994. Networks and Economic Life. In *The Handbook of Economic Sociology*, ed. R. Swedberg and N.J. Smelser, 368–403. New York: Russell Sage Foundation.

Power, M. 1991. Educating Accountants: Towards A Critical Ethnography. *Accounting Organizations and Society* 16 (4): 333–353.

Power, Michael. 1997. *Audit Society, The: Rituals of Verification*. Oxford: OUP.

———. 2000. The Audit Society—Second Thoughts. *International Journal of Auditing* 4: 111–119.

Preble, E., and J. Casey. 1969. Taking Care of Business: The Heroin Users Life on the Streets. *International Journal of the Addictions* 4 (1): 1–24.

Preda, A. 2005. *The Sociology of Financial Markets*. Oxford: Oxford University Press.

Pryce, K. 1986. *Endless Pressure: A Study of West Indian Life-Styles in Bristol*. 2nd. ed Bristol Classical.

Punch, M., and S. Gilmour. 2010. Police Corruption: Apples, Barrels and Orchards. *Criminal Justice Matters* 79 (1): 10–12.

Punch, Maurice. 1996b. *Dirty Business: Exploring Corporate Misconduct: Analysis and Cases*. Thousand Oaks, CA: Sage Publications.

Quirke, B. 2010. Fighting EU Fraud: Why Do We Make Life Difficult for Ourselves? *Journal of Financial Crime* 17 (1): 61–80.

Rauch, J.E., and P.B. Evans. 2000. Bureaucratic Structure and Bureaucratic Performance in Less Developed Countries. *Journal of Public Economics* 75 (1): 49–71.

Rawlinson, P. 1996. Russian Organised Crime: A Brief History. *Transnational Organised Crime* 2 (2–3): 28–52.

———. 2008. Mission Impossible? Researching Organized Crime. In *Doing Research on Crime and Justice*, ed. R. King and E. Wincup. Oxford: Oxford University Press.

———. 2010. Look Who's Talking: Interviewing Russian Criminals. *Trends in Organised Crime* 11 (1): 12–20.

Reed, M. 2005. Beyond the Iron Cage? Bureaucracy and Democracy in the Knowledge Economy and Society. In *The Values of Bureaucracy*, ed. P. Du Gay. Oxford: Oxford University Press.

Reiner, R. 1992. *The Politics of the Police*. 2nd rev. ed. Hemel Hempstead: Harvester Wheatsheaf.

Répássy, Helga, and David Symes. 2008. Perspectives on Agrarian Reform in East-Central Europe. *Sociologia Ruralis* 33: 81–91.

Reynolds, P.D., and S.B. White. 1997. *The Entrepreneurial Process: Economic Growth, Men, Women, and Minorities*. Westport, CT: Quorum Books.

Richardson, G.B. 1972. The Organization of Industry. *Economic Journal* 82: 883–896.

Rijkeghem, C. Van, and B. Weder. 1997. *Corruption and the Rate of Temptation: Do Low Wages in the Civil Service Cause Corruption?* Washington, DC: International Monetary Fund.

Ritzer, G. 1998. *The McDonaldization Thesis: Explorations and Extensions*. London: Sage.

Robins, D., and P. Cohen. 1978. *Knuckle Sandwich: Growing Up in the Working-Class City*. Harmondsworth: Penguin.

Romanelli, E. 1989. Organization Birth and Population Variety: A Community Perspective on Origins. In *Research in Organizational Behavior*, ed. M. Staw and L. Cummings. Greenwich, CT: JAI Press.

Rona-Tas, A. 1994. The First Shall Be the Last? Entrepreneurship and Communist Cadres in the Transition From Socialism. *American Journal of Sociology* 100 (1): 40–69.

Rose-Ackerman, S. 1978. *Corruption. A Study in Political Economy*. London/New York: Academic Press.

———. 1999. *Corruption and Government. Causes, Consequences and Reform*. Cambridge: Cambridge University Press.

———. 2006. Corruption. In *International Encyclopedia of Economic Sociology*, ed. J. Beckert and M. Zafirovski. London: Routledge.

Rosenhan, D.L. 1973. On Being Sane in Insane Places. *Science* 179 (4074): 250–258.

Roth, G. 1978. Introduction. In *Economy and Society: An Outline of Interpretative Sociology*, ed. M. Weber. Berkeley: University of California Press.

Rothschild, J., and T.D. Miethe. 1999. Whistle-Blower Disclosures and Management Retaliation: The Battle to Control Information about Organization Corruption. *Work and Occupations* 26 (1): 107–128.

Roy, D.F. 1959. 'Banana Time' Job Satisfaction and Informal Interaction. *Human Organization* 18 (4): 158–168.

Ruef, M., H.E. Aldrich, and N.M. Carter. 2003. The Structure of Organizational Founding Teams: Homophily, Strong Ties, and Isolation among U.S. Entrepreneurs. *American Sociological Review* 68: 195–222.

Ruggiero, V. 1996. *Organized and Corporate Crime in Europe. Offers that Can't Be Refused*. Aldershot: Dartmouth Publishing.

———. 2007. It's the Economy Stupid! Classifying Power Crime. *International Journal of the Sociology of Law* 35 (4): 163–177.

———. 2010. Dirty Collar Crime in Naples. *UN Freedom from Fear* 6: 29–31.

———. 2013. *The Crimes of the Economy. A Criminological Analysis of Economic Thought*. New York: Routledge.

Rumford, C. 2000. *European Cohesion? Contradictions in EU integration*. Basingstoke: Macmillan.

Ryan-Flood, Róisín, and Rosalind Gill, eds. 2010. *Secrecy and Silence in the Research Process: Feminist Reflections*. Abingdon, Oxon and New York, NY: Routledge.

Rytina, S., and D. Morgan. 1982. The Arithmetic of Social Relations: The Interplay of Category and Network. *American Journal of Sociology* 88: 88–113.

Sabel, C.F., and J. Zeitlin, eds. 1997. *World of Possibilities. Flexibility and Mass Production in Western Industrialization*. Cambridge: Cambridge University Press.

Sachs, J. 2005. *The End of Poverty: Economic Possibilities for Our Time*. New York Penguin Press.

Sahlins, M. 1972. *Stone Age Economics*. Chicago: Aldine.

Sajo, A. 1998. Corruption, Clientelism and the Future of the Constitutional State in Eastern Europe. *East European Constitutional Review* 7 (2): 37.

Sandu, D. 2010. *Lumile Sociale Ale Migratiei Romanesti In Strainatate*. Iasi: Polirom.

Sampson, S. 2010. The Anti-corruption Industry: From Movement to Institution. *Global Crime* 11 (2): 261–278.

Santiso, C. 2009. *The Political Economy of Government Auditing. Financial Governance and the Rule of Law in Latin America and Beyond*. New York: Routledge.

SAR. 2011. *Raport Anual. Romania in 2011*. Bucuresti: SAR.

Sartori, G. 1987. *The Theory of Democracy Revisited. Part 2*. Chatham NJ: Chatham House Publishers.

Sassen, S. 1991. *The Global City: New York, London, Tokyo*. Princeton, NJ: Princeton University Press.

———. 1997. Informalization in Advanced Market Economies. In Issues in Development. Discussion Paper 20. Columbia University, New York.

Savona, E.U. 1999. *European Money Trails*. Amsterdam: Harwood Academic Publishers.

Saxenian, A.L. 2000. Networks of Immigrant Entrepreneurs. In *The Silicon Valley Edge: A Habitat for Innovation and Entrepreneurship*, ed. Chong-Moon L. Miller, G.M. Hancock, and H.S. Rowen, 248–268. Stanford, CA: Stanford University Press.

Schneider, M., and P. Teske. 1992. Towards a Theory of the Political Entrepreneur. *American Political Science Review* 86: 737–747.

Schumpeter, J.A. 1934. *The Theory of Economic Development*. Cambridge, MA: Harvard University Press.

———. 1939. *Business Cycles: A Theoretical, Historical and Statistical Analysis of the Capitalist Process*. New York: McGraw-Hill.

———. 1942. *Capitalism Socialism and Democracy*. London: Allen and Unwin.

———. 1947. The Creative Response in Economic History. *Journal of Economic History* 7: 149–159.

Schütz, A., and T. Luckmann. 1974. *The Structures of the Life-World*. London.

Schwendinger, H., and J. Schwendinger. 1970. Defenders of Order or Guardians of Human Rights? *Issues in Criminology* 5 (2): 123–157.

Scott, J.C. 1972. Handling Historical Comparisons Cross-Nationally. In *Political Corruption. A Handbook*, ed. A. Heidenheimer, M. Johnston, J. LeVine, and V. Tanzi, 129–145. London: Transaction Publishers.

———. 1985. *Weapons of the Weak. Everyday Forms of Peasant Resistance*. New Heaven and London: Yale University Press.

———. 1998. *Seeing Like a State. How Certain Schemes to Improve the Human Condition Have Failed*. New Haven and London: Yale University Press.

Selznick, P. 1949. *TVA and the Grass Roots*. Berkeley and Los Angeles: University of California Press.

Sennett, R. 1998. *The Corrosion of Character*. London: W. W. Norton.

Shahzad, U., and T. Hopperb. 2001. A Bangladesh Soap Opera: Privatisation, Accounting, and Regimes of Control in A Less Developed Country. *Organizations and Society* 26: 643–672.

Shane, S., and S. Venkataraman. 2000. The Promise of Entrepreneurship as a Field of Research. *The Academy of Management Review* 25 (1): 217–226.

Shaxon, N. 2011. *Treasure Islands. Uncovering the Damage of Offshore Banking and Tax Heavens*. New York: Palgrave Macmillan.

Shleifer, A., and R.W. Vishny. 1993. Corruption. *The Quarterly Journal of Economics*: 599–617.

Shover, N. 1973. The Social Organisation of Burglary. *Social Problems* 20: 499–514.

———. 1985. *Ageing Criminals*. Beverly Hills: Sage.

———. 1996. *Great Pretenders*. Boulder, CO: Westview Press.

Shover, N., and D. Honaker. 1991. The Socially Bounded Decision Making of Persistent Property Offenders. *The Howard Journal* 31 (November): 276–293.

Simmel, G. 1907/1978. *The Philosophy of Money*. Trans. Tom Bottomore and David Frisby, Ed. David Frisby. 3rd ed. vol. 1. New York: Routledge. Original edition, 1907. Reprint, 1978.

Slapper, G., and S. Tombs. 1999. *Corporate Crime*. Harlow: Longman.
Smart, C. 1976. *Women, Crime and Criminology*. London: Routledge and Kegan Paul.
Smelser, Neil J., and Richard Swedberg. 1994. The Sociological Perspective on Economy. In *The Handbook of Economic Sociology*, ed. R. Swedberg and Neil J. Smelser, 3–27. New York: Russell Sage Foundation.
Smelser, N.J., and R. Swedberg, eds. 2005. *The Handbook of Economic Sociology*. 2nd ed. Princeton, NJ: Princeton University Press.
Smith, A. 1826. *An Inquiry into the Nature and Causes of the Wealth of Nations*. 4th ed. London: W. Strahan and T. Cadell.
Sneath, D. 2004. Property Regimes and Sociotechnical Systems: Rights over Land in Mongolia's Age of Market. In *Property In Question. Value Transformation In the Global Economy*, ed. K. Verdery and C. Humphrey, 161–182. Oxford: Berg.
Snider, L. 2000. The Sociology of Corporate Crime: An Obituary. *Theoretical Criminology* 4 (2): 169–206.
Solway, I., and J. Waters. 1977. Working the Corner: The Ethics and Legality of Ethnographic Fieldwork Among Active Heroin Addicts. In *Street Ethnography*, ed. R. Weppner. Beverley Hills: Sage.
Sousa, L., P. Larmour, and B. Hindess, eds. 2009. *Governments, NGOs and Anti-corruption: The new Integrity Warriors*. New York: Routledge.
South, N. 1998. Corporate and State Crimes Against the Environment: Foundations for a Green Perspective in European Criminology. In *The New European Criminology: Crime and Social Order in Europe*, ed., V. Ruggiero, N. South, and A. Taylor. London: Routledge.
Spicker, P. 2011. Ethical Covert Research. *Sociology* 45 (1): 118–133.
Stark, David. 1996. Recombinant Property in East European Capitalism. *American Journal of Sociology* 101 (4): 993–1027.
Stanculescu, M., and Berevoescu, I. 2001. Coruptia Intre 'Cadou' Si Imbogatire 'Peste Noapte'. OSF.
Stefanou, C. 2010. Databases as a Means of Combating Organised Crime Within the EU. *Journal of Financial Crime* 17 (1): 100–115.
Stinchcombe, A.L. 1959. Bureaucratic and Craft Administration of Production. *Administrative Science Quarterly* 4: 194–208.
———. 1965. Social Structure and Organizations. In *Handbook of Organizations*, ed. James G. March, 142–193. Chicago, IL: Rand McNally.
———. 1985. Contracts as Hierarchical Documents. In *Organization Theory and Project Management*, ed. A.L. Stinchcombe and C. Heimer, 121–171. Oslo: Norwegian University Press.
Stoica, C. A. 2006. Once upon a Time There Was a Big Party: The Social Bases of the Romanian Communist Party. Part II. *East European Politics & Societies August* 20 (3):447-482.
Suchman, M.C., D.J. Steward, and C.A. Westfall. 2001. The Legal Environment of Entrepreneurship: Observations on the Legitimation of Venture Finance in

Silicon Valley. In *The Entrepreneurship Dynamic*, ed. B. Schoonhoven and E. Romanelli, 349–382. Stanford, CA: Stanford University Press.

Sumner, C. 1994. *The Sociology of Deviance: An Obituary*. Buckingham: Open University Press.

Sutherland, E. 1937. *The Professional Thief.* Chicago, IL: University of Chicago Press.

———. 1944. Is 'White Collar Crime' Crime? *American Sociological Review* 10 (2): 132–139.

Sutherland, Edwin H. 1983. *White-Collar Crime: The Uncut Version*. Yale: Yale University Press.

Sutter, A. 1966. The World of the Righteous Dope Fiend. *Issues in Criminology* 2 (2): 177–222.

Suttles, G. 1968. *The Social Order of the Slum*. Chicago, IL: University of Chicago Press.

Swedberg, Richard. 1994. Markets as Social Structures. In *The Handbook of Economic Sociology*, ed. R. Swedberg and N.J. Smelser, 255–283. New York: Russell Sage Foundation.

Swedberg, R. 2000. The Social Science View of Entrepreneurship: Introduction and Practical Applications. In *Entrepreneurship: The Social Science View*, ed. R. Swedberg, 7–44. Oxford: Oxford University Press.

———. 2003. *Principles of Economic Sociology*. Princeton and Oxford: Princeton University Press.

Syal, R. and Ball, A. 2011. One in Five Pass-Holders in Lords Linked to Lobbying. *The Guardian*, November 9.

Sykes, G.M., and D. Matza. 1957. Techniques of Neutralization: A Theory of Delinquency. *American Sociological Review* 22 (6): 664–670.

Szarek-Mason, P. 2010. *The European Union's Fight Against Corruption : The Evolving Policy Towards Member States and Candidate Countries*. Cambridge: Cambridge University Press.

Szlelenyi, I., K. Beckett, and L.P. Likng. 1994. The Socialist Economic System. In *The Handbook of Economic Sociology*, ed. R. Swedberg and N.J. Smelser, 234–255. New York: Russell Sage Foundation.

Tanzi, V. 1998. *Corruption Around the World: Causes, Consequences, Scope and Cures*. Washington, DC: International Monetary Fund.

Taylor, A. 1993. *Women Drug Users: An Ethnography of a Female Injecting Community*. Oxford: Clarendon Press.

Taylor, I., P. Walton, and J. Young. 1973. *The New Criminology*. London: Routledge and Kegan Paul.

———, eds. 1975. *Critical Criminology*. London: Routledge and Kegan Paul.

The Economist. 2012. https://www.economist.com/blogs/easternapproaches/2012/06/eu-funds-absorption-romania

Thomas, William Isaac. 1967. *The Unadjusted Girl. With Cases and Standpoint for Behavioral Analysis*. New York; Evanston; London: Harper & Row.

Thompson, H. 1966. *Hell's Angels: The Strange and Terrible Saga of the Outlaw Motorcycle Gangs*. New York: Random House.

Thompson, E.P. 1971. The Moral Economy of the English Crowd in the Eighteenth Century. *Past and Present* 50: 78–98.

Thompson, G., J. Frances, R. Levacic, and Jeremy Mitchell, eds. 1991. *Markets, Hierarchies and Networks. The Coordination of Social Life*. London, Thousand Oaks, and New Dehli: Sage.

Thornton, P.H. 1999. The Sociology of Entrepreneurship. *Annual Review of Sociology* 25 (1): 19–46.

Thrasher, F. 1927. *The Gang*. Chicago, IL: University of Chicago Press.

Thrift, N. 2001. 'It's the Romance, Not the Finance, That makes the Business Worth Pursuing': Disclosing A New Market Culture. *Economy and Society* 30: 412–432.

Tombs, S. 1999. Death and Work in Britain. *Sociological Review* 47 (2): 345–367.

Tonkiss, F., and A. Passey. 1999. Trust, Confidence and Voluntary Organisations: Between Values and Institutions. *Sociology* 33 (2): 257–274.

Torsello, D. 2012. The New Environmentalism? Civil Society and Corruption in the Enlarged EU. *Urban Anthropology*, ed., G. Prato and I. Pardo. Surrey: Ashgate.

Transparency International. 2000. *TI Sourcebook. Confronting Corruption: The Elements of a National Integrity System*. Berlin: Transparency International.

———. 2011. *Raportul Naţional asupra Corupţiei Octombrie 2009—Februarie 2011*. Bucuresti: Transparency International.

Treisman, D. 2000. The Causes of Corruption: A Cross-National Study. *Journal of Public Economics* 76 (3): 399–457.

Tsebelis, G., and G. Garrett. 2001. The Institutional Foundations of Intergovernmentalism and Supranationalism in the European Union. *International Organization* 55 (2): 357–390.

Tupman, W. 2010. Keeping Under the Radar: Watch Out for 'Smurfs'. *Journal of Financial Crime* 17 (1): 152–162.

Turk, A.T. 1969. *Criminality and the Legal Order*. Chicago, IL: Rand McNally.

United Nations. 2004. *Anti-corruption Toolkit*. New York: UN.

United Nations Development Programme. 2004. *Anti-corruption Practice Note*. New York: UNDP.

Uzzi, B. 1997. Social Structure and Competition in Interfirm Networks: The Paradox of Embeddedness. *Administrative Science Quarterly* 42: 35–67.

Van Klaveren, J. 1999. The Concept of Corruption. In *Political Corruption. A Handbook*, ed. A. Heidenheimer, M. Johnston, and Tanzi V. LeVine, 25–29. London: Transaction Publishers.

Van Maanen, J. 1995. *Representation in Ethnography*. London: Sage.

Van Maanen, J., and S. Barley. 1984. Occupational Communities: Culture and Control in Organizations. In *Research in Organizational Behavior*, ed. M. Staw and L. Cummings, 287–365. Greenwich, CT: JAI Press.

Verdery, K. 2004. The Obligations of Ownership: Restoring Rights to Land in Postsocialist Transylvania. In *Property in Question. Value Transformation in the Global Economy*, ed. K. Verdery and C. Humphrey, 139–159. Oxford: Berg.

Verdery, K., J.C. Chesnais, H. David, C. Karnoouh, S. Nancy Leys, and V. Tismaneanu. 1996. Post-1989 Intellectual Cooperation and Intellectual Property Rights: A Romanian Case. *East European Politics and Societies* 10 (2): 328–332.

Verdery, Katherine. 1996. *What Was Socialism, and What Comes Next?* Princeton, NJ: Princeton University Press.

Verdery, K., and C. Humphrey, eds. 2004. *Property in Question. Value Transformation in the Global Society.* Oxford: Berg.

Von Hayek, F. 1989. Spontaneous ('Grown') Order and Organized ('Made') Order. In *Order—With or Without Design?* ed. N. Modlovky, 101–123. London: Centre for Research in Communist Economies.

Walby, S. 2003. *Modernities, Globalisation and Complexity.* Vol. 1. London: Sage.

———. 2006. *Complex Social Systems in a Global Era.* London: Sage.

Watson, T.J., ed. 2008. *Sociology, Work and Industry.* 5th ed. London: Routledge.

Watts, J. 2002. Heritage and Culture in Archangel, Northern Russia. In *Markets and Moralities*, ed. R. Mandel and C. Humphrey, 53–75. New York: Berg.

Weber, M. 1949. Max Weber on the Methodology of the Social Sciences: Free Press.

———. 1968. *Economy and society.* Vol. 1. New York: Bedminster.

Weber, E. 1976a. *Peasants into Frenchmen. The modernization of Rural France.* Stanford: Stanford University Press.

———. 1976b. *Protestant Ethic and the Spirit of Capitalism.* London: Allen & Unwin.

Wedel, J. 1986. *The Private Poland.* New York: Facts on File Publications.

———. 2001a. *Collision and Collusion: The Strange Case of Western Aid to Eastern Europe, 1989–1998.* New York: Palgrave.

Wedel, Janine R. 2001b. *Corruption and Organized Crime In Post-Communist States: New Ways of Manifesting Old Patterns. Trends in Organized Crime* 7 (1): 3–61.

Wedel, J. 2003. Clans, Cliques and Captured States: Rethinking 'Transition' In Central and Eastern Europe and the Former Soviet Union. *Journal of International Development* 15: 427–440.

Wedeman, A. 1997. Looters, Rent-Scrappers, and Divided-Collectors: Corruption and Growth in Zaire, South Korea and the Philippines. *The Journal of Developing Areas 31* (4): 457–478.

Wei, S.-J. 1997a. *How Taxing Is Corruption on International Investors.* NBER Working Paper No. 6030. National Bureau of Economic Research, Cambridge, MA.

———. 1997b. *Why Is Corruption So Much More Taxing Than tax? Arbitrariness Kills.* NBER Working Paper No. 6255. National Bureau of Economic Research, Cambridge MA.

———. 2000. *Bribery in the Economies.* Washington, DC: Brookings Institution.
Weick, K.E. 1996. Enactment and the Boundaryless Career: Organizing as We Work. In *The Boundaryless Career*, ed. M.A. Arthur and D.M. Rousseau, 40–57. New York: Oxford University Press.
West, B.A. 2002. *The Danger Is Everywhere! The Insecurities of Transition in Postsocialist Hungary.* Prospect Heights, IL: Waveland Press.
Westmarland, L. 2000. Getting on the Door and Staying There: A Covert Participant Observational Study of Bouncers. In *Danger in the Field: Risk and Ethics in Social Research*, ed. G. Linkogle and S. Lee-Treweek. London and New York: Routledge.
White, H. 1970. *Chains of Opportunity: System Models of Mobility in Organizations.* Cambridge, MA: Harvard University Press.
White, S. 1999. Investigating EC Fraud: The Metamorphosis of UCLAF. *Journal of Financial Crime* 6 (3): 255–260.
———. 2010. EU Anti-Fraud Enforcement: Overcoming Obstacles. *Journal of Financial Crime* 17 (1): 81–99.
Whyte, W. 1943/1955. Street Corner Society: The Social Organisation of a Chicago Slum. Chicago, IL: University of Chicago Press.
Williams, T. 1989. *The Cocaine Kids.* Reading, MA: Addison-Wesley.
Williams, Karel, Colin Haslam, and John Williams. 1992. Ford Versus 'Fordism': The Beginning of Mass Production? *Work, Employment and Society* 6 (4): 517–555.
Williams, T. 1992b. *Crack House.* Reading, MA: Addison-Wesley.
Williamson, O.E. 1975. *Markets and Hierarchies: Analysis and Antitrust Implications.* New York: Free Press.
Willis, P. 1977. *Learning to Labour: How Working Class Kids Get Working Class Jobs.* London: Saxon House.
Wilson, J. 1989. Corruption: The Shame of the States. In *Political Corruption: A Handbook*, ed. A. Heidenheimer. London: Transaction Publishers.
Winlow, S. 2001. *Badfellas: Crime, Tradition and New Masculinities.* Oxford: Berg.
Wolf, D.R. 1991. *The Rebels : A Brotherhood of Outlaw Bikers.* Toronto: University of Toronto Press.
Wolf, M.A. 1992. *A Trice-Told Tale: Feminism, Postmodernism and Ethnographic Responsibility.* Stanford, CA: Stanford University Press.
Wong, B. 1998. *Ethnicity and Entrepreneurship: The New Chinese Immigrants in the San Francisco Bay Area.* Boston, MA: Allyn and Bacon.
Woodiwiss, M., and Dick Hobbs. 2009. Moral Panics and the Rhetoric of Organised Crime Policing in America and Britain. *British Journal of Criminology* 49: 106–128.
World Bank. 2000. *Anti-corruption in Transition.* World Bank: A Contribution to the Policy Debate. Washington.
Wright, R., and S. Decker. 1994. *Burglars on the Job: Street life and Residential Break-ins.* Boston, MA: North Eastern University Press.

———. 1997. *Armed Robbers in Action: Stick-Ups and Street Culture*. Boston, MA: North Eastern University Press.

Wright, R., S. Decker, A. Redfern, and S. Smith. 1992. A Snowballs Chance in Hell: Doing Fieldwork with Active Residential Burglars. *Journal of Research in Crime and Delinquency* 29 (2): 148–161.

Xanthaki, H. 2010. What Is EU fraud? And Can OLAF Really Combat it? *Journal of Financial Crime* 17 (1): 133–151.

Yang, M. 1994. *Gifts, Favours and Banquets. The Art of Social Relations in China*. London: Cornell University Press.

Young, J. 1973. *The Drugtakers*. London: Paladin.

Zahariadis, Nikolaos. 2014. The Shield of Heracles: Multiple Streams and the Emotional Endowment Effect. *European Journal of Political Research* 54 (3): 466–481.

Zajda, Joseph. 2003. The Politics of Rewriting History: New History Textbooks and Curriculum Materials in Russia. *Internationa Review of Education* 49 (3): 363–382.

Zelizer, V. 1997. *The Social Meaning of Money. Pin Money, Paychecks, Poor Relief, and Other Currencies*. Princeton, NJ: Princeton University Press.

———. 2004. *Circuits in Economic Life*. Working Paper Esterni.

Zerilli, F. 2005. Corruption, Property Restitution and Romanianness. In *Corruption: Anthropological Perspectives*, ed. D. Haller and C. Schore, 83-102. London: Pluto.

Zorbaugh, H. 1929. *The Gold Coast and the Slum*. Chicago, IL: University of Chicago Press.

Notes

1. http://ec.europa.eu/dgs/home-affairs/what-we-do/policies/organized-crime-and-human-trafficking/corruption/anti-corruption-report/index_en.htm.

Index[1]

A

[1]Note: Page number followed by 'n' refers to notes.

R. Bratu, *Corruption, Informality and Entrepreneurship in Romania*, Political Corruption and Governance,
https://doi.org/10.1007/978-3-319-66667-9

D

The manufacturer's authorised representative in the EU is Springer Nature Customer Service Centre GmbH, Europaplatz 3, 69115 Heidelberg, Germany. If you have any concerns regarding our products, please contact ProductSafety@springernature.com

Printed and bound by CPI Group (UK) Ltd, Croydon, CR0 4YY
22/09/2026
02220948-0003